RECOLLECTIONS

RECOLLECTIONS

BY

WASHINGTON GLADDEN

Eugene, Oregon

Wipf and Stock Publishers
199 West 8th Avenue, Suite 3
Eugene, Oregon 97401

Recollections
By Gladden, Washington
ISBN: 1-59244-605-1
Publication date 3/17/2004
Previously published by Houghton Mifflin, 1909

CONTENTS

I. VESTIGES OF INFANCY 1
II. FARM LIFE AND SCHOOL LIFE 17
III. VILLAGE LIFE AND APPRENTICESHIP . . 40
IV. THE CHOICE OF A CALLING 55
V. COLLEGE DAYS 67
VI. PUTTING ON THE HARNESS 85
VII. THE BURSTING OF THE STORM 99
VIII. DARK DAYS 118
IX. THE END OF THE WAR 136
X. AMONG THE HILLS 158
XI. THE FOOLISHNESS OF RECONSTRUCTION . 176
XII. FROM STUDY TO SANCTUM 182
XIII. THE TWEED RING 197
XIV. THE GREELEY CAMPAIGN AND THE CREDIT MOBILIER 209
XV. THE SWING TRIAL 223
XVI. NEWSPAPER ETHICS 232
XVII. BACK TO NEW ENGLAND 239
XVIII. HERESY HUNTING 259
XIX. POSTMERIDIAN 282

CONTENTS

XX.	The Industrial Revolution	294
XXI.	A Widening Vocation	316
XXII.	The Municipal Problem	328
XXIII.	Bouquets and Brickbats	353
XXIV.	The Negro Problem	366
XXV.	A Political Retrospect	377
XXVI.	Partnership with Plunderers	398
XXVII.	October Sunshine	410
XXVIII.	Looking Backward and Forward	422
	Index	435

Note. — The frontispiece portrait is from a photograph by the Baker Art Gallery, Columbus, Ohio.

RECOLLECTIONS

RECOLLECTIONS

CHAPTER I

VESTIGES OF INFANCY

> O joy! that in our embers
> Is something that doth live,
> That nature yet remembers
> What was so fugitive!
> *William Wordsworth.*

THE story which I have undertaken to tell is that of an average American. It holds no such wonders of achievement as that of Booker Washington; it follows no such romantic paths as those in which Jacob Riis has led us; it climbs to no such altitudes of dignity and power as those to which we have rejoiced to follow Carl Schurz. It will take us along country roads, and through the busy thoroughfares of cities; it will observe, and try to interpret, the life of all sorts and conditions of American men and women. Its interest, if it has any, will not be found in any exploits of the narrator, but in whatever power he has possessed of looking sympathetically at the things he has seen and of accurately reporting them.

My life began in the little hamlet of Pottsgrove, in central Pennsylvania, in the angle made by the two branches of the Susquehanna River, and not far from their junction at Northumberland. My father, whose name was Solomon, was the teacher of the country school in this district. He was a native of Southampton, Massachusetts, the second of a family of twelve children. His father, Thomas Gladden, was a shoemaker by trade, though he found occasional employment in the harvest season in working upon the neighboring farms. That kind of work was most congenial to him, for he was a stalwart man, and the toil of the field was more welcome than the confinement of the shop.

My father's boyhood had, therefore, been spent in the lowliest conditions. It would not be true to say that he sprang from the proletariat, for in those days there was no such thing. My grandfather lived in his own house, had his own small garden in which he raised a large part of the food for his family, worked at his trade in the winter and on the farms in the summer, was never in want or in debt, and no sooner than any other sovereign would have taken a tip or accepted charity. His father, Azariah, had been a soldier of the Revolution. He enlisted from New Britain, Connecticut, in the summer of 1777, and was, I suppose, in the army of Washington at Valley Forge during that bitter winter. It is the family tradition, which I know no reason to dispute, that he was one of Washington's body-guard; a big brass button has descended to me, which has stamped upon it the legend that it once adorned a military coat worn by the great commander. My father heard from his grandfather many stirring tales of the days when he was with Washington, which helps to explain the name I bear.

My great-grandfather's name was Gladding. By what process it became changed, in the next generation, from a present participle to an active transitive verb I do not know. I suppose that my great-grandfather, who was born at Norwich, Connecticut, was a descendant of John Gladding, who came to Plymouth, Massachusetts, in 1640, and afterwards settled in Bristol, Rhode Island, but of this I have no definite proof. The Gladdings of that vicinage are descendants of John, and I have assumed that I belong among them.

Most of the boys and girls of my grandfather's family found employment on the farms and in the farmhouses of the vicinage. It was a plain countryside, lying west of Mount Tom and not far from its base — the quietest and most decorous neighborhood, I suppose, in all the world, and so they called it Bedlam. I remember, very well, my father's talk about his old home, — his glowing pictures of Mount Tom, over whose brow the sun rose every morning, and whose rocky slopes were infested with rattlesnakes.

My father's health, in his youth, was frail; he was unable to do the rough work of the farms, and the family seems to have determined to make a scholar of him. There was an academy of some note at Southampton, and thither he was sent; he worked for his board in the family of a good physician, who took special interest in him, and thus gained his equipment for the work of a teacher. Before he was of age he began teaching in the country towns of Hampshire County; when I lived in the Connecticut valley, in later days, I used to meet men, now and then, who had been his pupils, and who carried his name in grateful memory.

What started him on his way westward I never knew; but some time in the early thirties he turned his face toward the setting sun, and found his first halting-place in southern central New York, in the town of Owego, on the Susquehanna River, where he taught a country district school for one winter only. Thence he moved southward, following, perhaps, the Susquehanna, and landed in the neighborhood where the rest of his life was to be spent. Pennsylvania was just then getting ready to establish a free-school system, which went into effect in 1834; probably he thought that a market would thus be created for the wares of the schoolmaster. I suspect that he must have gone down the river on one of the lumber rafts which carried the white-pine lumber of the Owego forests, on the spring floods, down to the Pennsylvania farms.

The transition from the rocky ridges and sandy plains of western Massachusetts to the rich and fertile fields of the lower Susquehanna valley, and from the staid severities of New England Puritanism to the free and unconventional manners of the Pennsylvania Dutch, must have been to my father an interesting experience. Northumberland County, in Pennsylvania, was farther then from Hampshire County, in Massachusetts, than the heart of Africa now is from the middle of the continent. Measured by the standards of the postal service, it was five times as far away; for a five-cent stamp will carry a letter from Columbus to Congo, to-day, while the letter from which I am about to quote, sent from Pottsgrove to Southampton, in 1832, cost the receiver twenty-five cents. The civilization which my father encountered in his new home was full of novelties for him. "What first attracts the attention of a New England man" —

thus he writes to his brother at home — "is the wagons of enormous bulk, to which six horses are frequently attached, and generally as many as four. The driver always mounts one of the horses to guide the others. The management of the farms is also different from the New England method. No oxen are used. The hoeing of the corn is accomplished by the plow and harrow. The women are accustomed to work in the fields in many places, and generally in the time of haymaking and harvesting. On public days or times when the militia or the volunteers meet, the parade-ground swarms with women peddlers. Perhaps the women are not possessed of quite as much modesty as your Yankee ladies." And then he proceeds to animadvert on certain social customs which, to his severe morality, verged on the scandalous. He doubts whether he shall be content to find a permanent home among such people.

But there is quick demand for such trained faculty as he possesses, and he is soon at work; within a few days after his arrival he is installed as master of the district school in the little hamlet of Pottsgrove. Six months later he writes to his brother: —

I have a small school, no more than thirty scholars at present; but if I continue to teach here through fall and winter, the number will be much greater. I shall be urged to continue longer than this quarter, but it is uncertain that I shall. The honest Dutchmen prefer the Little Yankee to the drunken Englishman who taught here last winter, or to the dissipated and profane characters who have generally taught here.

You wished me to give you all the interesting information of this section of the country. But that which is interesting news to me would be uninteresting to you. If I should tell you that Judge Harper fell from his horse and broke his thigh last week, or that Dr. James Dougal continues to drink wine to excess, it could not be gratifying at all to you. And news of a public character — the desolation occasioned by cholera or the savage barbarities of the Blackhawks upon the frontier of Illinois — you receive by the public papers.

These bits of my father's letters give some hint of his intellectual habit. I have but a few of them, but his clear round handwriting, not unlike that of Abraham Lincoln, is a fitting vehicle for the accurate and felicitous English in which his thought finds expression. There is a touch of humor now and then, but the prevailing mood is one of deep seriousness. To his younger brother he gives a great deal of fatherly advice. He fears lest his brother may be corrupted by the vices of the countryside, whose contamination he has watched with solicitude, and he urges as a wise prophylactic the occupation of the mind by higher interests. "Treatises of natural history," he says, "are well calculated to produce pleasure in reading and a desire to improve the intellectual powers. Nor should the study of the sciences be neglected by any individual who does not wish to exclude himself from human society." The high valuation here placed on scientific study was not common in those days. Yet most of my father's books which have come down to me are of this character — astronomy, chemistry, and natural history evidently had a fascination for him; and while he had no occasion to teach these subjects in the schools of Pennsylvania, he was pushing his explorations in this field.

One of my father's pupils in the Owego school was a country girl by the name of Amanda Daniels. It would appear that she also, having graduated from the district school, had found employment as a teacher in her own neighborhood. Correspondence followed: I have the sacred fragments of the letter in which my father told my mother his love and besought her to share his life. He brought her to Pottsgrove in the summer of 1833, and they at once began to teach in adjoining districts, setting up their home in a house which stood midway between the two schoolhouses.

My mother's father was also a shoemaker, who stuck to his last in the winter, and wielded the scythe and the hoe in the summer, on a little farm of his own. One of John G. Saxe's poems contains a stanza which I have not found it difficult to remember: —

> Depend upon it, my snobbish friend,
> Your family thread you can't ascend
> Without great reason to apprehend
> You may find it waxed at the other end,
>   By some plebeian vocation.

Both strands of my "family thread" were undeniably treated after this manner at a period quite within my own remembrance, which fact makes it superfluous for me to claim identification with the working-classes. It has never been possible for me to forget the fact, and I am not conscious of having tried to do so. I have never found it necessary to cultivate sympathy with the people who work with their hands. My mother was also one of twelve brothers and sisters; race suicide was not in those days an imminent peril.

After two or three terms of teaching in separate schools my parents found one schoolhouse enough for the family, and my mother was fain to content herself with the care of one small pupil at home. It was on the 11th of February, 1836, that this charge was laid upon her.

The records of the next few years are meagre. My mother, who was, I believe, an accurate chronicler, told me in after years that my education began at a very early day; that when I was two years and a half old I was able to read, in turn with the others, my verse in the Bible at family prayers. Of learning to read and to write and to perform the rudimentary operations of arithmetic, I have no recollection. I faintly recall committing certain spelling lessons against the return of my father from school, and memorizing the etymological definitions in Kirkham's Grammar; this must have been before I was four years old. My father was evidently bound that I should know how to use the English language.

This process of cram, administered to the mind of a young child, was, of course, highly unscientific and altogether reprehensible; the only advantage to me was that it gave me a firm hold on my father's memory. He died before I was six years old, but he has always been a distinct figure in my recollection. His form, his face, his voice have always been with me; many of the scenes in which he appeared have returned to me continually through all my life. He died before the days of the

VESTIGES OF INFANCY

daguerreotype, so that I have had no other portrait of him than that which is stamped upon my memory. That one could carry clear sense-impressions from such an early age through a long life, I would not have believed if I had not experienced it.

For the last two years of his life, after my brother was born, I must have been my father's nearly constant companion; I remember the larks I had with him: toddling to school in the winter on the crust of the deep snow, which held me when he broke through at every step and I laughed merrily at him; sitting on the back of our black moolley cow, where he held me firm and laughed at me; walking to church in the summer time down a long hill in Washingtonville, on the slope of which our house stood, and hearing him tell a neighbor who walked with us that a church which we passed was a Christ-ian church, with the i in the first syllable long. One memory, naturally more distinct than most others, is that of a savage surgical operation by which the removal of enlarged tonsils was attempted. There were no adequate instruments in those days for the treatment of such cases, and anæsthetics were not yet. The first attempt was unsuccessful, and I remember my father's effort to reassure and hearten me for the second operation; some of the words that he used in that conversation are distinctly in my memory to-day, and I know that no one has ever assisted me in recalling them. All these things happened before I was four years old. I record them here, because they may have some psychological value, in indicating the backward reach of memory.

One very vivid memory, which dates from about this

time, gives me the clearest impression of my father's face. It is a scene at a religious meeting, at a country schoolhouse, in the evening. My father had been reared a Congregationalist, but he had not connected himself with the church in Southampton. In Pennsylvania there were no Congregational churches, and the stiff Calvinism of the Pennsylvania Presbyterians being too strong doctrine for him, he had allied himself with the Methodists. I often went with him to camp-meetings and revivals, and have never forgotten how the more boisterous demonstrations of those services seemed to affect him.

On the night of which I speak, he was standing behind the schoolhouse desk, taking part (for he was what they called a local preacher) in the conduct of the service. There was only one candle in the room; it stood before him on the desk and lit up his face. Some powerful evangelist had been preaching, and the physical effects which frequently followed such appeals were in full view. Men and women were prostrate on the floor, groaning and screaming frantically; some were trying to pray; some were shouting "Glory!" the excitement and confusion were indescribable. I sat on a low seat near my father and looked into his face; he stood perfectly silent; there were tears in his eyes, but the expression on his countenance was one of intense pain.

It must have been early in my fifth year that my parents removed to the smart village of Lewisburg, on the opposite shore of the Susquehanna, where my father became head master of one of the village schools. I am sure about the date, for I remember that it was in the

VESTIGES OF INFANCY 11

yard before our house in Lewisburg that another infantile politician and myself were shouting "Hurrah for Harrison!" The other youthful Whig, as I distinctly remember, could not roll his r's; they had the force of y's.

In Lewisburg my father's merits as a scholar and teacher were speedily recognized; in the church and in the community he must have been held in high respect and honor. It was more than fifty years after his death that I first revisited Lewisburg, and it was grateful to me to find his name held by numbers of his old pupils in affectionate remembrance.

It was in the late summer of 1841 that my mother took me with her on a visit to Danville, thirty or forty miles away. We went by the canal packet, and on our return, after an absence of a few days, as we drew near to Lewisburg, on the opposite side of the river, my mother noted that the curtains of our house, which stood near the bank, were not lifted. "I fear," she said, "that your father is sick." His haggard face, as he met us at the door, confirmed her apprehension.

It was an acute attack of some enteric malady, and the end came soon. How vividly it all comes back to me: my father's broken words to me — they were his last words, I shall never lose them if I live a thousand lives; the droning, dreadful days at a neighbor's while we waited for the funeral; the solemn procession, on foot, to the church, and the burying-ground; the scene at the grave; the many nights that I cried myself to sleep. Childish sorrows are short-lived, we say; but this one was not. It has never let go of my heart; the pain of it is poignant yet. This man had so wound himself into the life of this child that they could not be torn apart without lasting suffering.

After my father's death, my mother took up the work which he had laid down, teaching, for some months, the school of which he had been principal; but late in the following winter she returned, with her two boys, to her home in Owego. That journey is another vivid memory. My uncle had come to Pennsylvania for a load of cloverseed, for which he found market among the farmers of his neighborhood, and we were passengers on his heavily freighted sleigh. The desolateness and terror of that long winter journey through the interminable, lonely woods, and by narrow roadways cut in the mountainsides and overlooking abysses, kept me, for several days, in a state of nervous tension, from which the safe landing at my uncle's farmhouse was an unspeakable relief.

As I recall the experience of that journey, I am brought face to face with the amazing contrasts between the country as my childish memories recall it, and that in which we are living to-day. Here is an American who refuses to be counted among the aged, and what tremendous changes in the physical and economic conditions of this nation his recollection spans!

The country of those earliest memories was primitive and rude and simple, almost beyond the conception of those who are now young. In all the eastern and eastern-central states there were many well-tilled acres and comfortable homes, a considerable number of thriving towns, and a few smart little cities. But a large share of all this broad land was still primeval forest or virgin prairie. Every mountain brook was full of trout,

VESTIGES OF INFANCY

and the great game, deer and bears and wolves and panthers and foxes, roamed all over the mountains. It was no uncommon thing, when I was living on my uncle's farm, to see deer appear in our clearings; bears I never saw wild, but foxes were frequent, and catamounts were not rare.

A few short railways, in different parts of the country, were venturing upon the dubious experiment of steam transportation, but I suppose that not one in ten thousand of all the people of the United States had seen a railway car. Steamboats were beginning to ply upon the inland waters, but no vessel propelled entirely by steam had yet crossed the ocean.

When my life began there were but twenty-five states — Missouri, the last to be admitted, having added her star to the flag in 1821. Arkansas was admitted in 1837. In the first geography which I studied, Michigan, Iowa, and Wisconsin were territories. What is now Minnesota was part of Iowa territory. In the year of my birth Iowa had 10,500 inhabitants and Wisconsin 31,000. All these great central states were wildernesses, and the population had not gone far beyond the Mississippi River. New York city, by the last census before I was born, had a population of 202,589. Chicago had been three years incorporated as a town; it began with 175 houses and 550 inhabitants.

These facts show how little had been done toward the development of the resources of this great country, seventy years ago. The population was sparse, the apparatus of civilization was rude; tools were primitive, machinery had hardly begun to be used in agriculture.

Industry was still largely domestic; the clothing of the great majority of the people was spun and woven in their own homes. There were few large factories of any kind. Cotton had begun to be spun and woven to a considerable extent, but for the most part the mechanical work of the country was done in small establishments employing but few hands. Employers generally worked with their men in small groups, and all ate at the same table; there were no social distinctions between capitalists and laborers.

There had been, before my day began, a few chartered companies in which capital had been combined for industrial purposes, but each of these, I think, had been created by a special act of the legislature; the industrial corporation, in the form in which we now have it, had not been invented. It was during the year 1837 that Connecticut passed a general law empowering groups of persons to combine their capital for business purposes. Other states followed the example. Thus this mighty engine of finance, with such vast capacities for service and such enormous powers of spoliation and oppression, has sprung into existence and taken possession of the earth during a lifetime.

The decade of which I have just been speaking seems, indeed, to have been the beginning of a new era in industrial development. "This homely rural nation," says President Woodrow Wilson, "which in 1828 chose Andrew Jackson to be its President, was about to produce a vast and complex urban civilization. Its old habits were about to be broken up. Its railways were to produce a ceaseless movement of population, section

VESTIGES OF INFANCY 15

interchanging people with section — opinions, manners, and purposes made common and alike through great stretches of the land by reason of constant enterprise and united effort. The laboring classes, who had hitherto worked chiefly on their own initiative and responsibility, were now to be drawn together in large factories, to be directed by others, so that dangerous contrasts both of fortune and of opportunity should presently be created between capitalist and employee. . . . The first signs of a day of capitalistic combinations and of monopoly on the great scale began to be visible. . . . The aggregate material power of the country was to be greatly increased, but individual opportunity was to become unequal; society was to exchange its simple for a complex structure, fruitful of new problems of life, full of new capacities for disorder and disease." [1]

This was, indeed, what was to be, but nobody living at that time could have begun to divine it; these secular movements of social evolution are never predictable by any clairvoyance that we can summon. But this, for substance, is what has been happening since that winter ride over the Alleghanies. It almost staggers one to try to span the experience of a single life.

I have seen the forests disappear from a large part of the continent, sometimes in a ruthless and disastrous slaughter; I have seen the wild game which once roamed everywhere driven to a few sanctuaries in the western mountains, where they cannot long survive; I have seen the population spreading through the Mississippi valley and over the plains and mountains of the great North-

[1] *Division and Reunion*, p. 103.

west; I have seen a mighty empire spring to life upon the Pacific coast, and great cities, scores of them, rise from the heart of the forest or the sedges of the lake or the bosom of the prairie; I have seen the land, from ocean to ocean, covered with a network of steam and electric railways, whose veinings give to almost every hamlet in the land immediate and cheap access to all the rest of the world. All the marvels of electricity in its application to human needs have appeared within this time; when I was a lad it was a curious toy. I remember well the first telegram; the first ocean cable was laid when I was in college; the telephone, the electric light, the wireless telegraph, the Roentgen rays are later prodigies. I have seen, also, as the result of multiplying machinery for shop and farm, the population steadily lessening on the farming lands and massing in the cities; and I have watched the whole of that ominous polarization of social classes — the organizers and employers of labor gathering their hoards together, and, over against them, the men who do the work becoming banded and regimented for a perennial struggle over the product of labor. Such a marshaling of classes for industrial war could never have been dreamed of in my boyhood.

Such a swift glance over the seven decades may make it seem worth while to pass leisurely through them, gathering up such incidents and impressions as may throw light upon the course of events and the stream of tendencies. For it is not in the economic realm alone that great movements have been in progress; in politics and science, in education and religion, the changes have been no less notable.

CHAPTER II

FARM LIFE AND SCHOOL LIFE

> Shades of the prison-house begin to close
>   Upon the growing boy;
> But he beholds the light, and whence it flows,
>   He sees it in his joy.
>
> *William Wordsworth.*

For a few months after my mother's return to Owego, I found a home in the farmhouse of my uncle, three miles from the village. The next autumn, one of the farmers of that neighborhood, who had emigrated from Southampton, in Massachusetts, proposed to return to his old home, and my mother seized the opportunity to send me with him, for a visit to my grandfather. The journey of perhaps two hundred and fifty miles was made in a one-horse buggy of somewhat spacious dimensions, which carried a small trunk behind the single seat whereon sat the farmer and his wife with a babe in her arms, and which admitted a round cheese-box next to the dashboard, that held the provisions for the journey and served as a seat for me. How many days we were on the road I do not remember; it must have been a week. What a weariness it was! The roads were rough, the inns primitive, the weather often harsh, and a small boy of seven who sat numb and cramped through all those days of torture might well be skeptical concerning the pleasure of travel. But I remember, with delight, some picturesque miles along the headwaters of the Delaware, and a glorious view from the top of the Catskills; and I recall the ferry, worked by horses in a treadmill, which carried us across the river at Hudson, and a restful Sunday spent at Old Stockbridge.

We had nearly reached the end of our journey before we had seen a railway train or a railway track; but somewhere in western Massachusetts we came upon the track of the Western Railroad, which connected Springfield with Albany. Presently a passenger train came speeding past us from the west. It was a sensation quite unforgettable. Our charioteer, with exorbitant faith in the speed of his nag, spurred him into a run to keep up with the train, but soon desisted. That was the only glimpse we had of a railway, in all this journey of two hundred and fifty miles, through the heart of New York and Massachusetts.

For nearly a year I lived with my grandfather and grandmother in their little old house on Bedlam Street. Mount Tom, of which my father had so often told me, lifted up his shaggy sides toward the sunrising; the little Manhan River, whose name was also familiar to me, greeted me like an old friend, and many memories of my father endeared the place. They took me to a nook in the woods near the house, where he had braided the branches of pine trees into a bower for the diversion of his sister, who was an invalid; near by was his "seat," where he had fitted a plank between two contiguous oak trees and had used it as an outdoor study, to which he was wont in the summer to resort with his books. The seat was broken down, but bits of the plank were there; the trees had grown about the ends of it and

FARM LIFE AND SCHOOL LIFE 19

held them fast. Was it strange that I should like to sit between those old trees and listen to the whisperings of the forest?

I have always had reason to be grateful for the impressions made upon my life by the contact which this year in Massachusetts gave me with the Puritanism of the New England countryside in the first half of the nineteenth century. There was a flavor in it, easily enough perceptible to a boy of eight, altogether unlike that of central Pennsylvania or central New York. Living in a new community is a little like learning a new language: it gives you a new set of windows, through which to look out on life. The Yankee way of seeing things is distinctly unlike that of the Dutchman or the New Yorker, and a child unconsciously adopts the mental attitude of the people among whom he lives.

I attended school for two terms in the Bedlam schoolhouse; I knew all the people in the neighborhood; I worked in the fields of the farmers and sat at their tables, and all their life became familiar to me. The first money I ever earned was in a harvest field on Bedlam Street. We were getting in the rye, and, with a larger boy, who belonged upon the farm, I toiled hard from early morning till sunset, encouraged by the promise of wages for my work. A wiry boy of eight can heap together a good many sheaves of rye in twelve hours, and I was made to feel, all day long, that I was helping famously. When the even was come, like the men in the parable, I was called to receive my hire, and instead of getting what the men in the parable got, "every man a penny," my compensation was a half-cent. Such a coin was then in circulation. The use of it I could not quite understand, for there was nothing in the world for which you could exchange it. Nobody would sell you less than a cent's worth of anything. I kept my half-cent for some time as a souvenir, but nobody gave me another, and it finally disappeared, leaving, perhaps, an incipient sensitiveness respecting the conduct of those "who oppress the hireling in his wages."

The agricultural methods of the Connecticut valley were still very primitive in 1844; no farm machinery had yet appeared; the field work was all done by oxen, and though the grain cradle was employed, the sickle was still in use for harvesting. I have a scar on the little finger of my left hand which is the record of my first lesson in reaping.

Altogether my year in New England was a profitable year of my childhood; the schooling which one gets in such an experience counts for much in after-life.

In October, 1844, my grandfather's brother was returning to western New York from a visit to Southampton, and it was arranged that I should go, in his care, as far as Syracuse on my homeward way. My grandfather was to take me and my few belongings over the hills to Chester, on the Western Railroad, where I should meet my great-uncle, and go with him by rail to Albany. That ride of twenty miles, in my grandfather's buggy, half of the distance before daybreak, and the railway journey in a second-class car, which was a box without springs, and whose seats were benches without cushions or backs, is another leaf in my experience of the tortures of travel. I had not slept a wink the night

FARM LIFE AND SCHOOL LIFE 21

before; I had sturdily held myself awake, listening to the clock, for fear that my grandfather might oversleep; and what with the loss of rest and the long drive over the rough roads, and the din and jar and dust of this horrible railway passage, I gained about as vivid an impression of the Inferno as I have ever had. It is hard to realize, to-day, that the discomforts of railway travel ever could have been what they sometimes were in the first half of the nineteenth century.

At Albany we were drawn by a stationary engine up a heavy grade, and then let down by gravity to Schenectady, where we embarked on a canal freight-boat for Syracuse. The journey must have taken four or five days; the boat made slow progress; the passenger packets, which often overtook us and passed by us, probably made the journey in half the time. But it was not a fatiguing journey; we sat upon the deck, in the sweet October sunshine, and had time a plenty to study the landscape and chat with the natives on the farms and in the villages. There was always a mild excitement in passing the locks, and the encounters of drivers on the towpath sometimes lent spice to the dull stream of conversation.

At Syracuse my great-uncle commended me to the care of the coachman, and I set out alone on the last stage of my journey. The first night we spent at Cortland, where, in the early evening, I fell in with an ardent politician of about my own age, who was dancing about a hickory pole just erected on the public square, with a banner inscribed to Polk and Dallas flying from the top of it. From this point onward my attention was attracted to the hickory poles and the white-pine poles, by which partisans proclaimed their loyalties in the political contest then so hotly waged. Now and then we came upon an outdoor assembly listening to some fervid orator, arguing for "Polk and annexation," or for "Clay and a protective tariff"; and we had glimpses of those enormous teams of oxen by which each party, gathering at the hustings, sought to symbolize its strength. This was the first political campaign whose incidents I remember, and the proposed annexation of Texas, with the probable resulting war, gave even to a juvenile politician some cause for solicitude.

For it was in this very year, 1844, that the first effective political organization based upon opposition to slavery made its appearance in this country. There had been, a few weeks before this date, a convention at Buffalo which had nominated a candidate for the presidency on a platform which declared "that human brotherhood is a cardinal principle of the democracy as well as of pure Christianity; and neither the political party which repudiates it, nor the political system which is not based upon it, can be truly democratic nor permanent." Thus was born the "Liberty Party," the nucleus of the Republican Party. A small boy, listening to the talk of men on the decks of canal-boats and in the stage-coaches, was made aware that the question which was disturbing men's minds was the question of the extension of slavery; that Texas was wanted by the people of the South because it would give them more slave territory; and that the whole question of the rightfulness of slavery was thus forcing itself upon the conscience

FARM LIFE AND SCHOOL LIFE 23

of the people. The small boy was listening to the first notes of that "irrepressible conflict" which was to rend the nation in twain and deluge the land in blood.

On my return from Massachusetts, my mother, who had been married again and was living in the village of Owego, thought it best to place me in the care of my uncle, Ebenezer Daniels, on the farm where I had lived after my father's death. For the next eight years that farm was my home. It was understood that I was adopted into my uncle's family; that he was to give me the advantages of the common school; that I was to work for him upon the farm until I was twenty-one, and that I should then receive a good suit of clothes and either a good horse or one hundred dollars in money. Such were the ordinary terms of apprenticeship on which boys in those days were received into farmers' families.

My uncle was then a young man, under thirty; he had a rather stony hill farm of forty acres — afterward increased to eighty — on the banks of the Little Nanticoke Creek, three miles east of Owego, and a mile north of the Susquehanna. He was a sturdy figure, a little under six feet in height, with black hair, already thin, and blue eyes, a broad forehead, and a fine, strong, benignant face. He had had but the most meagre educational advantages; he had been a pupil of my father in the district school, and had such scant knowledge of the three R's as boys could get in three or four winter terms. But the first of the three R's for him should be writ large. A Reader he was, with a capital letter; books were the one recreation and solace of his laborious life. The supply of them was, indeed, limited; there were a few in the house that had descended from former generations, but the store was soon exhausted. We had, however, a school district library, furnished at that time by the State of New York to each school district — a most humane and enlightened provision. The district elected a librarian at the annual school meeting, and the library was thus located in one of the farmhouses near the centre of the district, and was accessible to all who chose to use it. Ours was but a limited collection — perhaps less than one hundred and fifty volumes; and there was very little fiction in it, and no poetry at all, so far as I can now remember; it was made up mostly of books of history and travel. Occasionally a few new volumes were added. This library, to a man like my uncle, was a godsend; I doubt if any other family in the district used it half as freely as ours did. Besides, we had access to two Sunday-school libraries, in which books of value were sometimes found; and the New York "Observer" and the New York "Weekly Tribune" kept us somewhat informed respecting the doings of both sides of the greater world.

In the little farmhouse a small sitting-room adjoined the kitchen, in which was an open fireplace; and one of my daily duties, from the beginning of my life on the farm, was to fill the wood-box every winter day with fuel for the evening fire. After the chores were done and the supper was cleared away, the family always resorted to this room, and there were often two hours for reading before our early bedtime. My uncle was the reader in the earlier years, and he always read aloud, sometimes by the light of pine-knots, of which we usually had a good supply, but most often by a tallow dip which he held close to the page. He was an admirable reader; of the arts of the elocutionist, happily, he knew nothing, but he easily caught the author's meaning, and interpreted it with great skill and accuracy. His voice was mellow and musical, he was sensitive to rhetorical beauty, and his tones grew sonorous or tremulous as the lines rose to passion or fell to pathos.

Thus we had, in the poor little farmhouse, our own *noctes ambrosianae*, with the firelight from the open hearth making flickering shadows on the lowly walls, and our minds traveling with Taylor up the Nile or with Hannibal over the Alps. My memory often goes back to those evenings with gratitude for the kind providence that guarded me from the mental debaucheries of sensational fiction, and led me so kindly into the delights of more sober literature. Many things, indeed, I missed, of which no boy ought to be defrauded, — the pageantry of Scott, the romantic adventure of Cooper: these did not come to me until my days of hero-worship were past; in the meantime, however, I had gained something which the average modern boy, with whole libraries of fiction open to him, generally fails to get.

As I grew older, my uncle occasionally drafted me into service as reader for a part of the evening, and in that practice I learned most of what I have known of the art of oral expression. There was very little criticism of the performance; all my teacher required of me was to speak distinctly, and to know and convey the meaning of the author. A beautiful art is this, the art of reading; and not as much cultivated, I fear, in these days as in the days of my boyhood. We have very little time for such employments; what with our shows and our social functions, and our fraternities and sororities, and all the rest, few families ever get a chance to spend an evening together, and such pleasures as those with which, in the plain old country farmhouse, we were fain to solace ourselves, are far from the thoughts of most of our contemporaries. Yet it might be worth while to try to recover such a lost art as the art of reading aloud, and even to find or furnish occasion for it in the family life. Perhaps, one of these days, it may be the fashion to entertain one another in this way. Instead of installing a talking-machine in a corner of the drawing-room, and listening to uncanny reproductions of other people's voices in speech or song, we may learn to find a higher pleasure in giving fitting and natural utterance, by our own voices, to fair fancies and kindling thoughts, preserved for us in the great literatures.

The life into which, on my uncle's farm, I was now introduced, was by no means a life of ease or luxury. It was only by the most tireless and constant labor, early and late, in which every member of the family was required to take part, that we were able to win from the intractable soil the means of livelihood, and to meet the payments which were due upon the land. My uncle was a man of prodigious industry; long before daylight in the winter mornings he would be away with his team to the woods to haul saw-logs to the mill or cord-wood to the village; all the year round he wrought with tireless patience, and he expected of all his household a similar diligence. At once certain definite tasks and

FARM LIFE AND SCHOOL LIFE 27

responsibilities were assigned to me, in the provision for the household fires, and in the care of the stock; gradually these burdens were increased. Very early I was initiated into all the manual arts then practiced by the farmer; I learned to use the axe and the saw, the hoe and the spade and the rake; the scythe and the plow and the grain cradle came into my hands as soon as I was strong enough to use them; before I was sixteen years of age I had learned to do all the kinds of work then practiced on the farm, and in most of them I was able to do a man's part. The labor was sometimes severe, but the outdoor life was, undoubtedly, the best possible regimen for me. When I was twelve or thirteen years of age a severe cold left some ominous symptoms of pulmonary injury, but the fresh-air cure was mine, without the formality of a prescription, and it did the business for me.

For schooling I had the advantages of the district school, which stood upon the corner of my uncle's farm, in which my father had once been a teacher and my mother a pupil. The building was a plain frame structure, into which fifty or sixty boys and girls were crowded during the winter term. All ages were represented in it: young men and women of eighteen or twenty and little children of five or six. In the first years of my attendance there were no classes, except in reading and spelling, because there was no uniformity of books; each pupil brought and studied the arithmetic or geography or grammar which had descended to him from his forbears; the people deemed themselves too poor to purchase new books for their children. The teacher came to each pupil's seat every day, and heard him recite what he had learned, giving him his lesson for the following day. Eager and ambitious pupils could go as fast as they chose; dull ones were not driven beyond their capacity. Like every other bad system, this had the advantages of its defects.

Our writing-books we constructed for ourselves, of foolscap paper folded once and stitched together, a sheet of brown paper being added for the cover. The schoolmaster "set the copy"; it was his handwriting that we were all required to imitate. One of the chief accomplishments of the "master" of the period was penmanship. Another was skill in pen-making, for steel pens had not appeared in that locality; the gray goose-quill was still the implement of letters, and the master, with his sharp penknife, was daily called to mend the pens of the writers.

I have described what was true of the first year or two of my pupilage in this country school; but some time in the late forties, my uncle, who was the school trustee, had the great good fortune to secure a teacher who had ideas about education, and who quickly succeeded in revolutionizing the methods of teaching. From this time forward this country district school offered advantages of no mean order. After my eighth summer my help was needed on the farm, and I was never able to attend the summer term, which was always taught by a woman. The winter term lasted never more than four months, beginning with November and ending with February; but in this limited time I was able to get, before the completion of my sixteenth year, a good training in arith-

FARM LIFE AND SCHOOL LIFE 29

metic (completing Thomson's Higher Arithmetic), an excellent knowledge of geography, a thorough drill in English grammar (we used Goold Brown's Elementary Grammar); a fair mastery of algebra, through quadratic equations, with daily practice in "intellectual algebra"; some insight into the elements of physics, as given in Parker's Natural Philosophy, and a delightful acquaintance with Mitchel's School Astronomy. Added to this was some weekly practice in declamation and in the writing of themes — "compositions," we called them. Most of this was gained in the last four or five winters. Up to my eleventh or twelfth year I had made very little progress. It would seem that my father had forced the season in my mental development, and the reaction came. I wanted to read all I could lay my hands on, but I could not apply my mind to study. But the teacher to whom I have referred, after some discouraging failures, succeeded in kindling my ambition. My debt to him is greater than I could ever hope to repay. His name was Horace Lee Andrews; he was a medical student, teaching winter schools to meet the expenses of his education; he graduated, later, in medicine, and practiced but a few years, dying very young. He might have been a good physician; he would certainly have been a great teacher. His power of arousing and inspiring students, of appealing to all that was best in them, of making fine ideals of conduct attractive to them, was quite exceptional. He found me a listless and lazy pupil; he left me with a zest for study and a firm purpose of self-improvement. It was a clear case of conversion; and when any one tells me that character cannot be changed through the operation of spiritual forces, I know better.

I am disposed to believe that this country district school, under the leadership of Horace Andrews and of one or two less notable successors, must have been of a better sort than the average of those days. What I have recorded concerning my own work before I was sixteen (and there were several boys and girls who did substantially the same work) may indicate that, with all our modern pedagogical methods, we are not getting ahead much faster than our fathers did. The output of our physical machinery has vastly increased production; our intellectual machinery has made no such astounding advances. It is even a question whether the progress of the more capable pupils is not often retarded by our highly graded educational machinery; whether there is not a tendency to level down to the dullest. If I had been compelled to travel at the gait of the modern school curriculum, my early education would have amounted to very little, and I never could have gone to college.

Life in this rural district was, for the most part, strenuous and toilsome; there were not many idlers, and no paupers. Some there were who would have been ready enough to live upon the labor of their neighbors, but they were not allowed to do it; their true condition and needs were too well known to permit them to impose upon us. The "ne'er-do-wells" never stay in the country; they always move to the city. It always amuses me to hear charitable people exhorting persons of this class to move into the country. For the industrious poor it

FARM LIFE AND SCHOOL LIFE 31

may be good counsel, but not for those whose occupation is looking for work. The country is the last place in the world for them.

We had our diversions and festivities. The Little Nanticoke, in those days, was well stocked with fish, and sometimes a "stent" — that was what we called it — could be worked off in time for an hour or two of fishing in the early evening. After the harvest we had our berrying parties, and sometimes, in the autumn, our husking bees and apple-paring bees. Spelling-matches between adjoining districts were not uncommon. I remember very well one evening when we went over to the "river district," a mile away, for a bout with the boys and girls of that neighborhood. I distinctly recall the stalwart figure of the "master" of that school, standing in the middle of the room with a spelling-book in one hand and a tallow dip in the other, and gallantly leading his host to ignominious defeat. "Frank" Tracy we called him then; he has since been Secretary of the Navy.

Once, in the last winter of my residence in this district, our school contests rose to the dignity of a debate. It was the early winter of 1852, and the reverberations of the great discussion in Congress over the compromise measures of 1850 were still sounding in our ears. That debate had made upon my own mind a deep impression. The New York "Weekly Tribune" gave us fair reports of it; but some one told me that the members of Congress would send me their speeches, and a few letters to Washington brought from Seward and Wade and Hale and Giddings and others copies of their speeches, which

I read and studied with the deepest interest. The great speeches of Clay and Webster and Benton were well reported in the newspapers. When, therefore, a debate on the repeal of the Fugitive Slave Law was proposed and I was asked to lead the affirmative, with the "master" as the leader on the other side, I was quite ready for the fray. I suppose that I was as keenly alive to the importance of that contest, in a little country schoolhouse, as college men have sometimes been over a 'varsity rowing-match or a football fight. At any rate, I went into training for it. Every morning, for three or four weeks, I was up as early as four o'clock, digging into the Constitution of the United States, conning the undesirable statute, section by section, getting all the light I could from every quarter. The fact that my side won the debate did not signify much; a more important fact, to me, was that I had taken a strenuous lesson in forensics, the value of which I never forgot.

If I have left to the last the religious phases of my life upon the farm, it is not because they were to me the least significant portions of my experience. Indeed, I am sure that while nobody who knew me suspected it, the one deepest interest of my life through all that period was religion. I was keenly alive to all the good things of this world; I had a boy's appetite and a boy's love of play, and a boy's craving for companionship; but underneath it all was an increasing craving for that spiritual experience of which I heard others testifying, and which I believed to be the supreme good. My early childhood had been bathed in an atmosphere of piety; every memory of my father wore the halo of sainthood;

FARM LIFE AND SCHOOL LIFE 33

and in my uncle's household religion was a vital element. It was never thrust upon me; my personality was respected, perhaps, too carefully; but it was commended to me in conduct whose sincerity I never could question.

Nor was there any lack of church privilege. We lived three miles from the village, yet I dare say that no family connected with the Presbyterian church in Owego was in its pew as many Sundays of the year as ours. Rain, snow, mud, were no hindrances; we went to church as regularly as we went to dinner. The lumber farm-wagon carried us for several years; rough boards laid across the box, and cushioned with horse-blankets, furnished our chariot. Later, we attained to the luxury of a spring wagon. There were two Sunday services, separated by a recess of an hour and a half, during which the Sunday-school held its session. This gave us a little nooning for the luncheon which we brought from home, and for an enlivening stroll, in the pleasant weather, through the adjoining graveyard. I could have passed an examination, *magna cum laude*, on those epitaphs.

I will not deny that those sermons were often a weariness of the flesh. A keen theological argument would have been interesting, but it was largely a restatement of platitudes; it hardly ever touched life in the remotest way. Now and then a preacher came along whose enthusiasm kindled me; there was a man from Binghamton, a pale and slender young preacher, by the name of Humphrey, whose occasional appearance in our pulpit was a refreshment; I would have walked the three miles, on the stormiest day, to hear him. But, as a rule, the tax upon the attention of a growing boy was rather exorbitant; need enough was there of the delectable dill and the consoling caraway, on which we were wont to nibble, to keep ourselves awake.

There was always the possibility, too, of something really rewarding. The choir, in that village church, was better than the ordinary run of village choirs; there was one soprano voice of great beauty, and the little chorus was intelligently led; so that when, at the close of the sermon, the minister sometimes said, "The choir will close with a piece of their own selection," boys who had been nodding began to sit up and listen. I suppose that I shall never hear any music which will touch me quite as deeply as some of those old anthems did: "How Lovely is Zion!" "By the Rivers of Babylon," "When the Worn Spirit wants Repose." I have n't the least idea who wrote them; I have never seen the music, but the melodies haunt me yet.

There were other churches in the village, but they had no more dealings with one another than the Jews had with the Samaritans. Sectarian jealousies were fierce; ministers of the different churches were hardly on speaking terms; an exchange of pulpits was a thing never heard of. While, therefore, I had as large an experience of church-going in my boyhood as most boys can recall, I cannot lay my hand on my heart and say that the church-going helped me to solve my religious problems. In fact, it made those problems more and more tangled and troublesome. I wanted to find my way into the peace of God, into the assurance of his friendship, and that I could not do. I understood that I, with all the

FARM LIFE AND SCHOOL LIFE 35

rest of mankind, had "by the fall lost communion with God and was under his wrath and curse, and so made liable to all the miseries of this life, to death itself and the pains of hell forever." Of the exact truth of this statement I had not the shadow of doubt. But I understood that there was a way by which I could escape from this curse and regain this lost communion. That was the one thing, above all others, that I wanted. I would gladly have exchanged for it not only every sinful pleasure, but all the pleasures that were not sinful. It will hardly be credited to-day, but I felt that being a Christian would mean, for me, giving up all my boyish sports, — ball-playing, coasting, fishing; and I was more than ready to make that sacrifice. So I kept trying, for years, to gain that assurance of the favor of God of which I heard people talking, and which, I felt sure, some of them must possess. I listened, in prayer meeting and revival meeting, to what they said about it; I noted with the greatest care the steps that must be taken, and I tried to do just what I was told to do. I was to "give myself away," in a serious and complete self-dedication. I suppose that I shall be far within the truth if I say that I tried to do that, a thousand times. But I understood that when I had done it, properly, I should have an immediate knowledge of the fact that it had been properly done; some evidence in my consciousness that could not be mistaken; that a light would break in, or a burden roll off, or that some other emotional or ecstatic experience would supervene; and when nothing of the kind occurred, the inevitable conclusion was that my effort had been fruitless; that I had failed to commend myself to the favor of God, and was still under his wrath and curse. It is not a good thing for any well-meaning soul to be left in that predicament. To feel that, in spite of your best endeavors, you are an alien and an outcast from the family of God is not encouraging to virtue; it tends to carelessness and irreverence. I have often wondered, in later years, that my faith did not give way; that I did not become an atheist. It was the memory of my father, and the consistent piety of my uncle, I suppose, which made that impossible. But that little unplastered room under the rafters in the old farmhouse, where I lay so many nights, when the house was still, looking out through the casement upon the unpitying stars, has a story to tell of a soul in great perplexity and trouble because it could not find God.

All this time I was studying the Bible diligently. We read the whole book through, chapter by chapter, at family worship four or five times while I was living on the farm, and the reading was not wearisome to me. Once we waded through the whole list of names in the Chronicles; for what reason I am not clear, unless it may have been that of a genial friend of mine who once confessed to me that he had read them all, because, he said, "It occurred to me that I might meet one of those old chaps in heaven some day, and it would be embarrassing to have to own that I had never heard of him."

Besides the daily Bible reading, my Biblical education was well advanced by the memorizing, as Sunday-school lessons, of all the historical portions of the New Testament, and many of the Bible stories of the Old Testament. And that nothing might be wanting to my

FARM LIFE AND SCHOOL LIFE 37

theological outfit, I committed to memory also the whole of the Shorter Catechism of the Westminster divines.

It would be difficult to convey to most of those who will read these pages any adequate sense of the positiveness with which those doctrines were held in the circle in which my life was spent. We did not admit to ourselves the possibility of any error in their statement, and we guarded ourselves carefully against any influences which would tend to weaken our hold upon them. Alien from the commonwealth of the true Israel as I believed myself to be, I still held fast to the orthodox creed, and regarded with keen disapprobation any one who challenged it. A preacher of the Universalist sect made his appearance in our neighborhood, and two or three families became known as his followers; we tried to keep treating them neighborly, but it went hard to do it; we felt that a great gulf had been fixed between us and them. There was a funeral in one of these families, and the young Universalist minister came to preach the funeral sermon; we attended the funeral, but we remained outside the house, that we might not hear the dangerous doctrine. Shortly after this we began afresh the reading, by course, of the New Testament at family worship; and I followed the reading, pencil in hand, through the entire New Testament, marking the texts which in my judgment contradicted the Universalist doctrine.

I am careful to relate these circumstances because I wish to make it clear that my difficulty in finding the solution of my problem of personal religion was not due to any heretical tendencies. In fact, it was due partly to the rigidity with which I held the traditional beliefs, and partly to the misleading notion that no one could have any assurance of the divine favor which was not signalized by some marked and easily recognizable emotional experience. It was not until my eighteenth year that a clear-headed minister lifted me out of this pit, and made me see that it was perfectly safe to trust the Heavenly Father's love for me and walk straight on in the ways of service, waiting for no raptures, but doing his will as best I knew it, and confiding in his friendship.

I have told this history because it helps to illustrate the changes which have taken place within the last sixty years in our conceptions of what is essential in religious experience. Such hopeless endeavors to find peace in believing were by no means rare in my younger days. When my ministry began I found scores of men and women who were living blameless lives, and wanted to be the friends of God, but who had given it up as an impossibility. They had tried, over and over, and had always failed, and they knew that this felicity was not for them. It has been a good part of my work as a Christian teacher to get people out of that slough of despond; and those who have read the little book entitled "Being a Christian: What it Means and How to Begin" will find in these pages the reason why it was written. I sometimes hear people desiderating the type of religious experience which was common in former days. It was more intense, more fervid, more self-centred; but on the whole, I do not think that we should wisely seek to

FARM LIFE AND SCHOOL LIFE 39

restore it. It cannot be good for any human soul to be required or permitted to maintain the attitude before the Being whom he calls God and worships, which was the only possible attitude for me for ten years of my life. And one who has come to believe that religion is summed up in the word Friendship — that it is just being friends with the Father above and the brother by our side — often looks back with a pang to the time when such a conception, if it could have reached him, would have lifted a great load from his heart and filled the world with beauty.

CHAPTER III

VILLAGE LIFE AND APPRENTICESHIP

Beneath the shadow of dawn's aerial cope,
  With eyes enkindled as the sun's own sphere,
  Hope from the front of youth in godlike cheer
Looks Godward, past the shades where blind men grope
Round the dark door that prayers nor dreams can ope,
  And makes for joy the very darkness dear
  That gives her wide wings play; nor dreams that fear
At noon may rise and pierce the heart of hope.
                    Algernon Charles Swinburne.

I HAVE explained that the farm was to have been my home until my majority. For the fact that it was not so, my uncle was mainly responsible. It was he who had kindled in me other ambitions. By the time I was sixteen years of age he became convinced that my aptitudes were leading me in other directions, and it was his own proposition that I seek for work in which they could find development. My judgment welcomed his counsel, but my heart shrank from it; I could not easily turn my back upon a home which, with all its hardships, had been very dear. Nor had I any definite plans of study: I had dreamed of the law; and I tried to find a place in a lawyer's office where I might support myself by copying and have time for reading, but no such opening could be found. Finally, one day, my uncle returned from the village with the tidings that the editor and publisher of the Owego "Gazette" wanted a boy, and that I could

VILLAGE LIFE AND APPRENTICESHIP 41

find occupation there. I sought that place, and was soon installed as a printer's apprentice.

It was a heavy heart that I carried away from the farmhouse, with the little trunk that held my few belongings, and the unpainted writing-desk which, on rainy days, I had constructed with my own hands. The homely picture, "Breaking Home Ties," which touched so many hearts at the Chicago Exposition, tells a story which has often been repeated.

My new home was to be with my employer, the editor and owner of the local Democratic journal, and a politician of considerable influence in his party. One window, with three small panes of glass, under the eaves, furnished all the light for my little bedroom; but I had the freedom of the kitchen, and a place at the family table. The term of my apprenticeship was to be four years, and my compensation for the successive years, in addition to my board and washing, was to be thirty, forty, sixty, and one hundred dollars. This was to suffice for clothing and for spending-money.

The removal from the comparative solitude of the farm to the bustle and stir of a smart county seat, with five or six thousand inhabitants, was an event of much significance in my life. Owego had been known to me for a decade, and I did not feel myself a stranger, but there was something very stimulating to the mind of the boy in this new contact with the life of the world.

It is easier for me than for most of my fellow citizens to reproduce the scenes of my youth; for this old home of mine has changed less, during the past sixty years, than most American towns. Owego was a beautiful village in my boyhood; it is fresher and fairer now than it was then, but it is no larger. It has kept its old features and its old character; it is quite conscious of its loveliness, but it is not ambitious to become a metropolis; it sits there, demurely, on the banks of the most beautiful river in the world, and rejoices in the strength of its guarding hills and the peace of its slumbering meadows. The clatter and rush of New York and Chicago seem very far away, and there are few communities of equal population in which the pleasures of the simple life are more accessible.

In my boyhood Owego was sometimes shyly advertised as a haunt of the muses. N. P. Willis had his home there, — Glenmary; it was a rustic cottage embowered in trees, just outside the village; near his door was the bridge over a ravine which gave title to his "Letters from under a Bridge." One or two members of the sometime famous artist family of Thompson also lived and painted there; the Susquehanna furnished them some charming landscapes. A little coterie of young men were practicing with their pens; sketches, poems, stories in the local papers, and elsewhere, were much talked about; there was quite a cult of Indian tradition. All this was highly exciting to a youth whose fingers had begun to tingle with the *pruritus scribendi*. So I took up my work in the printing-office with something other than the handicraft in sight. Perhaps Benjamin Franklin's gateway into letters was the best one open to me.

It was not, however, to literature that I was now apprenticed, but to a manual trade which gave me plenty of drudgery, and left in me, when the day's task was

VILLAGE LIFE AND APPRENTICESHIP 43

done, small impulse to woo the muses. The last comer in the printing-office had all the menial work to do, and there was enough of it. We had no power press; cards and circulars, as well as posters and newspapers, were all worked off on an old-fashioned Washington handpress; and a large part of every day was apt to be spent in the occupation of the roller-boy. Furnishing the fires, sweeping the office, cleaning the forms of type, and running on errands gave me exercise enough. But I was also furnished with a "stick" and a "rule" and given a chance to "work at the case," and this business of type composition and distribution speedily became interesting to me. It was manual labor, but it was manual labor "affected," as the jurists say, with an intellectual quality, or interest, as no other work had been to which I had set my hands. The study of language had always had a fascination for me, and we were dealing here with the physical framework of language, and all the technique of the types was significant. The artistic side of the work also attracted me; I liked to experiment with display type, and to study pleasing effects in cards and title-pages and advertisements.

A country printing-office, in the middle of the nineteenth century, offered a large opportunity for the study of human nature. The doings and the misdoings of the community were reported in it; it was the clearing-house of political and social gossip; it was the rendezvous of local politicians; and a large share of the subscribers, from town and country, dropped in to pay their subscriptions and have a chat with the editor or his assistant. All kinds of causes sought the advocacy of the paper; all sorts of cranks demanded a hearing; advice of every description was sought and volunteered, and personal grievances and bereavements were always knocking for admission to its columns. There were few phases of life or types of character with which the country newspaper did not come in contact. If any one wishes to know what manner of life it was, let him read Mr. Howells's delightful sketch of his own experience in his father's office, in Jefferson, Ohio. The years of his apprenticeship were the very years when I was learning my trade in Owego; the two communities were much alike, and the story, as he tells it, brought vividly home to me all the phases of my life as a printer's boy.

It was not many months after my entrance upon this novitiate that I ventured, one day, to leave upon the editor's table a more or less connected mélange of local news and hits and comments, a column or more in length. In a few minutes he brought it out to me, and bade me put it in type. From that time onward I was encouraged to use my pen whenever I preferred that to the composing-stick, and a considerable portion of the local work fell into my hands.

I have spoken of politics as one of the chief interests of the newspaper office, but the politics of that period were not of an inspiring sort. The political prejudice which I had inherited was for the Whig Party, and when my uncle left me in the sanctum of the Democratic editor he said to him, "You'll never make a Democrat of him." But there was not, in those days, in either party much to inspire the enthusiasm of a young idealist. When I entered the office the campaign of 1852 was

VILLAGE LIFE AND APPRENTICESHIP 45

drawing to its close; and it is doubtful whether a less vital issue has ever divided political parties in this country than that over which the followers of Franklin Pierce and General Winfield Scott were divided. The compromise measures of 1850 were supposed to have settled the slavery question for all time, and both of the old parties, eager to hold on to their southern constituencies, were emphasizing their loyalty to the terms of that settlement. Both of them were exhausting their rhetoric in their asseverations that what had been done in that compromise could never, no never, be undone. And both of them took pains to specify the Fugitive Slave Law as one of the terms of that compact which must not be disturbed.

But this was just where the shoe was pinching. It had gone hard with many of the northern people to consent to that provision; not a few of the more intelligent and enterprising slaves had escaped from their masters, and were living inoffensive and industrious lives in northern communities; most of their neighbors were glad that they had got away, and were in no mood to help in sending them back. The agitation of the abolitionists, the discussions provoked by the compromise measures themselves, above all, the powerful arraignment of the system in "Uncle Tom's Cabin," had kindled in the minds of the people of the North a strong sense of the essential wrong of slavery; and most of them revolted at the thought of rebinding its chains on any who had broken them. The law which commanded them to assist in this business, and made it a crime for them to refuse, was a law for which they could have no respect. Most of them felt that because it was the law of the land they must not resist it, but obey it they would not; they would honor it by suffering its penalty.

Certainly it was dubious policy for the slave-owners to press the enforcement of a law like this upon the people of the North; they would have consulted their own interest if they had forborne to exact the pound of flesh which the contract awarded them. But there had been, in many sections, aggravating and heart-rending instances of the enforcement of this law; and the conscience of the North was beginning to testify impatiently against it.

When, therefore, the two great parties, ignoring this uprising of the moral sense of the nation, competed with each other for the southern vote, by insisting, in their platforms, that the Fugitive Slave Law must be enforced, there were not a few who were ready to cry, "A plague o' both your houses," and to demand some new alignments of the political forces to meet the new issues.

It is interesting now to recall the growth of the anti-slavery sentiment. The rapidity of this movement was something phenomenal. I am sure that nobody thought so then; we all felt that the mills of the gods were grinding as slowly as is their wont; we were often crying out, "How long, O Lord, how long!" But we can see now, when we look back and count the years, that opinion was moving forward at a prodigious speed.

When the second half of the nineteenth century began, the anti-slavery sentiment of the country was almost a negligible quantity. It was only a year or two before this that the young minister of our Presbyterian

VILLAGE LIFE AND APPRENTICESHIP 47

church ventured, one day, to pray that we might "remember our brethren in bonds, as bound with them." I well recollect how the faces of some of the elders, standing in prayer time, grew red as they listened to the petition. It looked as though he must be an abolitionist. Called to account, he failed to clear himself of the imputation, and he had to go. We wanted no such incendiary praying as that in our pulpit. That was a fair sample of the ruling sentiment of the most respectable classes of the North as late as 1850. Abolitionists were a kind of vermin. The slaves were better off where they were. Were they not fulfilling the divine decree? How about Canaan? Were not the negroes his descendants, and had it not been said of him, "A servant of servants he shall be unto his brethren"? And what would become of them if they were set free? Did we want them overrunning the North? This was the moral plane on which the thoughts of most of us were ranging through the second quarter of the nineteenth century. But before we were aware of it, a new feeling had begun to pervade the community. It came, as the spring comes in the high latitudes, almost without premonition. In the midst of this languid campaign of 1852, the conviction was deepening that slavery had got both of the great parties manacled and muzzled, and that the time had come to put an end to slavery. But consider that it was only eight years after this that Abraham Lincoln was elected, on a platform which promised that there should be no more slave states. Can any one estimate the distance which public opinion traveled between 1852 and 1860? The psychological change in the mind of the nation is something prodigious. When one recalls the sentiments and judgments which were finding expression in the press and the pulpit and in private conversation in the campaign of 1852, and compares them with the utterances which had come to be habitual in the autumn of 1860, he gets a startling impression of the possibility of change in a democracy. One who has lived through such a renaissance as that is prepared to believe that while "the good can well afford to wait," it is not always doomed to long delay. There are days when "the dawn comes up like thunder."

What set the car of progress spinning "down the ringing grooves of change" was the repeal, in 1854, of the Missouri Compromise. It was the astute and masterful Douglas who was responsible for that. He wanted to be President, and it was plain that since the South was in the saddle, his only hope of gratifying his ambition was to make himself very serviceable to the South. The bill admitting Missouri to the Union as a slave state had expressly provided that slavery should be forever excluded from the territory west of Missouri and north of the parallel which constituted its southern boundary. That was a solemn compact. Mr. Douglas's proposition to repeal it, and permit the people of those territories to establish slavery in them, if they chose to do so, was a most flagrant repudiation of a pledge which ought to have been held sacred. As President Woodrow Wilson, himself a southern man, has testified: "The healing work of two generations of statesmen was destroyed at a stroke. . . . It was, in fact, matter of revolution."

If, at this distance, such seems to a southern historian

VILLAGE LIFE AND APPRENTICESHIP 49

to have been the nature of this transaction, it can hardly be wondered at that the indignation of the North was kindled by it. At any rate, the North was up in arms. The temper of the time is well reflected in an editorial which appeared in the Springfield (Massachusetts) "Republican," on February 8, 1854. The "Republican" had supported the Compromise of 1850, and had sharply reproved the popular uprisings by which the Fugitive Slave Law was set at naught. "The North," said this witness, "had acquiesced in these compromises; it sustained them and abided by them. But the South and its northern political allies have broken the peace of the country. They make fresh and monstrous demands. These demands will arouse the whole nation; they will widen and deepen the anti-slavery feeling of the country as no other conceivable proposition could. The signs are unmistakable. No mere party or faction will array itself against the Nebraska scheme. The whole people are against it. The moral force of the North, the influence, the learning, the wealth, and the votes of the North are against it, and will make themselves effectively heard, ere the agitation, now reopened by the insanity of the slave-holding interest, and in behalf of the schemes of ambitious partisans, shall have ceased. *The South and its allies have sown the wind, — will they not reap the whirlwind?*"

We were not, even in Owego, so far from the madding crowd that its tumult did not reach our ears. Our own representative in Congress voted for the Nebraska Bill. A protest was served on him, but he ignored it and followed his party leader. The popular wrath broke out in an indignation meeting, at which "Frank" Tracy, erstwhile the schoolmaster of the "river district," but now a promising young lawyer in the village, made one of the principal speeches, urging that the time had come for the formation of a new party to resist the extension of slavery. I reported that meeting for the "Gazette," and I fear that the report was somewhat irreverent. For reform, in its incipient stages, is wont to bring together a fine assortment of people with wheels in their heads, and this assembly had its humorous aspects. But it was a very serious purpose, after all, that found expression in it; the conflagration which Mr. Douglas had kindled on the prairies of Kansas was sweeping over the land.

Political issues, however, about this time, fell into a very complicated condition. Reform was the word of the hour, but reform had many irons in the fire. The temperance issue had invaded politics. Maine had enacted her prohibitory law in 1851, and Vermont and Massachusetts had followed her lead in 1852; New York was getting ready to repeat the experiment. In the summer of 1852, before I left the farm, my uncle and I came to the village one day to hear a rousing speech by Neal Dow on the public square. His fluent and fervid rhetoric and his impassioned appeal made a strong impression on my mind. No prohibition party had been organized in New York, but the champions of prohibition were learning to act together; they often held the balance of power, and used it effectively in procuring nominations and carrying elections. The order of Good Templars had sprung into existence in central New York and was spreading rapidly; soon after my eighteenth birthday I

VILLAGE LIFE AND APPRENTICESHIP 51

became a member of the local lodge and was made secretary, conducting the correspondence with other lodges of the country, by means of which we joined our forces for the fall campaign of 1854. Our candidate for the legislature was elected, and he voted, the next winter, for the prohibitory law which, for a year or more, had a name to live on the New York statute-book.

Thus began, at an early day, my apprenticeship to practical politics. There was keen satisfaction in playing the game; it was good to be in it, and to know that you were helping to bring things to pass. I have not forgotten the gratification I felt when, at two or three o'clock of the morning after election, after a ride of twenty-four miles through the rain and mud in a doctor's sulky, I was able to hand to "Frank" Tracy the returns from the most distant townships by which his election as district attorney was assured. It seems almost incredible now that so large a hand could have been taken in politics by a boy so much under his majority. It is a slight indication of one change which has taken place in social conditions. Boys were in the habit of doing many things fifty or sixty years ago which they would hardly be expected to do to-day. I am sure, however, that I suffered no injury whatever from my contact with politics at this callow age. Nothing dishonorable was required of me; there were no signs of bribery or corruption; for the political work which I did I never received a penny, nor dreamed of such a thing. It must have taken very little money in those days to carry elections. Tioga County, New York, has since been supposed to be one of the centres of dubious politics, but it was clean enough in those old times.

52   RECOLLECTIONS

Further to complicate the political situation, there entered, about this time, the agitation against citizens of foreign birth. The Irish famine, and the unsuccessful revolutionary movements of 1848 upon the European continent, had greatly stimulated immigration to the United States; and many Americans had begun to feel alarm respecting the possible encroachments of foreign ideas and influences. This fear had long been simmering; it came to a boil in the organization, about 1852, of an oath-bound secret order, popularly described as Know-Nothings, whose purpose was the exclusion from citizenship and from political office of all persons born outside the United States. The antipathies appealed to were partly racial and partly religious. With some the fact of foreign birth was the reason for ostracism; with others the attachment to the Roman Catholic Church was the ground of condemnation. Indeed, the crusade divided on this issue. Another order appeared whose votaries were called Know-Somethings; the difference between the two being that the Know-Somethings proposed to disfranchise all Roman Catholics, no matter where born; and the Know-Nothings to disqualify all those of foreign birth, no matter of what religion. The Know-Somethings gained but a small following; but the Know-Nothings, in a year or two, overran the land. "In the autumn of 1854," says Woodrow Wilson, "they elected their candidates for the governorship in Massachusetts and Delaware, and put close upon a hundred members into the Federal House of Representatives. In the autumn of 1855, they carried New Hampshire, Massachusetts, Rhode Island, Connecticut, New York,

VILLAGE LIFE AND APPRENTICESHIP 53

Kentucky, and California, and fell but a little short of majority in six of the southern states." [1]

There is not much to flatter our national self-complacency in the contemplation of such an episode as this in our history. Prejudices so rank and noxious ought not to grow upon American soil. Even if the suspicions on which they were based were justified, it ought to be evident to those who have breathed this free air all their lives that the methods of secrecy are not the methods by which liberty may best be safeguarded. I very well remember the feeling of the atmosphere created by this clandestine propaganda; it was sultry and fetid with distrust and resentment; it was distinctly anti-social. No one knew what plots against his freedom might be hid in the breast of any neighbor whom he might meet. Such a state of things is simply intolerable. Liberty would stifle in an air like that. Whatever may be said of secrecy in relations which are purely fraternal or social, there is no room for it in political or civil affairs. Here everything must be out in the open. No man has any right to be plotting public policies which are to be carried by concealment and stealth; for such policies affect the interests of all his neighbors, and they have a right to know all about them. Secret political orders in a free country can never be anything but a curse. It is the first duty of every patriotic citizen to denounce and oppose them, no matter at what cost to himself.

It is not altogether cheering to reflect that in a country which boasts of universal education, this elementary principle should have been so feebly grasped; that there

[1] *History of the American People*, ii, 171.

could be in Congress a hundred representatives who had been chosen by dark-lantern methods, and who were pledged to the disfranchisement of all such men as Carl Schurz and John Ireland.

What gave free course to this epidemic, at this time, was, undoubtedly, the political disintegration which followed the election of Pierce in 1852. The Whig Party was done for, there was no doubt of that; and the repeal of the Missouri Compromise was forcing a new combination of the elements. The logical outcome was foreshadowed by the Free Soil Party, which had had its candidates in the field for the last two campaigns; but the leaders were reluctant to take that plunge. While they stood shivering on the brink, this wave of nativism swept over the country. But there was, of course, no future for an organization whose strength was in its antipathies and whose ways were subterranean. As Mr. Greeley shrewdly said, it held about as much promise of permanence as an anti-cholera or an anti-potato-rot association. The Know-Nothings were very confident, in 1855, that they would elect the next President; in fact, they carried the State of Maryland, and had eight votes in the electoral college. It is not comforting to remember that the American people harbored such a conspiracy as this, even for a brief space; but it is reassuring to recall the promptness and decisiveness of the judgment by which they put it out of existence. It would have been well if they had made an end of it then, but that kind of bigotry has as many lives as a cat, and we shall meet it again before the end of our story.

CHAPTER IV

THE CHOICE OF A CALLING

Not to fawn on wealth and state,
Leaving Lazarus at the gate;
Not to peddle creeds like wares;
Not to mutter hireling prayers;

Nor to paint the new life's bliss
On the sable ground of this;
Golden streets for idle knave,
Sabbath rest for weary slave!

Not for words and works like these,
Priest of God, thy mission is;
But to make earth's desert glad
In its Eden greenness clad;

And to level manhood bring
Lord and peasant, serf and king;
And the Christ of God to find
In the humblest of thy kind!
John Greenleaf Whittier.

IT would not be fair to myself to permit the impression that the period of my newspaper apprenticeship was devoted wholly to politics. Other interests claimed a large share of my attention. I must confess that during the first new months of my residence in the village I spent a good many of my Sundays elsewhere than in church. I cannot say that this was a reaction against the compulsion of earlier years, for there had been no compulsion; if there had been pressure upon my life, it had been as unobtrusive and inevitable as the pressure of the atmosphere; I had gone to church without questioning. But when the influence was removed, I found my own inclination hardly sufficient to move myself in that direction. In fact, my garments were a little shabby; that excuse was sufficient for some weeks, and when it was no longer serviceable I had already formed the habit of staying away from church; and such a habit, as I discovered, is easier formed than broken. With the strict notions about the use of Sunday in which I had been reared, I could never have devoted the day to ordinary pleasure-seeking; I usually spent it in the printing-office, reading and writing; often promising myself that I would resume the church-going habit, but easily finding reason for delay as the Sundays came round.

That brief experience has thrown some light for me on the question of church neglect. We are all creatures of habit; church-going and staying at home are largely matters of habit. It would have been easy enough to attribute my absence from church to intellectual or theological or social causes; in fact, it was due to inertia. And it is safe to conclude that a large share of the church neglect for which earnest men in these days are trying to account is chargeable to indolence rather than to unbelief.

The voice that called me back to my accustomed ways was that of an evangelist, somewhat famous in those times, the Reverend Jedediah Burchard, D. D., who was conducting a series of services in the Congregational church. Dr. Burchard was a man of keen intellect and vivid imagination; his theology was a mild Calvinism,

THE CHOICE OF A CALLING 57

but his notion of Christian experience was simple and sensible; and he cleared away, with a breath, the fogs which had so long been obscuring the way of discipleship. I connected myself at once with the church, and found myself deeply enlisted in its work. As the months went by these interests laid stronger hold upon me, and gradually brought me to reconsider my plans of life. In the early months of 1855, a way was unexpectedly opened to me to begin my preparation for college, and after teaching a brief term in a country school, I found myself, in April of that year, in the Owego Academy with my face set toward the work of the Christian ministry.

Church life, in the middle of the last century, was much less highly developed than it is to-day. The activities of the church were summed up in the two Sunday preaching services, the Sunday-school, and the midweek prayer-meeting. Social meetings were rare, the young people were not organized, an occasional sewing-society or mothers' meeting sufficed to express the religious zeal of the women. Worship, in the non-Episcopal churches, was the reverse of ornate. Usually the hymns were sung by a mixed choir, and the people took no part in the singing; there were no hymn-books with tunes; the choir was provided with tune-books, of which "The Dulcimer," "The Shawm," and "Carmina Sacra" are well remembered. Sometimes the key was found by the chorister's tuning-fork, and the hymns were sung without accompaniment; generally, however, a small melodeon sustained the voices. Here and there was a pipe organ. The more ambitious choirs ventured, occasionally, upon an anthem. Of course all this service was voluntary.

The preaching was, for the most part, theological, and it was often controversial. The Calvinistic doctrines were much debated, the Presbyterians and the Baptists affirming, and the Methodists denying. The doctrine of predestination was, of course, the one around which the contention raged most hotly; but the fatalistic inferences drawn from it were warmly repudiated by the New School Calvinists. Indeed, there were many, even then, in the Calvinistic churches, who were inclined to say with Mr. Beecher, "The elect are whosoever will, and the non-elect are whosoever won't."

Baptism was also, in our neighborhood, a frequent theme of controversy. The Baptists were very enterprising evangelists, and they pushed their distinctive plea with relentless logic, and enforced it by immersing scores of candidates, every winter, in openings cut through the ice of the river.

The preaching, in all the churches, when it was not controversial, was almost wholly evangelistic. The conversion of sinners was supposed to be the preacher's main business. Respecting the eternal punishment of those who die impenitent, and the impossibility of repentance beyond the grave, there was no difference of opinion among evangelical Christians, and the immense importance of saving men from this fate overshadowed all other interests. The appeal was, therefore, almost wholly individualistic. It constantly directed the thoughts of men to the consideration of their own personal welfare. The motive of fear was the leading

THE CHOICE OF A CALLING

motive, but the bliss of the heavenly life was also vividly portrayed. That hell was a veritable lake of fire and brimstone was hardly questioned by any one. My memory holds many such representations. I was accustomed to hear, in my boyhood, the famous Jacob Knapp, one of the most popular evangelists of the central states; and I shall never forget some of his descriptions of the burning pit, with the sinners trying to crawl up its sides out of the flames, while the devils, with pitchforks, stood by to fling them back again. It was intended, of course, to frighten sinners; probably it had that effect on many, but I wonder whether it was, on the whole, even then, as telling as it was supposed to be. For myself, though a small boy, I distinctly remember that it made me angry.

Not many of the preachers of that time indulged in the sensational savagery of Elder Knapp; but the terrors of the future were steadily held before our minds. That fear was always haunting me in my childhood; my most horrible dreams were of that place of torment.

The expectation of the destruction of the world by fire was another nightmare. The Millerite horror was hanging over us in my earliest days; I remember well a lecture, in the Baptist church, when I was only seven years old, in which the lecturer, with figures drawn from the prophecy of Daniel, proved with chalk upon a blackboard that the world was going to be burned up in 1843. I could add up those figures for myself; there they were in black and white, and the correct sum was 1843. Was it not a demonstration? There was a blazing comet, too, in the sky that winter, — "wonders in the heaven above, and signs on the earth beneath," the preacher said; and I could see the comet, through my window, every night. I shall not be blamed for hiding my head under the coverlet, from the terrible portent.

When the last days of 1843 had passed, and the sun was bright on the New Year's morning of 1844, I was delivered from a great horror, but the peril was only postponed, for it was admitted by all that that catastrophe was inevitable, and that probably the day was not distant. My greatest relief came from a conclusion reached in a conversation of men standing about the well one hot summer day. They were seriously pondering the discredited prediction of Miller; they agreed that while he had missed in his calculation, the conflagration was coming; and they were inclined to accept a statement which one of them had seen, that it was likely to take place about 1860. That lifted a load from my heart. If the disaster was to be deferred to such a remote futurity, — if the world had a good seventeen years yet to endure, — there was no need of worrying. I went back to my play.

Still, the dates were all uncertain, and with such a peril impending one could not always resist the onset of sudden fears. Any unusual appearance in the sky was likely to quicken the pulse. I remember one October day, five or six years later, when the haze grew dense and yellow, and the air was filled with the odor of smoke, and there were lurid spots in the sky. I was working alone in a back lot, and fear took possession of me; I thought that the Great Day had come.

I do not think that subjective conditions such as I

THE CHOICE OF A CALLING 61

have described were rare in those days; they were the natural product of the prevailing teaching. The business of religion was to fill the hearts of men with fear. The fear was a personal fear; it concentrated the thoughts of men on their own danger, and their own safety. It cannot be argued that this is the normal regimen of the human soul. If force and fear are moral motives, they are certainly among the lowest moral motives; the conduct which they inspire must be an inferior kind of conduct. And it must be admitted that the aspects of religion which were most commonly presented to men from the pulpit in those days were not such as tended to develop an altruistic habit.

This is not saying that all religious people were egoists. Far from it. Though the motive which was most often addressed in leading men into the religious life was the motive of self-interest, when they were brought into the Christian life they were required to put themselves under the tuition and leadership of Jesus Christ. That was the meaning of discipleship. And if, through the four Gospels, they made themselves acquainted with him, — if they took his yoke upon them and learned of him, — they would soon find themselves under the sway of very different motives from those which first turned them toward discipleship. So it is true that the religion of the Christian church has always been immeasurably more Christian than its theology. Christ is a Saviour in more senses than one; he has always been saving his own church from the blighting consequences of a bad theology, and helping his disciples to be a great deal better people than, by their own theories, they would or could have been.

I have been speaking of the conceptions and tendencies which were prevailing in the Protestant churches of this country up to the time when my mind was turned to the Christian ministry. But I ought to explain that, about this time, some very marked signs were appearing of a different temper and tendency. The interest which the churches were taking in the temperance reform and the anti-slavery reform was an indication of a new spirit. The ethical and altruistic note was being struck now, in many pulpits, with clearness and vigor. That mighty change, of which I have spoken, which passed upon the popular mind in the sixth decade of the nineteenth century, was felt in the churches as deeply as anywhere else. By the middle of that decade it was finding voice everywhere. Some churches responded to this influence more promptly than others. The Episcopalians and the Presbyterians, always conservative, were slower to answer to it. The Baptists in our neighborhood were most hospitable to the new humanitarian impulse; I heard Gerrit Smith speak more than once from their pulpit, and they welcomed colored preachers and lecturers speaking in the interest of their race. The Methodists, generally, were enthusiastic advocates of the new gospel of freedom, yet here and there were contrary tendencies. The local Congregational church, to which I had become attached, was, from the first, in the front rank of this ethical movement. It had originated, indeed, in a protest against the conservatism which forbade the church to identify itself with the interests of

THE CHOICE OF A CALLING 63

humanity. Its first pastor was the young minister who had been compelled to leave the Presbyterian church because he had dared to pray for the slaves; after he had returned to New England, a number of his former parishioners seceded from the Presbyterian church, formed themselves into a Congregational church, and called him back to be their pastor. He was in his place in the church on the day when I was received into its membership, though his health was broken, and his work was done. I think that that was the last time he ever appeared in the pulpit.

A church with such an origin was not likely to occupy an ambiguous position in such a time as that; and the members of this church, though not many of the mighty and the noble were among them, were men who had the courage of their convictions, while their pastors were brave and faithful leaders. Doubtless there were, in those days, Congregationalists who were timid and hesitant in confronting the issues of the hour, but our church was not of that school. The New York "Independent" was the paper we all read, and Mr. Beecher and Dr. Cheever and Dr. Thompson of the Broadway Tabernacle were the leaders with whom we found ourselves in closest sympathy.

Such, then, was the soil in which my purpose to enter the ministry took root. It was not an individualistic pietism that appealed to me; it was a religion that laid hold upon life with both hands, and proposed, first and foremost, to realize the Kingdom of God in this world. I do not think that any other outlook upon the work would have attracted me. I had known the history of this little Congregational church from its beginning; I had been in keenest sympathy with all for which it stood, and the ethical thoroughness with which it committed itself to the cause of freedom when the gage of battle was thrown down by the repeal of the Missouri Compromise called out all my enthusiasm. I wanted to be — if I could make myself fit — the minister of a church like that. I could not think of any life better worth living.

The next year and a half was a strenuous period. There was no time to waste in my work of preparation for college. Happily the methods were so flexible both in the Owego Academy and in a boarding-school near the village, between which schools my time was divided, that it was possible for one who wished to advance rapidly to go at his own gait. Much of the time I was studying alone, and my teachers gave me every possible assistance and encouragement. I think that I gave, on an average, fourteen or fifteen hours a day to study, for six days in the week; on Sunday the rest was absolute.

Of all the days I had known, these were the happiest. The mathematical studies had no special interest for me, though I had no serious difficulty with them; but the languages and the literatures of Greece and Rome, into which I was now getting an introduction, were full of fascination. Perhaps my linguistic bent was due to the early training of my father; at all events, I have always found the keenest pleasure in such pursuits, and it has been a life-long regret that I have found so little time to give to them. These years in which I was getting acquainted with the rudiments of the Latin and the

THE CHOICE OF A CALLING 65

Greek were, therefore, delightful years; and I confess that I am never able to get the point of view of those educational reformers who propose to deprive American boys of this kind of pleasure. The days and the nights that I spent in tramping through Gaul with Julius Cæsar, or delving, with Titus Livius, into Roman antiquities, or following the fortunes of Vergil's hero, or marching with Cyrus against the Persians, or debating with Socrates against the Sophists, are memorable days and nights. Do you tell us, my masters, that there are to be no more of them; that our boys are nevermore to know the joy of turning one of Homer's sonorous hexameters into resounding English, or of finding the just right word for one of Horace's dainty epithets? It may be that you will have it so, but some of us will be glad that we lived in a better day.

Absorbing as these occupations were, other matters were forcing themselves upon the attention of the busiest of us. These months of 1855 and 1856 were witnessing some portentous political movements. The struggle for the possession of Kansas was going on, and exciting reports of the collision between the free state forces and the border ruffians were reaching us by every mail, so that the wrath of Achilles and the perfidy of Catiline were mingled, in our musings, with the strenuousness of Stringfellow and the fanatical vengeance of old John Brown. The Congress which the northern reaction against the Nebraska Bill had sent to Washington was going through a protracted struggle to get itself organized; legislation was paralyzed while the House of Representatives fought for two months over the election of a speaker. The conflicting currents of public opinion which found expression in this contest were, however, gradually merged in a new political organization which called itself the Republican Party, and which chose John C. Frémont to be its leader. When such things as these were happening, it was sometimes difficult for a boy to give undivided attention even to the rhetoric of Cicero, or the dialectic of Socrates. Now and then I found myself enticed away to a mass meeting in the village; and with much trepidation I ventured to contribute a song — a parody on Saxe's "Rhyme of the Rail" — which served the Republican Glee Club through this campaign. The leader of the club, then taking his first lesson in politics, was Mr. Thomas C. Platt. I read, not long ago, in one of the magazines, a satirical description of the performances of Mr. Platt in this campaign; the satire was not meant to be malicious, but it was quite beside the mark, for the leader of the Glee Club was no such gawky personage as he is there painted. Whatever judgment we may entertain respecting Mr. Platt's career as a national politician, we need not deny that in these early days he was a well-mannered young gentleman, a good singer, and an effective conductor of his club.

CHAPTER V

COLLEGE DAYS

> Come, dear old comrade, you and I
> Will steal an hour from days gone by, —
> The shining days when life was new,
> And all was bright as morning dew.
> *Oliver Wendell Holmes.*

IT was for Williams College that my preparation had been made. When I entered the Academy I had never heard of it, and my thought had been directed toward Hamilton College, at Clinton, New York; but the principal of the Academy was an enthusiastic graduate of Williams, and he soon convinced me that that was my proper destination. In September, 1856, having, as I confidently hoped, made myself ready to enter the sophomore class at Williams, I turned my face again eastward. Many things had happened during the fourteen years which had elapsed since I traveled to Massachusetts in a buggy; the Erie railway connected Owego with New York, and a midnight train carried me to the metropolis. The sleeping-car was not yet, and the polluted air of the crowded coach, coupled with the sickening motion, made my first long railway ride a dismal memory. What a relief it was to stand upon the deck of the ferry-boat at Jersey City and breathe the salt air! The sky-line, as one looked eastward, was not what one sees nowadays; the spires of Trinity and St. Paul's churches punctuated the horizon; with architectural sublimities of such dimensions our souls could then be stirred, and there were buildings of five or six stories in height, the sight of which made us dizzy. But the great river was all there; and the beautiful bay with the small islands in the foreground, and the green slopes of Staten Island in the distance, with the shipping ranged along the wharves, and ocean steamers that seemed huge lying there at anchor, and the smaller craft plying to and fro, made a picture never to be forgotten.

A day in the metropolis, with glimpses of the grandeur of the Astor House and the St. Nicholas Hotel, and the other marvels of Broadway, with a peep into the offices of the "Tribune" and the "Herald," a wondering look at Barnum's Museum, and a brief stroll through the Battery, was ended by a sail up the East River on the Hartford boat, for I was going to take in Southampton, on my way to Williamstown.

It was a beautiful September evening, half an hour before sunset, when I mounted the Williamstown stage at North Adams; recent rains had freshened the meadows, the forests on the mountain-sides still wore their summer dress, the fleecy clouds touched with crimson, that rested upon the Taghkanics in the west, or crowned the Saddle profile on the south, set off the bluest of skies. I had never seen anything so beautiful as that Williamstown valley appeared to me that evening; and I cannot say that I have seen anything since that has robbed it of its charm.

The entrance examinations the next day were not formidable, and before night I was matriculated as a sophomore, and established in the southwest corner of

West College on the lower floor. Thus opens a chapter of this history which must have far more significance to the writer of it than it can have to any of its readers.

Williams College in 1856 was an institution of modest pretensions. Its faculty consisted of but nine members, all of them full professors, and the four classes averaged less than sixty each. There may have been half-a-dozen "special" students who were taking a partial course; but almost all were candidates for the degree of bachelor of arts. The curriculum was perfectly rigid; all the work was required; the only electives were in the junior year, when we were permitted to choose between French and German. The classes were not divided, the instructional force did not admit of that; the whole class met, three times a day, in the recitation-room; naturally a student became pretty well acquainted with all his classmates. There was some advantage in the fact that all the instruction was given by full professors; tutorial assistance had been called in, in former years, but there was none of it in my day.

The teaching was mainly by means of text-books and oral recitations; lectures were few; in the last two years there were a few courses, but note-books were not much used in my time. The range of teaching was not wide. In the first two years Greek, Latin, and mathematics took up nearly all the time; in the sophomore year there was a course in Weber's "Universal History." No English was required for entrance, and the only English work of the first two years was one or two themes each term, with an occasional declamation before the class. There was also a speaking exercise, every Wednesday afternoon at the chapel, which the entire college was required to attend, and there were two speakers from each class; seniors and juniors presented original orations, sophomores and freshmen declaimed. The president and the professor of rhetoric presided, and criticised each speaker at the close of his performance.

In the junior year there were lessened rations of Latin and Greek, and some elementary instruction in science was given, so that every graduate might have some notion of the groundwork of botany and chemistry and physics and astronomy and mineralogy and geology; a single term was sufficient for political economy, and the tale of the themes was slightly increased. The senior year was devoted largely to mental and moral science, logic, the elements of rhetoric, and criticism, and the evidences of Christianity, with Paley's "Natural Theology" and Butler's "Analogy." I have reproduced the curriculum wholly from memory, but I think that I have not omitted anything essential.

Something like this was, I suppose, the course of study in most of the New England colleges of that period. Compare it with the bulletins of any of them to-day, and it seems a meagre provision for a liberal education. Yet there was enough in this, if rightly used, to secure a fair amount of mental discipline, and to guide inquiring minds toward the things worth knowing.

Better than the methods of instruction was the personal contact with the instructors. Every student in college was personally known by every member of the faculty, and the personal interest of the teachers in the students was as paternal as the students would permit.

This is not, indeed, saying a great deal, for in that time there was much of that traditional antagonism which makes it a point of honor for a student to refuse all friendly relations with teachers, as members of a hostile class, and which stigmatizes as "bootlicks" all those who seek such relations. Nevertheless, the association between teachers and students was, of necessity, so close that the personal touch could not be wholly evaded, and most Williams men of that time are ready now to confess that the best gains of their college course came to them in this way.

The conspicuous figure of the college was its president, Mark Hopkins, one of the four or five great teachers that America has produced. In 1856 he was in his prime, fifty-four years of age, tall, with a slight stoop, but stalwart, with a swinging gait. Over the great dome which crowned the broad forehead, and which was now nearly denuded of its covering, long brown locks were coaxed; and the strong chin and the Roman nose, with the eyes that glanced from under beetling brows, made up a countenance of great dignity and benignity. There was but one opinion about Dr. Hopkins in college; among the students his intellectual prowess was not disputed, and the wisdom and integrity of his character were never questioned. Every man has his foibles, and those who stood nearest to President Hopkins must have known what were his; but the student body, generally quick enough to spy out inconsistencies and weaknesses, was always singularly unanimous and enthusiastic in its loyalty to the great president.

He preached, frequently, in the village church, whose

galleries the students occupied; and these extemporaneous discourses, delivered with great deliberation and dignity, while they always held our attention, were not apt to awaken our enthusiasm; but the baccalaureate sermon was always an event. That was fully written; its philosophical framework was strong, its logic was convincing, and it was delivered with a power and fervor which made a lasting impression.

It was in the senior year that the students came in touch with Dr. Hopkins; a large share of the work of that year was in his hands; the seniors met him every day and sometimes twice; in philosophy and ethics, in logic and theology, he was their only teacher. The tradition of his masterful instruction was always descending; the freshmen heard of it from all above them; it was the expectation of every student that, however unsatisfactory other parts of the course might turn out to be, there would be something worth while in the senior year. The expectation was not disappointed. There was nothing sensational in Dr. Hopkins's teaching; his method was quiet and familiar; his bearing was modest and dignified; but he was a past-master in the art of questioning; he knew how by adroit suggestion to kindle the interest of his pupils in the subject under discussion, and by humor and anecdote he made dry topics vital and deep waters clear. What his best students got from him was not so much conclusions or results of investigation, as a habit of mind, a method of philosophical approach, a breadth and balance of thought, which might serve them in future study. What Garfield said (and I heard him say it, at a Williams banquet at Delmonico's in New York) expressed the feeling of many another graduate of the Berkshire college: "A pine bench, with Mark Hopkins at one end of it and me at the other, is a good enough college for me!"

A unique exercise was the conversation on the Catechism every Saturday morning in senior year. Following the Westminster Assembly's Shorter Catechism, Dr. Hopkins led his seniors carefully over the whole field of theology. The questions and answers, while not furnishing in all cases an adequate statement of doctrine, served as a convenient guide in the investigation of the deep things of God; and there was no other exercise in which the peculiar quality of this teacher appeared more strikingly. These Saturday morning discussions would have been a good equivalent for a Seminary course in systematic theology.

President Hopkins's brother Albert was another great character in our faculty. With a figure as erect and lithe as an Indian's, a face like Sargent's Elijah, an eye that flashed from cavernous sockets, and a voice like a trumpet, "Prof. Al" was the one man in the faculty whose moral and religious influence was most positive and profound. Our respect for him amounted to awe. I have never known any one whose personality more perfectly filled my idea of a Hebrew prophet.

Other professors whose memory the students of that decade will recall were the jocose Tatlock, whose mathematical teaching was not much more than a joke; the versatile but somewhat irascible Chadbourne, who taught but a little botany and chemistry, but taught that little wonderfully well; the sprightly and vivacious

Lincoln, with whom Latin prose was a passion; the calm and scholarly Phillips, who helped us to feel the power of Sophocles and the glory of Demosthenes; and the enthusiastic Perry, whose warm heart won the affection of all right-minded men, and whose championship of free trade gave rise to controversies in the class which were sometimes very entertaining.

Of all the instructors, however, the one to whom I am most indebted was John Bascom, then professor of rhetoric, later, for many years, President of the University of Wisconsin, and now resting, after his long day's work, in his old home among the stately trees planted by his own hand in Williamstown. I was not a little irritated by my first interview with Professor Bascom; I had carried to him a theme for criticism; I thought it a meritorious performance, but his blue pencil seriously disfigured it. I went away much exasperated, but on looking it over, I had to confess that the points were well taken. Of that just and penetrating judgment I gradually learned to avail myself; before the end of the course, respect had deepened into affection, and all my life long my debt to that brave and veracious soul has been growing. The score of volumes of which Dr. Bascom is the author have had but a limited circulation; but there are few books of the last half-century, dealing with applications of philosophy to life, which are better worth knowing.

College life in that time was very simple. The college buildings were plainness itself, wholly devoid of architectural pretensions; the furniture of most of the rooms was far from luxurious; the expense of living was light.

My board, in a club, the first term, cost me two dollars and thirty cents a week; it never exceeded two dollars and seventy-five cents a week. The entire expense of my college course, for the three years, including clothing, was less than nine hundred dollars. Several of the students who boarded themselves, in their own rooms, brought the cost far within that figure.

Several Greek-letter fraternities were flourishing, and there was an anti-secret confederation which made war upon them, but was quite as clannish as they were. None of these societies had houses of their own; they were content with humble quarters, which they rented in private houses, or in lofts over village stores.

A large place in the life of the college was taken by the two rival literary societies, — the Philologian and the Philotechnian, — to the one or the other of which every student belonged. These societies had well-furnished rooms in one of the dormitories, with libraries of three or four thousand volumes each. Their weekly meetings were events of no little interest to the college community; the programme generally included one or two original orations, a debate, sometimes a poem, an essay or two, and the report of the censor upon the performance of the previous meeting. The two societies were united in the Adelphic Union, which gave three or four debates or exhibitions annually, in the chapel or the village church.

The summer vacation was short, not more than five or six weeks, and there was a long winter vacation, beginning at Thanksgiving and continuing into January, that students who were supporting themselves might teach in the winter terms of country schools. All my winters were thus employed.

Of the men in my time some names are well known. First among them was Garfield, of the class of '56, who was a senior when my class were freshmen, and whom, therefore, I did not personally know. The fame of him, however, was large when I entered college. He had distinguished himself as debater and orator; there were many reminiscences of his brilliant performances in the Logian forum and on the chapel stage. When my class graduated, he returned and took his second degree, delivering a "master's oration" on our Commencement stage. He had taken to himself a wife, who accompanied him to the scene of his former triumphs, and proudly witnessed his induction into the new honors. He was then President of Hiram College, in Ohio, and must then have been a candidate for the state senate at Columbus, to which, in October of that year, he was chosen. He was a fine, strong young fellow, with a ruddy face, a massive head, a cordial manner, and an air of mastership. The hour that I spent with him on this occasion gave me a large sense of his power. Few who knew him in those days were surprised at his swift ascent to the places of command.

In my own class, the man who was soonest to obtain distinction was the youngest man in the class, Ranald Slidell Mackenzie. He came to college a mere lad of fifteen, in a roundabout; he had a slight lisp and was extremely shy; but he was a good scholar, and a thoroughly likable boy. He was the son of Commodore Alexander Slidell Mackenzie, the distinguished naval

COLLEGE DAYS 77

officer and author, whose name had been made famous by the manner in which he had dealt, fourteen years before, with a mutiny on the brig Somers, of which he was commander. The ringleader of this mutiny was a youth named Spencer, son of John C. Spencer, then Secretary of War. After a brief trial on shipboard, Spencer and two others were hanged to the yardarm. It was a curious fact that a kinsman of Spencer's, Walter DeForest Day, was also a classmate of mine, and that Mackenzie and Day were members of the same Greek letter fraternity, and close friends. Mackenzie did not finish his course in Williams. In the middle of our junior year he received, through the influence of his uncle, Senator Slidell, of Louisiana, an appointment to West Point, from which he graduated with high rank in 1862, and immediately entered the Union army. Of his splendid work as a soldier the records of the service tell abundantly. He was shot to pieces again and again, but he always managed to pull himself together and get back into the field very speedily. "Among those who distinguished themselves," says Sheridan's dispatch after Cedar Creek, "was Colonel Mackenzie, twice wounded, but refused to leave the field." At Five Forks he was brevetted major-general on the field for gallantry, and it was he who outran Lee to Lynchburg, and checked the final retreat of the Confederate army.

Two of our best-known magazine editors, Mr. Henry M. Alden, of "Harper's Monthly," and Mr. Horace E. Scudder, of the "Atlantic," were contemporaries of mine at Williams. Alden's forte was metaphysics; he was supposed to be occupied mainly with interests purely transcendental, absorbed in investigating the "Thingness of the Here"; and if the Messrs. Harper had come to Williamstown inquiring for a young man who would be a skillful purveyor of short stories and poems and sketches for a popular magazine, the last man to whom they would have been sent was Henry Mills Alden. Nor is it probable that our veteran managing editor ever dreamed, at that day, of the kind of occupation in which he was destined to spend his years and to render to the world a service so high and fine. Just how Alden ever got down from cloudland to Franklin Square I have never been able to find out, but it is well for the world that he came, and perhaps the world has been the gainer by his early residence in cloudland. We get our best training for work in this world by living above it.

As for Scudder, whether he ever dreamed of editing the "Atlantic Monthly," I know not; he might, for his pen had a dainty nib, even then; we counted him one of our most graceful writers; what he wrote had an air of distinction and refinement to which undergraduate prose does not often attain. The "Atlantic," in those days, was in its pristine glory. Its life began in Scudder's senior year, and every number, with possible contributions from Emerson or Longfellow or Hawthorne or Lowell or Whittier, and with "The Autocrat of the Breakfast-Table" running its bright career, was an event in our little college community. How we canvassed those first numbers, guessing the authorship of the contributions, all of which were anonymous, and glorying in the new light that had arisen upon American letters!

Scudder was a shy and modest fellow; I doubt if he ever conceived of climbing into Lowell's seat.

Both Alden and Scudder practiced for their promotions by editing the "Williams Quarterly." I have six volumes of that stately periodical, and a comparison of it with undergraduate publications of the present day enforces the conclusion that the intellectual life was a larger concern in college fifty years ago than it is to-day. We were, indeed, so unfortunate as to have few interests which were not intellectual. Athletics were not yet; we sometimes kicked a football rather aimlessly about the campus, never having seen a football game; we played, among ourselves, an occasional game of what we called baseball — class against class; and in our senior year we had one match game with Amherst; but the interest in athletic sports was a negligible quantity. Some of our more adventurous spirits found vent for their surplus force in natural history expeditions to Newfoundland and South America, and an occasional picnic at Lanesboro Pond, or a tramp to the top of Greylock, gave zest to life. But for the most part, the subjects which claimed our attention were those which had some reference to the work of the college. The rivalry for college honors was keen; every man's chances of getting on to the "Moonlight," — the prize rhetorical contest, — or to the "Junior Exhibition," or to the Commencement stage, were freely canvassed by every other man; who was the best Grecian, the best Latinist, the best mathematician, the strongest writer, the finest speaker in any class, was a question on which differences of opinion were freely expressed.

College music at the middle of the nineteenth century was not of a high order. At Yale and Harvard there had been some singing; in the fresh-water colleges the repertoire of the singers was scanty. At Williams, in my sophomore year, two or three old Latin songs were occasionally sung, — "Gaudeamus Igitur," to a good German choral; "Integer Vitae," to Flemming's strong setting; and "Lauriger Horatius," to the air since better known as "Maryland, my Maryland." For the rest there was a meagre collection of nonsense songs, like the lines, set to Rousseau's "Greenville," "Go tell Aunt Nancy her old gray goose is dead," and several drinking songs, like "Landlords, fill your flowing bowls," and "Roll, roll, rolling home!" Longfellow's "Psalm of Life" was also chanted to a rollicking melody with the refrain of "Cocachelunk-chelunk-chelaly," which was a little like dressing up the Apollo Belvidere in a sweater and tennis shoes. Occasion for song had also been developed by the Biennial Examinations, which had been introduced not long before my day. After two weeks of written examinations on all the subjects of the first two years, the Sophomores were apt to feel the need of hilarity; and they were wont to serenade the professors of whom they were taking leave, and to celebrate the event in a supper at the Mansion House. For these festive occasions songs were written, and some of them were good enough to be preserved and transmitted.

During my junior year one or two men came to us from Yale, bringing some of the nonsense songs which were current there, and groups began to gather in the summer evenings on the benches in front of East College

COLLEGE DAYS

for the singing of these new songs. It must have been early in my senior year that a musical organization was formed which called itself "The Mendelssohn Society," of which I was made the conductor. This society made some ambitious attempts at glees and male choruses, giving, in the course of the year, a few concerts in the surrounding towns. By these various measures so much interest in college singing was awakened that I ventured to publish, at the close of our senior year, a collection of the "Songs of Williams." Most of the songs were written for the collection, and many of them were, of course, lyrically defective; it is not an easy thing to write a singable song. But I find in the latest Williams song-book fourteen numbers from my old compilation. How many of them are sung in these days I do not know. One of these I had the good fortune to write. I had been wishing that I might write a song which could be sung at some of our exhibitions; and one winter morning, walking down Bee Hill, the lilt of the chorus of "The Mountains" came to me. I had a little music-paper in my room in the village, and on my arrival I wrote down the notes. Then I cast about for words to fit them, and the refrain, "The Mountains, the Mountains!" suggested itself. I wrote the melody of the stanza next, and fitted the verses to it. We were soon to have a public debate, in the Chapel, for which the Mendelssohn Society was to furnish the music; we learned this song and sang it on that occasion. The next morning I heard the melody whistled by students in the halls and by town boys in the streets; it was evident that it had caught on. That it would be sung by fifty college classes, and become the accepted College Song, I could not, of course, have imagined. It is a simple and catchy melody, and the words serve to connect it with that which is most impressive and permanent in the environment of college life at Williamstown, and so it has established itself as one of the traditions of the college. I know not what greater grace could be given to any man than to become, for generations, the voice of the happy loyalty of the men of such a college as Williams. He would be a low man who would be proud of such a thing, but he needs not be ashamed to confess that it has given him not a little unalloyed pleasure.

A friendship of the greatest value to me was that which I formed during my college life with Samuel Bowles and Josiah G. Holland, then editors of the Springfield "Republican." My newspaper knack easily gained for me the place of college reporter for the "Republican," and after a while I ventured occasionally to send a poem or a story. One day I found, in the "Republican," a poem of mine, which I had written for delivery at a meeting of the Logian Society, printed with an editorial comment that quite took my breath away. It was the first recognition which had ever come to me from a literary source whose verdict was entitled to respect. How much it signified I shall never be able to tell. Any one who has committed his life to a venture which has been, hitherto, wholly problematical, is apt to be stirred by the first clear token of success. What these words told me was simply this, that there was good hope for me. I should wrong myself if I confessed that they nourished my self-conceit;

they made me humble; but they lifted up my heart with a great thankfulness.

Dr. Holland was then writing his "Titcomb's Letters," his "Gold Foil," and his "Bittersweet," and his writings had a great vogue, not only in the columns of the "Republican," but in the book form in which they were rapidly appearing. He was not the finest of our essayists, nor the greatest of our poets; but there was a wholesome good sense and a sound and sweet humanity in him that greatly endeared him to a multitude of American readers. How considerate and generous a friend he was to me, in the day when I needed friends, I could not fail to bear witness.

Mr. Bowles was a man of keener wit and more brilliant parts; to many persons he seemed to have a harsh temper and a biting tongue; but he, too, was quick in his appreciations, and ready and prompt to lend a hand to those in whom his interest was enlisted. During my senior year I visited Springfield and spent a Sunday with these two editors, and that was the beginning of a friendship that death has interrupted, but has not broken. For both of them it was my privilege to speak, after death, the last words of memory and affection. I think they both knew that the boy to whom, in his college days, they gave a strong right hand, was never forgetful nor ungrateful.

Commencement, in those days, was a high festival. It drew to the village all the people of the countryside, and there were booths for gingerbread and root beer, and sellers of whips and toy balloons, and the usual assortment of fakirs. Few of the hundreds of country people who flocked to the show paid much attention to the graduating exercises; the occasion simply supplied them with an out-of-door holiday.

The Commencement occurred during the first week in August, and the day was sacred to the graduating class. Out of a total of fifty or sixty, from thirty to thirty-five men presented original orations. The speaking began in the village church about nine o'clock in the morning, and continued until noon; after an intermission of two hours for dinner, the floodgates of oratory were reopened, and it was after four o'clock before the valedictorian made his final bow to the applauding crowd. With such powers of endurance were the audiences of those days endowed!

It was a heavy heart that I carried out of that valley when the Commencement festivities were ended, in the summer of 1859. I had tarried for a day after my classmates were gone; and I was alone on the train that bore me away to the westward that August afternoon. I sat at the window and looked backward till Greylock and Prospect were shut from sight, and I knew that the curtain had gone down on the happiest time that I had ever known. Not that there were no flies in the amber, for there were blunders and faults enough to recall; but the work had been congenial and the friendships inspiring, and there had been enough of achievement to kindle hope. To turn my back on all that care-free college life and face an unknown world cost a pang. I do not think I have ever had the same sense of the closing of a door upon the past as that which I experienced when the train carried me homeward from dear old Williamstown.

CHAPTER VI

PUTTING ON THE HARNESS

> Hark, hark, a voice amid the quiet intense!
> It is thy duty, waiting thee without.
> Rise from thy knees in hope, the half of doubt.
> A hand doth pull thee — it is Providence.
> Open thy door straightway and get thee hence;
> Go forth into the tumult and the shout;
> Work, love, with workers, lovers, all about.
> *George Macdonald.*

THE end of college life is apt to bring some sense of depression, but for me there was no time for regrets or deplorings. Something to do must be found, without delay. Half-a-dozen possibilities were in sight; but the three or four weeks in which I was canvassing them seemed a very long time. By the end of that period I had contracted to teach the principal public school in Owego, and had entered upon a life of continuous labor. Since that day I have never been "out of a job" for a minute. Always I have been somebody's hired man, under contract for service. There have been no pauses or interludes between occupations; I have never had a chance to know how it would seem to have nothing to do. Whether that day will ever come, I do not know; I rather hope that I may, one of these days, get a little time out of harness, but I am not sure that I shall know what to do with it.

Schoolmastering, however, was not my trade. The big school — seventy or eighty pupils in one room, where all my teaching had to be done — worried me. The instruction was a pleasure, and there was no sense of failure in the discipline, but the constant nervous strain wore upon me, and I began to doubt whether it would be possible for me to earn, by this calling, the funds needed for my professional studies.

In the meantime I was enjoying a most delightful companionship with a young man who had recently been called to the pastorate of our Owego Congregational church, the Reverend Moses Coit Tyler. He was a graduate of Yale and Andover, and was only a year older than I. We occupied adjoining rooms in the same boarding-house, and his friendship brought into my life a most stimulating influence. With him I began at once reading along theological lines; and at his request I preached my first sermon in his pulpit, not many weeks after my return from college. It was also at his rather urgent instance that I presented myself before the Susquehanna Association of Congregational Ministers, and was licensed by them to preach, Mr. Tyler's expectation being that I would exercise my gifts in schoolhouses and country meeting-houses as occasion offered. That was, probably, a very irregular procedure; the fact that the Reverend Thomas K. Beecher, of Elmira, was moderator of the Association may help to explain it. Mr. Beecher, to put it mildly, was not a stickler for ecclesiastical proprieties. My year in theology, under Mark Hopkins, may have given me some small outfit for such an examination, which, as I cannot help remembering, was not a shining exhibition of theological proficiency.

My certificate of licensure is in Mr. Beecher's hand-

PUTTING ON THE HARNESS 87

writing. The scribe of the Association, who was an illiterate blunderer, had written it and handed it to the moderator to sign; he glanced at it, and suddenly said: "What's this? 'The Susquehanna Association, having examined [So and so, in such and such things] commends him to the churches of Chr,' at the end of the line, with a hyphen, 'ist' at the beginning of the next line! Is Christ divided? Give me a pen and let me write a certificate that will not disgrace this body."

It was not the first time I had met Mr. Beecher. He was a familiar and picturesque personage in central New York through the second half of the nineteenth century. His ministry in Elmira began when I was in the printing-office, and he frequently came to Owego to preach or lecture. Once, when I was in the Academy, he came, at my request, to speak at an Academy exhibition, and on that occasion he drew me into his room at the hotel, and talked to me until a late hour, probing my purposes, and offering me counsel. He seemed most anxious that I should not venture into the ministry unwarned of its difficulties and discouragements. Above all, I must be sure of myself, and must stand on my own feet. "When I started out," he said, "a great many people seemed to think that I would sail in the wake of my relations, availing myself of their popularity; I have tried to let them see that I don't propose to be the copy or the echo of anybody else." Nobody ever accused him of that. He was a most original and independent character, often offending against conventions, and traveling wide of the beaten paths, but full of warm humanity and spiritual enthusiasm. His slender but graceful figure, his expressive countenance, and his sympathetic voice gave him exceptional power as a speaker; I have heard from him more persuasive and convincing speech than I ever heard from his more famous brother.

It so happened that there came to the meeting of the Susquehanna Association, which had so rashly turned me loose upon the churches, a supplication from a discouraged church, just over the Pennsylvania line, in Le Raysville, that some one be sent to help their minister in a series of special services, by means of which they hoped to resuscitate the enterprise. The Association, again throwing discretion to the winds, advised the church to send for me; and I, with no more prudence, resigned my school and accepted the invitation. This was early in January, 1860. Arriving in Le Raysville on Wednesday afternoon, after a stage-ride of twenty miles, I found myself announced to preach Wednesday, Thursday, and Friday evenings, and twice on the coming Sunday. For eight weeks this programme was extended, — five week-day services and two or three Sunday services. That it was very crude preaching hardly needs to be said; the theology was raw, and the rhetoric was ragged; the only thing that rescued it from contempt was the saving grace of a youthful enthusiasm and a real wish to help men find the way to a better life. Far more was done in the daily personal contact with old and young; and the result of the effort was not only a considerable addition to the membership of the church, but a deepening of my conviction that my best way to prepare for the ministry was in the work of the ministry. After preaching for a year or two I might

PUTTING ON THE HARNESS 89

hope to step aside for a year or two of theological study. That, as things had turned out, seemed to be the practicable programme.

After the work at Le Raysville was finished, invitations came to preach in three or four vacant churches of the neighborhood, and while I was considering these, a call came from Brooklyn, and by the beginning of May I was in charge of an organization which styled itself the First Congregational Methodist Church of that city.

I am entirely sure now that this was a place where angels would have feared to tread; that was why I rushed in. A more foolhardy undertaking it would be difficult to imagine. The church was the fruit of a secession from the Methodist body, arising in a quarrel about a minister; it had a small membership, with few men of substance, and an enormous debt incurred in the erection of its edifice; it had no natural constituency; the attempt of an untrained boy to carry such a load is not more astonishing than the fatuity of the people who asked him to undertake it. The fact that there was a theological seminary within easy reach, of whose advantages I might hope to avail myself, was one reason for accepting this offer. But that was a vain expectation.

Brooklyn, in 1860, was a comfortable city of about 275,000 people; it had not quite outgrown its bucolic traditions, and the Dutch flavor in the municipal life was quite perceptible. It was the City of Churches, and there was no lack of them; Mr. Beecher was, of course, the star of the first magnitude in the ecclesiastical firmament, but Dr. Storrs and Dr. Cuyler and Dr. Bartlett and others were also shining lights. In the midst of such a galaxy, the rushlight is not likely to miss the fact of its own insignificance. It seemed, indeed, a hopeless business, once it was fairly on my hands; but the people were kind, and I gave them the best that was in me.

The city, from the first day, was a thing stupendous and overpowering, a mighty monster, with portentous energies; the sense of its power to absorb human personalities and to shape human destinies was often vivid and painful. To one who had nursed his fancies for the greater part of his life in the solitude of a back country farm, and who had breasted no currents of life stronger than those which meander through the streets of a quiet village, the contact with the strenuous life of the great city was a revelation. One was standing in the centre of a galvanic field, with lines of force crossing each other in every direction. Everything was alive, yet there was a vivid sense of the impersonality and brutality of the whole movement, of the lack of coördinating intelligence. The Brooklyn ferries and street-cars were then a quiet scene compared with the volcanic torrents of humanity at the bridges and in the subways in these days; but the amount of titanic energy which was even then finding vent in the life of what we now call the Greater New York was enough to start a great many queries about how all this might be wisely handled, and whereunto it was likely to grow. One could not help wondering whether in liberating the force which gathers men into cities, and equipping it with steam and electricity, a power had not been created which was stronger than the intelligence which seeks to control it; whether such aggregations of humanity, with wills no better

PUTTING ON THE HARNESS

socialized than those of the average nineteenth-century American, are not by their own action self-destructive. I do not mean that I reasoned out this query, at that time; but some sense of the appalling nature of the municipal problem was certainly present with me. It signified much to me that I was forced to meet, on the threshold of my ministry, what Dr. Strong calls "the challenge of the city." I could not answer it then, and I cannot now; it has been a lifelong problem.

It was not, however, to municipal politics that the thought of the people was then turning. Other and what seemed more momentous questions were forcing themselves upon our attention. These were the days when opinion was moving swiftly toward the decision which plunged the nation into the Civil War. Buchanan's administration had resulted in consolidating the antislavery sentiment of the North; the struggle on the plains of Kansas had revealed the increasing purpose of the northern people to prevent the further extension of slavery; and the great debate between Lincoln and Douglas had practically completed the education of the people of the free states. Reports of that debate had been widely circulated; many of us had read all the speeches, and had found in the invincible moral sense of Lincoln the word of the hour. When I went back to Owego, after my first visit to Brooklyn, to close up my affairs and prepare for removal to the city, the Chicago convention was in session; every day brought exciting news; and it was on my return to the city, as the train stopped at Narrowsburg or Port Jervis, that the news came of Lincoln's nomination. Many of the New

Yorkers looked glum; Mr. Seward's state had been backing him heavily; but my cap went up in the air with a shout; the thing seemed too good to be true.

So it came about that my first year in the ministry was destined to be a momentous year. The free-state forces were rallying for an aggressive campaign, and there was a note of confidence in their appeal; the split in the other party gave them good ground for hope. The Wide-Awake movement was spreading; torch-light processions, and rallies in the wigwams, filled the summer nights with a boisterous enthusiasm.

Religious circles were less moved by this commotion than might have been expected; for the most part, the churches kept on the even tenor of their ways. Mr. Beecher, now and then, shot out a shaft of satire or invective; but there was very little reporting of sermons, and if less conspicuous men spoke on the issues of the day, few outside the immediate audience were likely to hear of it. There was, indeed, much solicitude, even among right-minded people, lest the pulpit should be desecrated by politics. There was apt to be in every congregation a contingent who were excessively sensitive on this point, and who were wont to hear the voice of political agitation in the most obvious Biblical commonplaces. I remember an occasion when a neighbor was preaching in my pulpit, and I had selected James Montgomery's hymn, "Daughter of Zion, from the dust." One of the stanzas of that hymn is a versified paraphrase of a passage in Isaiah, respecting the returning exiles: "I will say to the north, Give up; and to the south, Keep not back." The rhymed version runs thus:

> Rebuild thy walls, thy bounds enlarge,
> And send thy heralds forth;
> Say to the South, Give up thy charge,
> And keep not back, O North.

My neighbor in giving out the hymn, which is a long one, suggested the omission of this stanza. The next day there appeared in the daily paper an enthusiastic letter, praising this minister for having rebuked the pastor of the church, who was trying to foist upon the congregation an abolitionist hymn. It was an outrage, he said, to stir up sectional feeling by such inflammatory words, and the minister who had put down this sinister endeavor was worthy of all commendation.

One sermon which was preached in one of the most conspicuous pulpits of the city, during that summer, raised some excitement. The preacher was the Reverend Henry J. Van Dyke, one of the most honored and influential of the Presbyterian pastors, and the sermon was a closely-reasoned and forcible argument to prove that abolitionism and infidelity were synonymous terms; that no man could be an abolitionist without being an infidel. The argument, of course, was Scriptural; it was easy to show that slavery was a Biblical institution; that the holders of slaves had in many cases been inspired men; and that laws under the imprimatur of Jehovah himself had enjoined slavery; this was a demonstration that God had made Himself responsible for the institution, and that opposition to it was rebellion against Him. The logic was relentless; the conclusion was one of many monstrous results, which, upon the assumption of the inerrant authority of the whole Scripture, are inescapable. It was tragical to see a man of the acumen of Dr. Van Dyke writhing in the coils of such a conception.

The summer of 1860 was uneventful. As the prospect of Lincoln's election grew more clear, the threats of disunion were more frequent and passionate, but they were regarded, for the most part, as rhodomontade; the actual rupture of the national bond seemed a thing incredible.

My own work went on without interruption through the summer; most of the churches, in those days, kept up all their services; the need of a two or three months' vacation had not yet been discovered by many of them. In the course of the autumn my church escaped from its anomalous independence, and entered the Congregational fellowship, and my own association with the ministers of that communion became increasingly pleasant. Those courses of study at the Union Seminary on which I had been fondly counting did not, however, materialize; two sermons a week, with all my pastoral cares, were enough to occupy my time; there was no space for systematic study. No phenomenal success could be reported in the work of the church; the gains were slow, but they seemed to be substantial; on the whole, there was reason for encouragement.

The sixth of November brought the eventful day when the fate of the nation was to be decided. That evening I spent in Printing-House Square, New York, watching the bulletins on the Tribune Building, and I did not return to my lodgings until the telegrams had made it sure that Lincoln was elected. What a night was that, my countrymen! And who that had been

PUTTING ON THE HARNESS 95

living eight years before, and breathing the political atmosphere of the commonwealth that chose Franklin Pierce to be its chief magistrate, could have believed that the same nation would now be shouting itself hoarse over the choice of a man who represented what Abraham Lincoln stood for?

For no man could help seeing that this political revolution registered an ethical advance in the American people. There had come about, during the eight years, a change in the moral feelings of the multitude. Their ideals had been, in some good measure, transformed; the public opinion of the masses held a larger infusion of altruistic sentiment. Their attention had been drawn to the question, "Who is my neighbor?" and they had learned to answer it more nearly in the sense of the good Samaritan.

Such changes as these in the habitual thoughts of the people, in their ruling ideas, are to be looked for; the hope of the world is in them. The notion that human nature is a fixed quantity; that men always act from the same motives; that the troglodyte in his cave and the philanthropist in his laboratory respond in the same way to the same moral stimuli is sufficiently absurd, on the face of it; but such a transformation of the moral feelings of a whole population as occurred in the eight years of which we are speaking ought to put an end to all such pessimistic reasoning. "Human nature," says Arnold Toynbee, "is not always the same. It slowly changes, and is modified by higher ideals and wider and deeper conceptions of justice. Men have forgotten that though it is impossible to change the nature of a stone or

96   RECOLLECTIONS

a rock, human nature is pliable, and pliable above all to nobler ideas and to a truer sense of justice." The instance to which Toynbee points, in support of this contention, is "that great change of opinion which took place in England with regard to slavery."[1] In England, as well as in America, the entire attitude of the people upon a great question of morals was changed within a generation.

It is well to bear such facts in mind, for they help to show that the function of the prophet and the moral teacher is not superfluous; that the destiny of mankind is not wholly shaped by physical and economic forces; that Confucius may prove to be as much of an empire builder as Alexander or Genghis Khan — perhaps a more enduring builder. "If," says Toynbee, "such a rapid change as that relating to slavery could take place in our moral ideas within the last hundred years, do you not think it possible that in the course of another hundred years English employers and English laborers may act upon higher notions of duty and higher conceptions of citizenship than they do now?" Theories of social reform which rest upon the skeptical notion that human nature is irreformable appear, therefore, to be unscientific.

The verdict of the North was decisive; what would be the answer of the South? That question was on the mind of every thoughtful man at the North, when he read in the dispatches of November 7 the news of Lincoln's election. And there were not many among us who gave the correct reply. The North did not believe that

[1] *The Industrial Revolution*, p. 175.

PUTTING ON THE HARNESS   97

the South would secede, and the South did not believe that the North would fight to resist secession. A tremendous disillusion was in store for both sections. If the North had taken the southern threat of secession seriously, would not strenuous efforts have been made to patch up some kind of compromise? If the South had known that the North would have an army of half a million men in the field within a few months, would not even the hot-headed South Carolinians have been a little less precipitate in their haste to fling themselves out of the Union? Perhaps not. Perhaps the conflict was irrepressible, and had to be fought out. Perhaps the vast infidelity of the nation in harboring slavery — a crime in which both sections were implicated — had to be atoned for by the frightful retribution of the Civil War.

I doubt if there were many men in either section who were looking for war, on the morning of the seventh of November. But our optimism was rudely shaken before many days. On the tenth of November the Legislature of South Carolina called a State Convention to dissolve the union of that state with the Federal Government; within a day or two both her senators at Washington resigned their offices, and their resignations were accepted by the Legislature; and steps were taken at once to secure a similar action in several of the other cotton states.

It was in the midst of these ominous and exciting events that a council was called by my church for my ordination to the ministry. That was no part of my own plan; but the church insisted that it must have the services of a fully qualified minister, and that I must accept ordination. The council convened on November 15; the moderator was Dr. Richard S. Storrs, who gave me the right hand of fellowship; the sermon was preached by the Reverend William Alvin Bartlett, and the address to the people was given by my former pastor, Reverend Moses Coit Tyler, who was then in the Congregational church of Poughkeepsie. It was an eminently respectable and learned council, and now that all the members of it have passed to their reward, I may express my wonder that they should have been willing to proceed, unanimously, with the ordination of one whose examination must have exhibited in a strong light his lack of preparation for so great a work. It can be explained only by imputing to them a large measure of the charity that covereth a multitude of deficiencies, or of the faith that judges a man less by what he is than by what he hopes to be.

Perhaps I was dealt with less judicially, because the hearts of the men composing this council must have been full of a great solicitude respecting the state of the country. In every assembly of serious-minded Americans that interest was uppermost; the ominous possibilities were gathering like a sullen cloud all along the southern horizon.

Another event which followed close upon my ordination was my marriage, in my own church, on December 5, to Miss Jennie O. Cohoon, who had been a schoolmate in the Owego Academy, and was at that time a resident of Brooklyn.

CHAPTER VII

THE BURSTING OF THE STORM

> Peace hath her not ignoble wreath,
>   Ere yet the sharp, decisive word
> Light the black lips of cannon, and the sword
>   Dreams in its easeful sheath;
> But some day the live coal behind the thought,
>   Whether from Baäl's stone obscene,
>   Or from the shrine serene
>   Of God's pure altar brought,
> Bursts up in flame; the war of tongue and pen
> Learns with what deadly purpose it was fraught,
> And, helpless in the fiery passion caught,
> Shakes all the pillared state with shock of men.
> *James Russell Lowell.*

JUST two weeks after my ordination services came Thanksgiving Day, and as it was known that Mr Beecher would speak on the national issues, I went to hear him. The great church was crowded to the doors, and the air was quivering with suppressed excitement. I think I have never been in any orderly assembly in which there were more signs of intense feeling. Before the preacher had been speaking very long, some trenchant utterance started a ripple of applause, which was quickly suppressed by the indignant "Sh-h-h!" of the regular worshipers, who had no mind to have their sanctuary profaned by such noises. Mr. Beecher paused a moment, and with a quick glance about him, said quietly, "'T ain't Sunday!" That let the audience loose. From that moment onward the address was punctuated with vociferous applause. It was a scene long to be remembered.

The sermon is printed — the bones of it — in Mr. Beecher's "Freedom and War," under the title, "Against a Compromise of Principle." It is, after all, but a meagre outline of the passionate plea to which we listened on that memorable day. Yet that was the substance of it: compromise is fatuous; the nation must stand fast upon the principles to which it is now committed. "The North," cried the orator, "loves liberty, and will have it. We will not aggress on you. Keep your institutions within your own bounds; we will not hinder you. We will not take advantage to destroy, or one whit to abate, your fair political prerogatives. You have already gained advantages of us. These we will allow you to hold. You shall have the Constitution intact, and its full benefit. The full might and power of public sentiment in the North shall guarantee to you everything that history and the Constitution give you. But if you ask us to augment the area of slavery; to coöperate with you in cursing new territory; if you ask us to make the air of the North favorable for a slave's breath, we will not do it! We love liberty as much as you love slavery, and we shall stand by our rights with all the vigor with which we mean to stand by justice toward you."

With one sentence of this declaration the southern man would have joined issue. The intimation that no slave can breathe northern air contradicts, he would have said, the constitutional provision for the return of fugitive slaves. "So long," he would have urged, "as you refuse to send back our slaves, you are insincere in

THE BURSTING OF THE STORM 101

telling us that we shall have the Constitution intact and its full benefit." That, indeed, was one of the serious complaints of the southern people, and it must be admitted that not only by the personal liberty laws enacted by several of the northern states was the spirit of the Constitution violated, but that the public sentiment of the North practically nullified the Federal statute by which this constitutional provision was enforced. Here, if anywhere, the people of the North were failing to keep their part of the compact. And in the anxious days that followed the election, many among us were inclined to confess this default, and to try to make amends for it. The personal liberty laws were, in fact, mainly repealed, and there was a disposition on the part of some conservative statesmen to get the Fugitive Slave Law so amended that it might be enforced.

All this, however, was futile. The moral sentiment of the North had reached a stage at which the return of fugitives to slavery was a thing no longer possible. That provision of the old compact was dead, and could never be resurrected. If secession could be averted only by that kind of guarantee, secession must take its course. And Mr. Beecher, in this tremendous sermon, told the South the exact truth about this.

Suppose you tell the people, then, that when their fugitives come North they shall be surrendered. Will you not please to catch them first? You know you cannot. There are five hundred men that run through the northern states where there is one that stops or is turned back. They know it, you know it, we all know it. The radical nature of the feelings of the North is such that they will hurry on the black man and trip his hunter. If the managers of parties, and heads of conservative committees, say to the South, "Be patient with us a little longer, do not punish us yet, let down the rod and the frown; spare us for a short season, and we will see that your slaves are returned to you," do you suppose there will be a fulfillment of the promise? You know there will not. I know there will not. I would die myself, cheerfully and easily, before a man should be taken out of my hands when I had the power to give him liberty and the hound was after him for his blood. I would stand as an altar of expiation between slavery and liberty, knowing that through my example a million men would live. A heroic deed, in which one yields himself up for others, is his Calvary. It was the lifting up of Christ on that hill-top that made it the loftiest mountain on the globe.

As the weeks went by, it became increasingly evident that the great majority of the people who had voted for Lincoln stood on this platform, and could never be moved from it. They believed that freedom was national and slavery sectional; they would suffer no further extension of slave territory. Nor would they bind themselves to send back fugitives.

And now suppose that South Carolina should make good her threat of secession, and that the other cotton states should follow her: what then? How should the nation meet that emergency? Mr. Beecher did not answer that question explicitly. But a day or two before, in Boston, in reply to the question, "Do you think the South will secede?" he had said: "I don't believe they will, and I don't care if they do." Such was

THE BURSTING OF THE STORM

the first response to the secession movement of many radical Republicans. The New York "Tribune," which was the Republican Bible, said, three days after the election: "If the cotton states shall decide that they can do better out of the Union than in it, we insist on letting them go in peace. The right to secede may be a revolutionary one, but it exists, nevertheless. . . . Whenever a considerable section of our Union shall deliberately resolve to go out, we shall resist all coercive measures designed to keep it in. We hope never to live in a republic whereof one section is pinned to the residue by bayonets."

Up to the middle of December this policy was tentatively advocated by a good many anti-slavery men. The reason of it was in the horror of war, and in the grave doubt whether such a question could be settled by force. Gradually these doubts were overborne, and the Websterian sentiment of the indissolubility of the Union began to prevail. The enormous difficulty of maintaining two nationalities upon this territory, with no natural frontier; the certainty of constant collisions and entanglements over economic and political questions; the intolerable consequence of having our natural access to the Gulf closed against us, — all these considerations soon began to get such possession of the northern mind that peaceable secession was practically dismissed, as a chimerical proposition.

Just how much of this conclusion was rational and how much of it was due to instinctive impulses and elemental passions, we may never know. It is useless now to speculate on what might have been, but one cannot help wondering what would have happened if General Scott's first impulse had been followed, and the "erring sisters" had been bidden to "go in peace." How many of them would have gone? The Gulf states, undoubtedly; but eastern Kentucky and Tennessee and western Virginia could hardly have been forced out of the Union. And the states thus seceding could have set up no claim to any of the territory of the nation, north or south; certainly, such a claim would never have been allowed. The new slave republic would thus have been inclosed within free territory, with little chance for expansion. Cuba would, no doubt, have been benevolently absorbed very soon; beyond that, the boundaries were not likely to be extended. That restriction would have meant economic feebleness and decay, for, as Cairnes had so cogently argued, the existence of such a system of unskilled labor depends on the constant enlargement of territory. Since the land which it occupies must needs be impoverished, it can live only by continual migration to fresh fields. This was the reason why the slave power was always so hungry for more slave territory: it was an economic necessity.

And there can be no doubt that the new republic, making slavery its corner-stone, and having no other obvious reason for its existence than the determination to perpetuate its peculiar institution, would have fallen under the ban of the enlightened opinion of the world. With the entire ethical evolution of modern society it would have found itself at war. It is not credible that a slave republic could long have maintained itself upon that territory. The stars in their courses would have

THE BURSTING OF THE STORM 105

fought against it. It would have been forced, before many decades, to face the problem of emancipation. And it is not improbable that that problem might have been worked out in a peaceful evolution, with results less disastrous than those which have attended the destruction of slavery as a measure of war. The relations between the races would have been less strained. It is not impossible that the freedmen and their masters might have dwelt together as amicably as they are dwelling in Jamaica to-day. Beyond a question, a large part of the race hatred which now exists in the South is due to the irritations and antagonisms engendered by the war.

When emancipation had been effected, there would be no reason whatever why the severed sections should remain apart, and they would be almost sure to come together. It is by no means improbable that we might, by this time, — at the end of a half-century after the rupture of the national bond, — have been negotiating for a restoration of the Union, with good hope of dwelling together again in peace and amity, with the race question settled, and the prospect bright of a new Saturnian reign.

What the northern nation might have become, by this time, if it could have devoted all the enormous sum which has been expended for the war, and on the pension list, in the development of its resources, in making its domain more fruitful and more beautiful, and in filling the homes of its people with the abundance of peace, I will not try to tell. Nor could any man compute the moral gain which might have accrued to the nation if the demoralization and corruption incident to such a war could have been avoided.

I know very well that quite another series of possibilities could be excogitated, as the result of peaceable secession, — possibilities as much more dire than existing conditions, as those which I have been imagining are more benign. And nobody will ever know which of these possibilities is the more probable. But, as I recall those anxious days of November and December, 1860, I cannot help wishing that the ethical passion of the North for liberty had been matched with a faith, equally compelling, in the cogency of good will. One or two sermons, yellow with age, bearing those dates, testify of a strong desire to find a better way out of the trouble than the horrible way of war, and I am not ashamed of the youthful faith that a better way was possible.

The dreadful winter dragged slowly by. Congress was trying to patch up a compromise, but the effort was nugatory. The southern states were completing their preparations for the formation of a southern Confederacy, and the shadow of a great calamity lay heavily upon the land. Commercial activities were prostrated; it began to be evident that the debts due from the South to northern merchants would never be paid; the money market was tight and panicky, and the social atmosphere was as dense and depressing as that which we sometimes breathe when an August thunderstorm is brewing.

In February Mr. Lincoln started from Springfield for Washington. The telegraph brought us daily tidings of his progress, and the reports were not, on the whole, reassuring. There was a tender genuineness about the speech to his old neighbors that touched all our hearts, but the other speeches seemed lacking not only in felicity, but in grasp and seriousness. There was little of the cogency and directness of the debates with Douglas; could we have been mistaken in our man? The possibility was appalling. I went over to New York to see him pass down Broadway. He stood in his barouche, bowing rather stiffly right and left to the throng that packed the sidewalks. There was more curiosity than enthusiasm. His face was wan and anxious; he must have known that his greeting greatly lacked cordiality. I stood upon the curbstone, and his carriage paused for a minute or two opposite the place where I was standing, so that I had a good look into his face. It was the only sight of it I ever had, except one brief glimpse of him on horseback, at City Point, in wartime. The face was strong and benign, but unspeakably sad; the burden of a nation was on his heart. Was he man enough for the hour? Some who had come into close contact with him felt confident. Thurlow Weed, the veteran editor, who was no sentimentalist, had had good opportunity to measure his mind, and his verdict was unhesitating; he told us that he was not only honest and true, but "capable — capable in the largest sense of the term. He has read much and thought much of government, inwardly digesting its theory and practice." It was good to get such assurance just then; in fact, we needed it. For, doubtless, in the hearts of millions who had watched this journey there was a painful misgiving that another brilliant editor's estimate of him, as "a simple Susan," might be nearer the mark.

For the dispersion of these fears we had not long to wait. The first inaugural address put them all out of our minds. The man who could meet a great emergency with such wisdom and courage and gentleness was a man whom we need not fear to follow. There was no need of making apologies for Abraham Lincoln, from the hour when the great responsibilities of office were placed upon his shoulders.

Soon came the crucial test of the national authority. The Confederate government, with seven states, had been organized at Montgomery; South Carolina was gathering an army in the environs of Charleston, and had occupied two of the forts in that harbor; but Fort Sumter stood there grim and defiant, with the United States flag flying over it, and a brave Federal officer commanding it. Should it be evacuated or defended? Mr. Lincoln said that it should not be evacuated, and sent supplies for the garrison. The Confederate authorities, hearing this, demanded its surrender. The demand was refused, the Confederate batteries opened on the national citadel, and after an unequal contest the garrison was compelled to abandon the fort. The war was begun, and there was no question as to who began it.

Mr. Lincoln had kept the promise of his inaugural address. "The power confided to me will be used to hold, occupy, and possess the property and places belonging to the government, and to collect the duties and imposts, but beyond what may be necessary for these objects there will be no invasion, no using of force against or among the people anywhere." Not a thing had been done "to coerce a sovereign state"; no troops

THE BURSTING OF THE STORM 109

had been sent even to strengthen the garrison at Fort Sumter; no act more warlike had been committed by the national government than the attempt to supply Major Anderson's soldiers with food. It was for this that the batteries of the seceders had opened on Fort Sumter; that the flag had been insulted and the authority of the nation defied. The patient Lincoln had won the game. This wanton attack upon Sumter gave him, in one hour, a united nation. "Had any one," said Lowell, "ventured to prophecy on the Fourth of March that the immediate prospect of Civil War would be hailed by the people of the free states with a unanimous shout of enthusiasm, he would have been thought a madman. Yet the prophecy would have been verified by what we now see and hear in every city, town, and hamlet from Maine to Kansas."[1] And George Ticknor, in a letter of April 21, bore testimony: "The heather is on fire. I never before knew what a popular sentiment can be. . . . Indeed, here at the North there never was anything like it; for if the feeling was as deep and stern in 1775, it was by no means so intelligent or unanimous, and then the masses to be moved were as a handful compared to our dense population now." The prompt call of the President for seventy-five thousand militiamen to defend the capital was greeted with exultation. The populations that had been hesitant, sullen, apathetic, sprang to their feet as one man.

Professor Shaler had a theory that the processes of development are sometimes mightily hastened; that there are critical instants which complete the work of

[1] *Atlantic Monthly*, June, 1861.

long periods, as when water on the verge of freezing is suddenly converted into ice by a slight blow on the vessel containing it. Such a crystallization was the work of the first gun fired at Fort Sumter.

Probably there was no place in the land where this change was more nearly miraculous than in the city of New York. Through the early months of 1861 New York had been by no means sure that it was not a city without a country. The New York "Herald," which was the paper of largest circulation, was in undisguised sympathy with the secessionists; the mayor of the city, in a message to the Council, had urged that if the South seceded, New York city should also declare itself a free city and dissolve its relations with the Federal Government; and there seems to be good evidence that a plot was incubating, in which a large number of "the most influential and wealthy citizens" were involved, "to throw off the authority of the Federal and State governments, to seize the navy yard at Brooklyn, the vessels of war and the forts in the harbor, and to declare New York a free city." To one who had been gasping in this stifling atmosphere for some months, the change which took place on the day when the bombardment of Fort Sumter began was exhilarating. It was like those sudden northwest breezes which sometimes come down upon the city in the torrid days of August and drive the humidity out to sea.

I went over to the city nearly every day; it was like a bath of oxygen to mingle with the crowds on the ferries and in the streets. One morning, as I went up Fulton Street from the ferry, a crowd appeared, coming up

THE BURSTING OF THE STORM 111

Nassau Street from the south. Some one told me that they were visiting the offices of sundry newspapers, whose attitude upon national questions had been equivocal. They had just come from the office of the "Journal of Commerce," and in response to their suggestion the flag had been displayed on the building of that newspaper. They were by no means a rough crowd; they were making no noise, but there was determination in their looks, and many of them had brickbats or paving-stones in their hands. They had paused in front of the office of the New York "Herald," on the corner of Fulton and Nassau streets, and some one had gone up the stairway on the Fulton Street side. Presently a boy in his shirt-sleeves came down the stairs and ran toward Broadway, returning, in a few moments, with a long parcel, wrapped in brown paper. Immediately a window was opened, and the American flag was thrust out. The crowd cheered it, dropped their brickbats, and dispersed, with some merriment. I had the "Herald" in my hand at the time; its leading editorial was an exasperating plea for affiliation with the South. The next morning its loyalty was unequivocal. "War," it declared, "will make the northern people a unit." I felt that I had been the witness of a conversion which for suddenness quite eclipsed that of Saul of Tarsus.

The next day the Sixth Massachusetts Infantry marched down Broadway, through crowds that rent the air with shouting. What a different temperature from that through which Lincoln had passed not many days before! But in the midst of all this exaltation there came terrible moments of depression. I shall never forget the sickening sense of the reality of it all which came over me as those Massachusetts boys tramped by. They were not all hilarious: on the faces of the more thoughtful there was a strained look; they knew that they were not out for a holiday. I had seen soldiers on parade many times, but this was something else; ball cartridges were in these belts, and these men were marching to dreadful war; before the next noon, some of them would be lying dead in the streets of Baltimore.

It was the next day that our own crack regiment, the Seventh, started for Washington. The massacre in Baltimore had hastened their departure. The metropolis again went wild. Theodore Winthrop, whose life was laid down but a month or two later, was in those ranks. "It was worth a life, that march," he wrote. "Only one who passed, as we did, through that tempest of cheers two miles long, can know the terrible enthusiasm of the occasion."

Not many days after, a great war meeting was held in Union Square. The whole space was packed with tens of thousands of shouting patriots; there were half-a-dozen speaking platforms, and the orators of Gotham were out in force. The "Tribune" was probably justified in saying that it was the greatest crowd ever gathered upon this continent. Leading Democrats were among the speakers, and Archbishop Hughes sent an enthusiastic letter. Mayor Fernando Wood, who a few days before had been counseling alliance with the Confederates, made a vehement speech, in which he answered the boast of the Confederate Secretary of War, that the rebel flag would soon be flying over the national

THE BURSTING OF THE STORM

capital and Faneuil Hall, by declaring that to get Boston they would have to go over the body of every citizen of New York, and that the capture of the capital would mean the enlistment in the army of "every man, woman, and child in the North." New converts are always zealous.

The instances show that the blood of the North was up. The leaders at Charleston and Montgomery must have been astounded. They had reliable advices from well-informed secret service agents in New York that the metropolis was all ready to range itself on their side. Something must have happened.

Yet, in the midst of the tumult and the shouting, the hearts of thoughtful men were very sad. Men like Seward, whose optimism was almost flippant, could talk of ending the war in ninety days, but that was a fond imagination. That bloody years were before us seemed a dreadful certainty. In the "Century War Book,"[1] is a testimony by General J. D. Cox, which reveals the undertone of feeling: —

> The situation hung upon us like a nightmare. Garfield and I were lodging together at the time [in Columbus], and when we reached our sitting-room, after an evening session of the Senate [of the Ohio Legislature], we often found ourselves involuntarily groaning: "Civil war in our land!" The shame, the folly, the outrage seemed too great to believe, and we half hoped to wake from it as from a dream. Among the painful remembrances of those days is the ever-present weight at the heart, which never left me until I found relief in the active duties of camp life at the close of the month. I went about my duties (and I am

[1] Vol. i, p. 87.

sure that most of those with whom I associated did the same) with the half-choking sense of a grief I dared not think of; like one who is dragging himself to the labors of life from some terrible and recent bereavement.

In fact, the labors of life, for people in general, were greatly interrupted. Business was at a standstill; the army of buyers from the South were of course not there, and remittances from that region had ceased; all over the country industry was paralyzed; men were standing idle in the market-place. And it must be confessed that this unwonted excitement did not prove conducive to the growth of churches. The congregations dwindled, the Sunday-schools were decimated, the whole work of the church seemed to have come to a sudden pause. Every Sunday, regiments from New England or northern New York were marching down Broadway on their way to Washington, and the crowds flocked over the ferries to see the spectacle. Our own church, which, in the autumn, seemed to be gathering up its forces, shared in these distractions, and the young pastor found himself struggling with conditions that were hopeless. Like many other enterprises in those days, the church was financially disabled, and the wolf was looking in at the door of the parsonage.

The strain of the work and the anxiety, intensified by the conditions of the national life, were quite too much for a constitution which had hitherto recognized no limitations upon its endurance, and a nervous collapse left me in a crippled condition. It was clear that this work must be abandoned; it was not clear, for a few weeks, that any other work could soon be undertaken.

THE BURSTING OF THE STORM 115

But it happened that there was a little church in Morrisania, two miles north of the Harlem River, which was just then vacant, and it was a good Providence that drew me into that quiet suburb. The people were willing to let me do what I could, which was little, at the beginning; and the light labor was probably better for me than any enforced leisure would have been. So it came about that without a week's interruption my work went forward in this new field.

The territory now included in the borough of the Bronx which stretches north and east from the Harlem River was then parceled out among a number of sprawling villages, Mott Haven, Melrose, Morrisania, Tremont, Fordham, and West Farms, — access to which from the city was given by the Harlem Railroad, and by a line of little steamboats plying between Peek Slip and the Harlem River. From Harlem Bridge a line of rickety stages ran north to the various villages through bottomless mud in the wet seasons, and clouds of dust in the dry. The Third Avenue horse-cars also crawled from the City Hall to the bridge in an hour and twenty minutes. Yet I am persuaded that life was more restful in those days for the inhabitants of that region than it is in these. The sail of forty-five minutes up the East River was very refreshing; the torment of the stages was brief; and we found ourselves at the end of our journey in green country lanes, with no noise of wheels or whistles, with time to work in our gardens, and birds and bees and butterflies filling the air with life and color and music.

Our home in Brooklyn had been upon a street traversed by the Long Island market wagons, the din of whose wheels on the cobblestone pavements began soon after midnight and never ceased; and the silence of the first nights in Morrisania was so oppressive that we could not sleep. The nerves had to adjust themselves to the new conditions. It did not take long, however, and the stillness and sweetness of the rural life were very medicinal.

Through the years of the Civil War this was to be my home. In an hour I could be in the heart of the metropolis, but we were far enough from the madding crowd to escape the nervous wear and tear, and find space for reading and reflection. The little church offered me kindly and grateful associations. It was made up of young professional and business men, teachers, librarians, city officials, and the like; the average of intelligence was much higher than that of my Brooklyn congregation, and the people were disposed to be generous and considerate in their judgment of a young man's limitations.

Meantime the volunteers were pouring southward every day, and the troops of the insurgents were beginning to concentrate in the neighborhood of Washington. Early in July the "Tribune" began printing, under its editorial heading, in flaming capitals, this imperious demand: *Forward to Richmond! Forward to Richmond! The Rebel Congress must not be allowed to meet there on the twentieth of July. By that date the place must be held by the national army!* This language was repeated with the same emphasis, day after day. The newspaper supposed that it was giving voice to the national impa-

THE BURSTING OF THE STORM 117

tience; perhaps it was; but the time had been brief for the assembling and equipment of an army prepared to take the offensive in a country difficult of invasion. It was not long before the tidings came that McDowell was moving southward, in force, and our hearts stood still. On Sunday morning, July 21, as we gathered at the church, news came that the fight was beginning. That night and the next morning the word was all of victory; but before Monday noon we knew that the short-lived triumph had turned to disaster, and that our shattered and demoralized army had come huddling back into the fortifications about Washington. Will any one try to estimate the load that lay that night upon the heart of a loyal nation? There was no discouragement, and not a thought of turning back; the purpose of the people was stronger than ever; but the magnitude and the appalling seriousness of the work before us was brought home to us with terrible power. And it must be admitted that there was much rash and wild talk; the people were not yet sufficiently sure of themselves to bear such a reverse quite steadily. Scapegoats were sought for; the government at Washington was bitterly denounced for inefficiency; the "Tribune" went so far as to demand the immediate resignation of the entire Cabinet. It was well for us that the patient Lincoln was at the helm.

CHAPTER VIII

DARK DAYS

So long ago it seems, so long ago,
Behold, our sons, grown men since those great days, —
Born since the last clear bugle ceased to blow
Its summons down the valley; since the bays
Shook with the roar of fort and answering fleet, —
Our very children look into our eyes
And find strange records, with a mute surprise;
As they some curious traveler might greet
Who kept far countries in his musing mind,
Beyond the weltering seas, the mountain-walls behind.
    And yet it was this land and not another,
Where blazed war's flame and rolled the battle cloud.
In all this land there was no home where brother,
Father, or son hurried not forth; where bowed
No broken-hearted woman when pale Death
Laid his cold finger on the loved one's breath.
Richard Watson Gilder.

THE outstanding memories of all those days in Morrisania are, of course, the events of the war; but in the midst of arms the voices of the spirit were not wholly silent; our life went quietly forward, and other interests were not neglected. The little church gave me no financial worries, and there was time for study. An introduction to the librarian of the Astor Library gained me the freedom of the theological alcoves, and I spent much of my time in them. Professor Roswell D. Hitchcock and Professor Henry B. Smith, of the Union Theological Seminary, also kindly permitted me to attend their lectures, and I gave what time I could to these stimulating teachers. Of greater consequence, however,

DARK DAYS

than these influences, was the entrance into my life of Frederick W. Robertson and Horace Bushnell, — each of them through volumes of sermons which opened to me a new world. Here were men to whom spiritual things were not traditions but living verities; men who knew how to bring religion into vital touch with reality. What I found upon these throbbing pages was what Dr. Munger afterward described as "The Appeal to Life." I can never tell how much I owe to these two men — to Robertson, first, for opening my eyes; to Bushnell, chiefly, for teaching me how to use them.

Some one, to whom I was confessing my indebtedness to Bushnell, told me of an earlier book of his, — "God in Christ," — which I procured, and lived with for some months. The introductory essay, on Language, was, for me, a "Novum Organon," giving me a new sense of the nature of the instrument which I was trying to use, and making entirely clear the futility of the ordinary dogmatic method. And in the three great discourses which followed, delivered at New Haven, at Andover, and at Cambridge, I found an emancipation proclamation which delivered me at once and forever from the bondage of an immoral theology. That there was a gospel to preach I had no longer any doubt, for I had been made to see that the Judge of all the earth would do right. That was the foundation of Bushnell's faith; his heresy was the unfaltering belief that God is just. What he denied was simply those assertions and implications of the old theology which attribute to God injustice. He had found God, in his college days, by his insistence upon an ethical theology. And his entire quarrel with the traditional dogmas grew out of his determination to admit no explanations of the divine conduct which were in conflict with the fundamental principles of morals. That men should be judged and doomed before they were born; that men should be held blameworthy and punishable for what was done by their ancestors; that justice could be secured by the punishment of one for the sin of another, were propositions to him unthinkable. He dared to say so, and by his courage he opened the way to a larger liberty for a great multitude. Yet, at that day, he was still under the ban of his own denomination; the heresy-hunters had not been able to dislodge him from his church, but they had filled the churches with suspicions of him, and "Bushnellism" was a name with which no ambitious minister could afford to be branded. It was well understood that nobody suspected of that taint could hope for ordination over a Congregational church. Nevertheless, what he had taught seemed to me true, and it was hardly possible that I should hold my tongue about it. Gradually my own teaching reflected the new conceptions into which I had been led, but as they were not set forth controversially, nobody seemed to be greatly troubled by them.

One Sunday morning, after a sermon in which I had been more frank than ever before in the expression of the heretical theory, I found myself following up the street one of my most conservative parishioners, who had intimated to me, once or twice, his dissent from what he had been hearing. Naturally I hesitated to expose myself to his criticism, but he was walking

DARK DAYS

slowly and I found it difficult to avoid overtaking him. His greeting was: "That was a good sermon! I wish we might have more sermons like that." The good man would have been confounded if he had known that he had been listening to heresy. I did not enlighten him. Since the only bit of genuine heresy to which he had been exposed seemed so palatable to him, it would have been unkind to disturb his enjoyment of it.

The small chapel in which we were worshiping soon became too strait for us, and with much labor and sacrifice we succeeded in replacing it with a larger and more attractive church. That the church ought to serve all the higher interests of the community seemed to us a sound principle, and we opened the new church the first winter for a course of lectures which made no small stir in our quiet suburb. The course included Miss Anna E. Dickinson, then a popular speaker on political and social subjects, George William Curtis, Bayard Taylor, and Ralph Waldo Emerson. My first meeting with Mr. Curtis was when I called to invite him to deliver this lecture. He was then writing the editorials for "Harper's Weekly," and his work was done at a small pine table in the middle of the composing-room on the top floor of the Harper Building on Franklin Square. Here I found him, surrounded by printers working at their cases, intent upon his own task and quite oblivious of what was going on about him. It was a curious environment for a nature so fastidious. Mr. Curtis received me very genially, and cordially entered into my plans. I visited him more than once, after that, in the same place, and always brought away from the interview the impression of a man whose kindness was equal to his refinement.

With Bayard Taylor, too, I had two or three interesting interviews, in connection with this engagement. On the winter night after the lecture I joined him in a long walk, and he talked quite freely of his experiences in Egypt and in the Norse countries. He was a fine specimen of a man, with a frame fitted for such adventures as had made the staple of his life; and while his manner as a public speaker was not unpleasing, his talk was far finer. I had followed him round the world in the "Tribune," and it was a great pleasure to hear some of the stories from his own lips.

Emerson's simple and gracious ways were very winning. He chatted with me most naturally for a little while before the lecture, and I could easily understand how the farmers of Concord found him an agreeable companion. There was not a particle of affectation, and he met you on your own ground and talked about the things you were interested in. I do not think that his lecture was popular. I have forgotten, now, what he called it; it was one of his ethical essays — preaching, of course, of a high quality. But his manner was so quiet and deliberate, there was so little of what the reporters call "oratory," that most of the audience voted it rather tame. His manuscript, as was often the case, was a pile of loose leaves, which he turned over and turned back quite frequently, sometimes losing his place, and giving us a chance to reflect on what had been said. I remember a subsequent occasion in Boston, when the audience waited for a minute or two while he fumbled

DARK DAYS

with his leaves. At last he got what he had been looking for, and it was but a single sentence, — the last sentence of the lecture. As we came out of the hall an auditor said: "We had to wait a good while for that last word. But," he added after a pause, "it was worth waiting for."

One of my Morrisania parishioners was Mr. Robert Bonner, proprietor of the New York "Ledger," who had a summer home on the West Ridge, and who was wont to give me an airing, now and then, behind the swift steeds of which he was so fond. Mr. Bonner was then negotiating with Mr. Beecher about a story for the "Ledger," and had made him, undoubtedly, a munificent offer for such a production. He showed me, one day, a letter from Mr. Beecher, promising to undertake this work, and humorously imagining some future biographer referring to him as "this distinguished novelist (who sometimes preached)." Mr. Bonner was himself quite a character. Of sturdy Scotch sense and clean mind, there was nothing yellowish about his journalism. It may be admitted that the fiction on which he fed the multitude was not of the highest literary art, but it was as moral as a Bowery play. "I tell all my editors," he said, "that nothing must ever appear in the 'Ledger' which would trouble my Scotch Presbyterian mother if she should read it after prayer meeting."

All this life in Morrisania is so colored and flavored with memories of the war that it is hard to separate its fortunes from those of the nation during this period. Of course the national interest was the absorbing interest; the suppression of the rebellion, the preservation of the Union, was not only our business, it was our religion. The young men of our homes were given up with a consecration as holy as that with which any gift was ever laid upon an altar of sacrifice. And there was privation and suffering for those who remained at home, as well as for those who enlisted. When the price of gold kept mounting up until a dollar in gold would buy two dollars and a half in currency; when a yard of plain shirting cost thirty cents, and a pound of sugar twenty-seven, and a pound of rump steak twenty-five, people whose salaries had not been raised found themselves in exiguous circumstances. The rigid economies to which we were forced, the shifts we were compelled to make to supply our common needs, and keep ourselves presentable, were part of the price we had to pay for the life of the nation. Nor was it always grudgingly paid; we did not forget the heavier sacrifice of the men at the front.

I must not forget that I am not writing a history of the war, but it is hard to turn the pen aside from all that made life in those days memorable and significant. One recalls, with a sense of suffering, the long agony of the conflict in Virginia, with the frequent changes of commanders; the great expectations of McClellan, long cherished and often revived, but gradually sinking into hopelessness; the experiments with Pope and Hooker and Burnside; the heartsickness of hope long deferred which now and then overcame the nation. Through all these dark days the conviction was growing that the war could not end without the destruction of slavery. Lin-

DARK DAYS

coln's large statesmanship early pressed upon Congress measures for the compensated emancipation of the slaves of the border states; he believed that motives of economy as well as of justice would warrant the nation in assuming the burden; but his overtures met with scant encouragement from the people most concerned. The border states declined to move in the matter, and the President was driven to consider emancipation as a military necessity.

No single incident of those dark days of 1862 is more vividly impressed on my mind than Lincoln's answer to Greeley's "Prayer of Twenty Millions," for the emancipation of the slaves. Greeley's open letter to the President gave voice to the impatience of the nation; the war, which Seward was going to end in ninety days, had dragged itself through a year, and although some light had appeared in the west, the outlook was gloomy. McClellan's Peninsular Campaign had met with disastrous failure, and the spirit of discontent was abroad in the land. "We require of you," said the great editor, rather magisterially, "as the first servant of the republic, charged especially and preëminently with this duty, that you *execute the laws*. We think you are strangely and disastrously remiss in the discharge of your official and imperative duty with regard to the emancipating provisions of the new confiscation act; that you are unduly influenced by the counsels, the representations, the menaces of certain fossil politicians hailing from the border slave states; that timid counsels in such a crisis are calculated to prove perilous and probably disastrous. We complain that the Union cause has suffered and is now suffering immensely from your mistaken deference to rebel slavery." And there is much more, equally petulant and critical. It would seem that Mr. Greeley might have had a little more patience and charity; certain it is that not all of the twenty millions for whom he assumed to speak were equally skeptical of the President's purpose. But whatever may have been the popular disaffection when this letter appeared, the President's reply effectually extinguished it. Mr. Greeley probably never rendered the country a greater service than when he called forth that answer. It appeared in the "Tribune" itself, and probably every newspaper in the North printed it. Few American state papers have been more universally read, perhaps none ever made a more profound impression. I doubt if any battle of the Civil War helped more to win the final victory than did this short letter of Abraham Lincoln. It cleared the air. It silenced the croakers. It filled the whole North with a new spirit. It drew the hearts of hundreds of thousands to Lincoln with an affection and trust that from that day never wavered. There is room for it here; it is one of the great words that must not be forgotten.

If there be in it [your letter] any statements or assumptions of facts which I may know to be erroneous, I do not, now and here, controvert them. If there be in it any inferences which I may believe to be falsely drawn, I do not, now and here, argue against them. If there be perceptible in it an impatient and dictatorial tone, I waive it, in deference to an old friend whose heart I have always supposed to be right.

DARK DAYS

As to the policy I "seem to be pursuing," as you say, I have not meant to leave any one in doubt. I would save the Union. I would save it in the shortest way, under the Constitution. The sooner the national authority can be restored, the nearer the Union will be "the Union as it was." If there be those who would not save the Union unless they could at the same time save slavery, I do not agree with them. If there be those who would not save the Union unless they could at the same time destroy slavery, I do not agree with them. My paramount object in this struggle is to save the Union, and is not either to save or to destroy slavery. If I could save the Union without freeing any slave I would do it; and if I could save it by freeing all the slaves I would do it; and if I could save it by freeing some and leaving others alone I would also do that. What I do about slavery and the colored race I do because I believe it helps to save the Union, and what I forbear I forbear because I do not believe it would help to save the Union. I shall do less whenever I believe that what I am doing hurts the cause, and I shall do more whenever I shall believe doing more will help the cause. I shall try to correct errors when shown to be errors, and I shall adopt new views so fast as they shall appear to be true views.

I have here stated my purpose, according to my view of official duty; and I intend no modification of my oft-expressed personal wish that all men everywhere could be free.

How fine and large it is! Not a trace of resentment or impatience, not an ungracious tone; the calm utterance of a strong soul, who has learned the great prophetic word: "In quietness and confidence shall be your strength." And how perfect is the form of it! Were words ever handled more deftly? His sentences go like bullets straight to the mark.

And who could have guessed from anything here said that the Emancipation Proclamation was already written; that it had been lying for some weeks in his portfolio; that it had been submitted to his Cabinet and approved by them, and was withheld only from the feeling that the issuance of it in those dark days might seem like an act of desperation, and in the conviction that it would be better to send it to the country on the wings of victory? That was one of Mr. Seward's wise suggestions, which Lincoln had promptly adopted. How little ground there was for the accusation that Lincoln's policy was dictated by a "mistaken deference to rebel slavery"! It was just a month later, after the battle of Antietam, that the Proclamation was published; but this letter of August 23 put an end to the radical carping against Lincoln, and united the North in his support. "We are coming, Father Abraham, three hundred thousand more," was the answer of the people to this call of their leader. The enlistments went on with new spirit, and it was the revival of hope and courage in the Union army that gave us the victory of Antietam and prepared the way for the Proclamation.

I remember well that September day when the long-delayed blow was struck which destroyed slavery. The New York State Association of Congregationalists was in session at Syracuse; and the news was brought into one of our meetings. Immediately the order of the day was suspended, and the venerable Doctor Joshua Leavitt, then an editor of the "Independent," formerly

DARK DAYS 129

editor of the "Emancipator," and one of the original members of the "Anti-Slavery Society," was called upon to offer prayer. What a cry to Heaven it was — of thanks and praise, of penitence and humiliation, of hope and courage! This great soul had long been waiting for this hour, and probably never expected to see it. How many of those who had been seeking to awaken the conscience of the nation against slavery had ever cherished the hope that the end of it would come while they were on the earth? By most rational men such an expectation would have been counted visionary. It was pathetic to catch the note of surprise which mingled with the exultation of Dr. Leavitt's prayer.

The end was not yet. The moral victory was won, but there were yet dreary months before the tide of battle would turn. The disasters of Fredericksburg and Chancellorsville, and the dubious combat of Stone River, were yet to follow, while the irritating and disheartening opposition of such men as Vallandigham at the North was a heavy tax upon the patience and faith of loyal men.

It is hardly to be wondered at that General Lee, emboldened by his almost uniform successes in Virginia, and encouraged by what he believed to be the rapidly rising tide of opposition to the war in the North, should have resolved to carry the war into the enemy's country, to capture Harrisburg and Philadelphia, and to cut off the national capital from communication with the rest of the nation. That, he naturally thought, would bring the war to a speedy termination, and would secure the independence of the Confederacy. His bold advance into

Maryland and Pennsylvania, in the midsummer of 1863, was a stroke of strategy which the conditions seemed to warrant. But he was reckoning without his host. Gettysburg made it plain to him and to all the world that the will of the nation was unbroken.

The anxiety and suspense of those days are still, to a few of us, a vivid memory. When we knew that Ewell's corps was within four miles of Harrisburg; that the railway station between Harrisburg and Baltimore had been destroyed; that York had been occupied by the Confederate forces; that Philadelphia was threatened; that business was completely suspended; and that the people of the Quaker City — ministers and lawyers and merchants, among the rest — were working in the trenches to fortify the city against the invaders, — it can be imagined that for many of those who lived a little further north there was not much calm repose. Yet I cannot recall any symptoms of a panic. Those were anxious days, but they were not days of despondency or fear; and if it had been imagined that the appearance of a Confederate army on northern soil would be a signal for the rising of the disaffected elements in the North to welcome the invader, the expectation was rudely overthrown. Governor Seymour, of New York, had been one of the sharpest critics of the administration, but before Ewell could get to Harrisburg, Governor Seymour had nineteen regiments of New York militia in the trenches before that city. In the presence of this peril the divisions which had existed among the northern people disappeared. And when, in the critical and decisive struggle of the war, the Confederacy gathered up all

DARK DAYS

its strength and hurled it against the unflinching battle-line of Meade, only to shatter itself against that adamant, we all knew that the beginning of the end had come. What a Fourth of July was that, my countrymen, when we read in our morning papers these restrained but tender words! "The President announces to the country that news from the Army of the Potomac, up to 10 P. M. of the 3d, is such as to cover that army with the highest honor, to promise a great success to the cause of the Union, and to claim a great condolence for all of the many gallant fallen; and that for this he especially desires that on this day He whose will, not ours, should ever be done, be everywhere remembered and reverenced with profoundest gratitude."

Yes, we were alive, that day, some of us; and we have not all forgotten how the landscape grew dim with the mists of thankful tears, and how our voices choked when we tried to speak to one another the words of congratulation. If we could have known what news was traveling toward us, — that a dispatch from Grant, dated that very morning, was on its way to the nearest telegraph station, to let us know that Vicksburg had just surrendered, — the cup of our rejoicing would have been filled to overflowing.

It would seem that such victories should have resulted in rapidly recruiting the national army, but in fact volunteering had ceased, and the only resource of the government was the enforcement of the Conscription Act. In most of the states this measure, though very unpopular, was submitted to without resistance; but in New York city there were large elements of imperfectly

Americanized immigrants to whom this exaction was intolerable. And almost before the odor of the burnt powder of the Fourth of July rejoicings had faded from the air, there was insurrection in New York city against the enforcement of this law. The scenes of those draft riots one would gladly erase from the memory. Such an eruption of savagery has not often disfigured our civilization. For two or three days New York was under mob rule. The police were powerless; the militia regiments were away in Pennsylvania, resisting the invasion, and the lawless elements were let loose. Frenzied crowds stormed the saloons and demanded drink, and with their fury thus rekindled, roamed the streets, dealing death and destruction. The buildings in which the draft had been progressing were burned to the ground, and when the flames spread to other buildings it was difficult to secure the coöperation of the firemen to stop the conflagration, for they, too, were more or less bitten with the madness of the mob. The house of the mayor was assailed; the "Tribune" office was gutted; worst of all, the Colored Orphan Asylum, on Fifth Avenue, a philanthropic institution which was giving shelter to several hundred children, was sacked and burned. The negroes were the principal victims of the brutality of the mob. The rioters were inflamed with the notion that this was an abolition war, and that they were being drafted to fight to free the negro. They proposed, instead, to do what they could to exterminate him. A dispatch to Secretary Stanton at 9.30 on the night of Monday, July 13, informed him that small mobs were chasing individual negroes "as hounds would chase a fox."

DARK DAYS

We watched the city anxiously that night, from our home in Morrisania; the horizon was lurid with conflagrations. What would have happened before morning, it is difficult to imagine, if before midnight a tremendous rain had not begun to fall, putting out the fires and quenching the madness of the mob. The next morning, however, chaos came again. The bands of civilization were loosed, and arson and pillage were running riot. All the thieves and thugs in the region were set free to work their will. Men were held up and robbed in the streets. The omnibuses and horse-cars ceased to run. The Harlem and Hudson River tracks were torn up, and there was no access to the city from the north. Telegraph lines were cut. All business was suspended.

The little passenger boats on the East River continued to run, and by means of one of them I managed to make my way to the lower part of the city, which was not, perhaps, a prudent adventure. I looked in at the wrecked office of the "Tribune," and found the City Hall Park opposite filled with the mob. Governor Seymour, it was reported, was coming to the city, and would address the rioters. The throng was moving uneasily about, evidently with no leadership or concert of action, and there was little noise. While I stood there Governor Seymour appeared in the balcony of the City Hall, and made his famous address. I could hear his voice, but was not near enough to catch his words.

Much was made of the phrase, "My friends," with which the governor began his speech. That criticism is, perhaps, somewhat captious. Nevertheless, it was no time for persuasion. None but the most rigorous measures were adequate in that emergency. General Wool, with such regulars as could be spared from the forts in the harbor, and with such veterans as could be hurriedly organized for service, soon had a force which could make short work of mobs. With the return of the militia regiments from Pennsylvania, order was soon restored; not, however, until a thousand men had been killed and wounded, and a million and a half of property had been destroyed.

The suburbs, in the meantime, were largely unprotected, and the lawless depredators, checked in their operations in the city, were soon making incursions into the outlying districts. It became necessary to organize a Home Guard in Morrisania to perform police duty; and men of the vicinage volunteered for service, taking turns in patrolling the streets at night. With my next neighbor I served for several nights in this capacity, seeking to become a terror to evil-doers. A huge horse-pistol was the only weapon I could lay my hands on; it was never loaded, and I fear that I could not have discharged it without peril, but it was a formidable-looking piece of artillery, and I trusted that the sight of it might strike dread to the heart of any lurking footpad.

A curious comment it was upon the race prejudice which found such brutal expression in these draft riots, that while the ruins of the Colored Orphan Asylum were still smoking, Robert Shaw was leading the storming column of the Fifty-fourth Massachusetts colored regiment in the assault upon Fort Wagner. "Thirty-four years later," says Mr. Rhodes, "appeared on Boston Common the contribution of sculpture to this heroic

DARK DAYS

episode. The thought and skill of Augustus Saint-Gaudens portraying Shaw and his negro soldiers marching to Battery Wharf to take the steamer for the South, has forever blazoned the words of Lincoln: 'And then there will be some black men who can remember that with silent tongue and clenched teeth and steady eye and well-poised bayonet they have helped mankind on to this great consummation.'" [1]

From this time onward the hopeful symptom was the rapid enlistment of the negroes, and their good behavior on the battlefield. It began to look as though the necessity of conscription would be obviated by the replenishing of our armies from this source.

[1] *History of the United States*, iv, 333.

CHAPTER IX

THE END OF THE WAR

> Rushed the great drama on its tragic way
> Swift to the happy end from that tremendous day.
> Happy, indeed, could memory lose her power
> And yield to joy alone the glad, triumphant hour;
> Happy if every aching heart could shun
> Remembrance of the unreturning one;
> If at the Grand Review, when mile on mile
> And day on day the marching columns past,
> Darkened not o'er the world the shadow vast
> Of his foul murder — he the free from guile,
> Sad-hearted, loving, and beloved, and wise,
> Who ruled with sinewy hands and dreaming eyes.
> What soul that lived then who remembers not
> The hour, the landscape, ah! the very spot, —
> Hateful for aye, — where news that he was slain
> Struck like a hammer on the dazèd brain!
> *Richard Watson Gilder.*

THROUGH the autumn of 1863 victory seemed to be coming our way, but with hesitant feet. Chickamauga dulled our hopes, but Missionary Ridge and Chattanooga gave us a happy Thanksgiving. The appointment of Grant to the chief command in the next spring, and the resolute movement of the Army of the Potomac southward, brought us all new hope. But the battles of the Wilderness and Spottsylvania tried our faith, and the disastrous repulse of Cold Harbor sent our hopes down to zero. There was nothing between us and despair but the invincible determination of a man who did not know how to be beaten.

THE END OF THE WAR

It was four or five days after Cold Harbor that I received a letter, scrawled on the leaf of a blank-book, from my half-brother, who was a private in the Eighth New York Heavy Artillery, telling me that my only brother, who was a lieutenant in the same regiment, was missing, after that fatal repulse; he had fallen at the moment when his regiment retreated, and had been left upon the field. Securing an appointment for service in the Christian Commission, I started immediately for the front.

The scenes of that journey are fresh in my memory. From Baltimore I took passage on the transport for Fortress Monroe, finding on my arrival that Grant was moving his army to the south side of the James River. Transports laden with troops were coming down the Bay from the York River, and ascending the James; we heard that the bulk of the army was moving across the Peninsula between the two rivers, and would cross the James at Harrison's Landing. There was a delay of a day or more at Fortress Monroe, which I utilized in visiting Norfolk, and in passing the scene of the fight between the Monitor and the Merrimac. A flag marked the watery grave of the rebel ram.

It was on a hot morning, late in June, that we steamed away up the James, past the wrecks of the old wooden frigates that the Merrimac had destroyed, past Newport News and Jamestown Island. The Confederates had been amusing themselves by firing upon transports at various places along the south bank, which lent an element of expectancy to the rather dull journey. One surprise was the entire lack of cities and villages for a hundred miles of this navigable stream. The banks of the Hudson and the Connecticut, with which I was familiar, were lined with towns; where were the people?

An hour before sunset we found ourselves in the midst of stirring scenes. The river was full of craft of every size and shape lying at anchor; beyond this flotilla was a pontoon bridge over which troops were pouring south in ceaseless procession. We disembarked and climbed the north bank; from a bluff overlooking the river, and commanding the plateau which stretched away to the west and north, a spectacle was visible which one might travel far to see. The supply trains, the ambulances, and the artillery were parked there upon that plain, whitening the summer fields as far as the eye could reach; the lines of the soldiery came winding across the plain, and went filing down to the river-crossing. The men had been marching for days; they were grimy with dust and perspiration; their clothing had evidently been reduced to the minimum; yet they were apparently in good heart. I stood for more than an hour and watched them marching by, exchanging greetings with them, and almost all of them had a laugh or a jolly comment on things visible or audible. A ponderous old negro cook stood simmering over his evening fire, just south of the line; every man's head was turned toward him, and every variety of good-natured chaff was shouted at him. There was little to choose between officers and men so far as toilet was concerned, all were about equally disreputable; but the men were in good health, and, although they had just come from Cold Harbor, they were full of good cheer.

THE END OF THE WAR

After sunset we boarded a transport above the pontoon bridge on which a portion of the Sixth Corps was going up to Bermuda Hundred, and late that night were landed there, finding shelter in the hospital tent at Butler's headquarters. Here, and at City Point, on the other side of the Appomattox, I found my work for the next few weeks. The army was investing Petersburg, for the last long struggle of the war. Two or three corps had crossed the river; Grant himself had not yet arrived. His headquarters were soon established at City Point, and before his arrival I helped to pitch the first tents of the post hospital on the Appomattox, which, before I came away, had grown to be a city of eight or ten thousand sick and wounded men.

Immediately on my arrival I sought out my brother's regiment. At my first visit to the front I found it in the battle-line a mile or two from Petersburg. An aide at Hancock's headquarters showed me the field across which the trenches ran in which the regiment lay, but admonished me that no one could safely cross that field. Accordingly I betook myself to the field hospital into which wounded men were constantly being brought on stretchers and in ambulances. It was a farmhouse, with ample grounds and outhouses; in the shade and under the shelters two or three hundred wounded men were lying. It was my first experience of this kind of service. I had always supposed myself to be an exceedingly squeamish person, liable to be overcome by sights of blood and suffering, but, for some reason, the gruesome sights which here assailed my sense did not disturb me. There was work to do in caring for the needs of these suffering men; a cup of cold water was a welcome gift to many of them, and the cloths that had been laid upon their wounds needed wetting. I kept myself busy till near sundown caring for these sufferers, and then hurried through the woods to the headquarters of the Eighteenth Corps, where my blankets were, to find that that corps had been ordered to cross the Appomattox. It was a night's march of a dozen miles, and by the time we reached the end of it, I was ready to lie down by the roadside with no covering. For the next six hours I am sure that the heaviest cannonade would not have wakened me.

A day or two after this, a chaplain from my brother's division brought me word that the regiment was in an accessible place, and I hastened to learn what I could of the fate of the missing one. It was little that any one could tell me, but enough to make it probable that I should never see him again. The colonel of his regiment, Peter A. Porter, of Niagara, a man of large influence in New York, had fallen in the same charge. The regiment had gone into the Cold Harbor fight, eighteen hundred strong; the adjutant showed me his roster that morning, and there were less than six hundred names. Lieutenant-Colonel Bates was in command; I sat down and talked with him for a little while that Sunday morning about the experiences of the last few days. Within a week he was brought into one of my wards at City Point, mortally wounded. I cared for him until the end.

Those few weeks with the army were a rather important part of my educational opportunity. I learned several things which are not taught in the theological

THE END OF THE WAR

seminary; the close contact with men, under circumstances when pretense and insincerity were out of the question, was very illuminating. The men were exceedingly grateful for all that was done for them. The Sanitary Commission and the Christian Commission sought to render them a kind of service which the regular hospital workers could not always command. Under the advice of the physicians we prepared for the sick men various delicacies, we provided them with certain comforts which were not in the hospital supplies, and we endeavored to befriend them in many personal ways. We wrote letters home for them, we distributed to them papers and reading-matter, we sometimes read to them, we encouraged them to call on us for any help we might render. Sick men are proverbially selfish and exacting, but these men were not. "Serve that boy first, chaplain; he needs it more than I do." That was the rule. Men thought of the comfort and welfare of their comrades more than they thought of their own. It could not have been always so; there must have been selfishness and meanness among them; all I can say is that in all my work among them, I encountered almost none of it.

The memorandum-book which I carried in this hospital work contains many other items suggesting the kind of service needed. Joyce, in Ward 3, wants a pair of crutches, and Gysi, in 17, a pair of drawers, and O'Neill, in 18, a shirt; Anthony, in 8, craves mustard for his salt junk, and Ward, in 1, hankers for some cheese and a Testament; and Elmer, in 3, wants a comb, and Underwood, in 6, a pencil. All such supplies are in our store tent, and it is a great pleasure to provide them. A

Confederate soldier, in one of my tents, who cannot write, permits me to be his amanuensis. He wishes me to tell his wife that he is wounded in the left leg below the knee, and that the doctors hope to save it; in his first letter he requires me to say that he is treated "as well as he could expect to be." That is rather diplomatic. But before I write again he is ready to make it much less equivocal. The kindness with which he is surrounded is, evidently, a great surprise to him. We do a banking business, in a modest way; I find that I have charged myself with two hundred dollars which I have received from his chaplain, for Alexander McIvor, who has gone to Washington, and which I am to deliver to him there, on my return; and beneath it a receipt for the amount from a Christian Commission man in Washington, who undertakes to pass it over to McIvor. Confidence is not lacking.

One day, going hurriedly into the tent of one of the nurses, I met her coming out with a short man in a blue blouse and a slouch hat. Paying no attention to her guest, I did my errand, when she confounded me by saying, "Do you know General Grant?" I came to attention very promptly, and invited the general to go with me to the headquarters of the Christian Commission. We gave him a comfortable seat, and treated him to lemonade, and tried to learn from him something about the result of the hard fighting which had been going on for the preceding thirty-six hours. We learned very little. We had suffered some heavy losses, he said, — which was not news to us; but we had gained some decided advantages in position. But the general

THE END OF THE WAR 143

was more interested in the weather than in the details of military movements; he was evidently a man who could be silent in several languages.

Another day, going down to the landing, I saw quite a cavalcade coming out of Grant's headquarters. Pausing to let them pass, I saw that General Grant was accompanied by President Lincoln, mounted on a tall steed, and his little son Tad on a pony; Colonel Horace Porter was also of this party, and there were several staff officers. They were just starting for the front, seven or eight miles away. Lincoln was wearing a tall silk hat, and he was not a conspicuously graceful rider. It was Lincoln's only visit to the army before Petersburg. I was not at the front when he arrived, but Mr. Rhodes thus describes it: —

The President on horseback, wearing a high silk hat, frock coat, and black trousers, rode with Grant along the line. A civilian, mounted, was always an odd sight amid the crowd of uniformed and epauletted officers; and Lincoln, although a good horseman, was ever awkward, and now, covered with dust, presented the appearance of a country farmer riding into town, wearing his Sunday clothes. But the character of the man disarmed the keen sense of the ridiculous of the American soldiers, and as the word was passed along that "Uncle Abe is with us," he was greeted with cheers and shouts that came from the heart. He visited a division of colored soldiers who had won distinction by their bravery in Smith's assault on the works at Petersburg. They flocked around the liberator of their race, kissing his hands, touching his clothes for the virtue they conceived to be in them, cheering, laughing, singing hymns of praise, shouting, "God bless Massa

Lincoln!" "De Lord save Fader Abraham!" "De day of jubilee am come, shuah." His head was bare, his eyes were full of tears, his voice broke with emotion.[1]

The weather was sultry and dry, the water-supply was inadequate, and before the end of June it became evident that I should soon be an inmate of the hospital, if I did not hasten homeward. Very reluctantly I laid down that labor. My note-book bears witness to that regret, on the ground that "There is so much to do and so few who are willing to work, or who can work, effectively, for the *temporal* welfare of the soldiers." The underscoring of "temporal" would seem to have some significance, though I do not now distinctly recall the circumstances which justified it.

That homeward journey was a troubled dream. The malaria was burning in my veins, and the weariness and suffering of the passage by the fetid transports and the crowded railway cars are a horrible memory. For a day or two after I reached home I hoped to be able to resume my work, but the poison was in my blood, and a sullen fight of two months with a slow fever was ahead of me. The vital breath of the Berkshire Hills at length brought me back to life.

The last winter of the war dragged gloomily by; Sherman's army was raiding the South; Thomas and Schofield were striking deadly blows against the Confederacy in its western strongholds, and the Army of the Potomac was besieging Petersburg and waiting for the hour to strike when the long agony should be at an end. That it must come soon seemed probable; the

[1] *History of the United States*, iv, 492.

THE END OF THE WAR 145

resources of the South were well-nigh exhausted, and some of the Confederate leaders were beginning to talk of the terms of peace. But we had waited long, and hope was half-dead in our hearts. For four bitter, wasting, terrible years we had been carrying this load, and predictions of success were now always discounted by our fears.

When, therefore, in the beginning of April, we heard that the Army of the Potomac had moved south and west with the purpose of surrounding and capturing Lee's army, there was but a dull popular response to tidings which would once have been exciting. And when we learned that Sheridan, at Five Forks, had cut the enemy's army in two, and that Petersburg was taken, that was good news; but we had heard good news before, and we dared not permit ourselves to be elated. And when the dispatches made it clear that Lee was flying away toward the mountains, and that our own left wing was pushing ahead to circumvent him, we only wondered what mischance it would be that would dash these expectations. For a day or two the news was scanty and confused; but at last that bright Monday morning came which turned the long winter of our discontent to glorious summer.

I was working in my garden, and, looking up, I saw my next neighbor, who was a Wall Street broker, come striding down the street, his coat-tails flying. He had been down to the city, and at this early hour was returning, evidently in a very exalted mood. He rushed into his house without stopping to speak to me, and immediately came out with his flag, which he hoisted to the top of his flagstaff; then he ran back into the house and came out again with his revolver, which he began firing into the air. "What's the matter, MacArthur?" I shouted. "Lee has surrendered!" was all he had time to say. He went on with his shooting. At last he composed himself sufficiently to tell me that there was no business down town; that the Street had gone wild; that the people were frantic with joy. Mr. Rhodes's description revives the scene, which my neighbor that morning pictured to me with gleaming eyes and hilarious tones and profuse gesticulation: —

Business was suspended and the courts adjourned. Cannons fired, bells rang, flags floated, houses and shops were gay with the red, white, and blue. There were illuminations and bonfires. The streets of the cities and towns were filled with men who shook hands warmly, embraced each other, shouted, laughed, and cheered, and were indeed beside themselves in their great joy. There were pledges in generous wines and much common-drinking in bar-rooms and liquor shops. There were fantastic processions, grotesque performances, and some tomfoolery. Grave and old gentlemen forgot their age and played the pranks of schoolboys. But always above these foolish and bibulous excesses sounded the patriotic and religious note of the jubilee. "Praise God from whom all blessings flow" were the words most frequently sung in the street, the Board of Trade, and on the Stock Exchange. One writer records that in the bar-room of Willard's Hotel, Washington, when the news arrived, an elderly gentleman sprang upon the bar and led the crowd in singing with unwonted fervor the well-known doxology. "Twenty thousand men in the busiest haunts

THE END OF THE WAR 147

of trade in one of the most thronged cities of the world," Motley wrote, "uncovered their heads spontaneously and sang the psalm of thanksgiving, 'Praise God.'" [1]

Nor was there, in that outburst of thanksgiving, much of the exultation of the victor over the vanquished. The first impulse of the people, as I recall the impressions of the hour, seemed to be one of tenderness toward a fallen foe. I have found a soiled and faded sermon, which was preached on the Sunday after Lee's surrender.

There has been [says this old witness] in the hearts of the people who have been rejoicing, a sincere pity for the vanquished. With our joy for the victory there has been mingled a real sorrow for the army and the people of the South, — a sorrow not only because they are called upon to suffer so terribly, but that they are made to pass through such humiliation. If we could have saved their lives and their property and their pride and at the same time have saved the nation, I do not know who would not have chosen it. There is nothing like hatred or vengeance in the hearts of the people of the North toward the people of the South. There has only been a stern determination that they should not rend the nation asunder. . . . I most firmly believe that by a hearty and considerate kindness to the southern people we can restore the old relations of amity; nay, that we can establish new relations of friendship which shall be far closer and more enduring than the old ones were. But to do this will require the utmost gentleness and patience on our part. There must be no more angry disputings, no more ridicule, no more crimination and recrimination. Bygones must be bygones. Shame upon the northern man who would fling in

[1] *History of the United States*, v, 131.

the face of his southern brother a single taunt! Shame upon the northern newspaper that speaks of the southern people in any other terms than those of considerate kindness! Shame upon the Federal officer, whether civil or military, who will not do all in his power to lighten the load of humiliation under which the people of the South must come back into the Union! There is room now for the exercise of a true chivalry, — opportunity to show our southern friends that we know how tender a feeling is wounded pride, and how to treat it with the gentleness and the respect that are the only medicine adequate to its cure.

Such words as these reflected the temper in which many of the people of the North were disposed to bring to a close the bitter and bloody struggle. That Lincoln's great heart was full of this irenic purpose was soon manifest. What he said at his last Cabinet meeting was not known to the people till long afterward, but it was indicated in all his public utterances: "I hope there will be no persecution, no bloody work, after this war is over. No one need expect me to take any part in hanging or killing these men, even the worst of them. Frighten them out of the country, open the gates, let down the bars, scare them off. Enough lives have been sacrificed. We must extinguish our resentments if we expect harmony and union." [1]

None but those who bore the heavy burdens and the tormenting anxieties of those four years of war can understand the sense of relief that filled the hearts of the people in those April days. Every man seemed to be

[1] Rhodes, *History of the United States*, v, 137.

THE END OF THE WAR 149

drawing a deeper breath, and speaking in a calmer and more confident tone. It was over and gone — the horrible nightmare; our hearts were so buoyant that it did not seem as if we had ever known trouble. We read of the unfurling of the flag over the ruins of Fort Sumter just four years from the day on which it was lowered, with a deep and solemn gladness; there was no shouting or hilarity. The heart of the nation was filled with the abundance of peace.

Monday, Tuesday, Wednesday, Thursday, Friday — days fuller of well-being than some of us had ever known. Saturday morning I went out to my doorstep and picked up my morning "Tribune." It was black with mourning lines!

Merciful God! What a cry it was that went to heaven that morning! The disaster was appalling, but the grief was heart-breaking. There are many living yet who will not deny that they have never known a more poignant sorrow. Our President was more to us than the head of the government. He was the heart of it, too. Through all these years of agony and suspense he had been winding himself into the affection of every loyal man and woman, until those of us who had never spoken with him were conscious of a sacred sense of friendship for him. He had stood, more and more firmly, for all the things we cared for most. He had spoken, in darkest days, our deepest wishes, our dearest hopes. He had led us, safely and triumphantly, through the nation's sorest testing-time, and had restored to us our country, united and free. Not often, in history, has a bond so vital, so tender, so finely human, bound together ruler and people. And when was any nation ever so suddenly plunged from such a height of rejoicing into such a depth of sorrow?

That month of April seems, as I recall it, a month of years. The gladness and grief of a generation were crowded into its momentous days.

Most saddening of all was the sudden turn of the popular feeling from kindness to vengeance. At once there was a disposition to hold "the South" — that was the popular phrase — responsible for Lincoln's assassination. It was the impulse of the unthinking crowd; but alas! in such moments it is the unthinking crowd which speaks quickest and loudest. If, at the moment, we could have had a leader of clear moral sense and real magnanimity, — a man like Lincoln, — who could have spoken the sane and convincing word, how much misery and disaster might have been averted! But the leadership fell upon a man utterly incapable of discerning the great opportunity, who could do no better than catch from the mouths of the mob their cries of wrath and retaliation, and repeat them from the seat of authority; who vociferated that the day of mercy for rebels was now past, and that the voice of justice must be heard; that it was time now to say that treason was a crime, and that traitors must be punished and impoverished, and who, before Lincoln was buried, had issued a proclamation accusing the President of the Confederacy and other officers high in that government of having "incited and encouraged" the assassination. With such a man at the head of the nation there was little to stem the tide of unreasoning fury which swept over

THE END OF THE WAR

the land. In every city and town crowded assemblies listened to the voices of orators who clamored for vengeance upon "the South" for the murder of Lincoln. That was what the people wanted to hear; the fiercest denunciations and the most sweeping demands for a vindictive policy evoked the loudest applause. If there had been any evidence that this act of a desperado had been the result of a plot in which the southern leaders were implicated, such an outburst would have been justifiable; but no such evidence appeared, and the determination to hold "the South," and especially the southern leaders, responsible for this crime was one of the saddest illustrations of popular injustice that history records. Even level-headed men like Grant were swept away by this torrent of unreasoning anger, and he issued an order for the imprisonment of leading Confederate officers of state at Richmond, and for the arrest of "all paroled officers unless they take the oath of allegiance." "Extreme rigor," he said, "will have to be observed whilst assassination remains the order of the day with the rebels." But there was no proof, none that rational men in sober mind could have deemed worthy of a moment's consideration, that assassination had been made the order of the day by the rebels. And it seems one of the monumental wonders that strong men in the high places did not see the truth and speak to the raging populace the word of calmness and wisdom. Where were Sumner and Chase and Fessenden and Trumbull? Could they not see that just and magnanimous words, at this hour, were worth more to the nation than fleets or armies? Some of these men to whom we had a right to look for leadership were egging on Johnson, in his violent speeches, and intimating that the removal of Lincoln was providential, since a man was in his place from whom traitors need expect no mercy!

On Wednesday, the 19th of April, at the hour of the simple funeral in Washington, religious services were held in most of the towns and cities of the North. In most of these, as I remember, the demand for a rigorous policy in dealing with treason made itself heard. There were a few who did not feel that this was the word to speak at Lincoln's bier. My own little church in Morrisania was crowded that day, and I knew that most of those to whom I was speaking were listening for a very different message when I said to them: —

This assassination seems to have awakened in the breasts of all the people a disposition to use stern and severe measures to the end that such an act may not be repeated. My belief is that stern and severe measures, instead of preventing the repetition of such acts, will have a tendency to multiply them. But it is said that this assassination is itself an illustration of the futility of clemency. "President Lincoln showed a disposition to be forgiving to the rebels, and they have murdered him. Does not this prove that his policy will not work?" I answer, no. It proves nothing of the kind. This deed of a knot of desperadoes in Maryland and Washington cannot be fairly taken as an index of the feeling of the southern masses or even of the southern leaders at the present time. Do we forget that Mr. Lincoln went to Richmond, once, twice, and came home safely? No attempt was made to harm him there. No disrespect was shown him. Would

THE END OF THE WAR 153

it not be wise, before preaching a crusade against the southern people, to wait and hear what they have to say upon this matter? Some voices from the South have reached us already. General Ewell, on his way to Fort Warren, heard the news and burst into tears, declaring that it was the worst thing that could happen to the South. The word from Richmond is that the tidings caused universal sorrow. I do not learn that a single word has been heard from the South justifying or applauding.

The events of the last few days have tended to exasperate and inflame the public mind and to lead men to perpetrate vengeance, calling it by the more euphonious name of justice. The instinctive indignation that rises in men's hearts upon the perpetration of such a deed is deepened and strengthened continually by their contact in the excited crowds of cities, and it needs not to be nursed and stimulated. It is easy enough at such times to gain applause by falling in with the popular current. A man has only to shout, "Hang them! crush them! exterminate them!" and the ceiling will resound with cries of approval; but that applause is not worth having. Rather should the reason, the calm, unprejudiced reason, be appealed to; rather should these instinctive feelings be rigidly challenged and held in check.

Of the few hundreds who listened, a score may have been convinced; but a voice like this affected the raging of the populace about as much as the chirping of the swallows on the telegraph pole affects the motion of the Twentieth Century Limited.

Let us confess that it takes a stalwart optimism to stand up against such a spectacle as was presented to the eyes of the world in this emotional cyclone which swept a whole nation out of the ways of sanity, and practically destroyed the finer growths of tolerance and magnanimity on which the successful reconstruction of our national government so largely depended. To me, at least, there came, in those bewildering days, a sense of the possibilities of popular error and madness from which I have never been able wholly to free myself. For nothing is clearer than that the passions engendered by that tragedy have left their blight on the whole subsequent history of this nation. The bitter outbreak of anti-southern sentiment at the North blasted all possibilities of prompt reconciliation; it left the southern people angry and sullen; above all, it resulted in that complete ostracism of the southern men of character and influence which was the one ghastly and fatal blunder of the reconstruction policy. Nothing short of a wholesale execution of the southern leaders would satisfy the sentiment of the multitude in those fierce days. Out of that hot demand came forth the ugly progeny of measures by which it was attempted to revitalize the southern body politic by eliminating its brains. To this dire result President Johnson abundantly contributed, — first by his intemperate utterances respecting the rebel leaders; then by his complete *volte-face*, within a month, in the interest of the class which he had been denouncing. But it must be confessed that, with all this muddling at the White House, there was also a plentiful lack of sane and firm leadership at the other end of the avenue.

"That nothing walks with aimless feet," in the great movements of divine Providence, is my deepest faith;

THE END OF THE WAR 155

and I am sure that in some way the death of Lincoln must be working, through long lines of hidden causes, for the ultimate good of mankind; but I know of no great historical event which it is so hard for me to reconcile with the doctrine of a wise and good Providence. So far as I am able yet to see, the effect of it was wholly calamitous. It removed from the head of the nation, at the hour when he was most needed, the man who was supremely qualified for its leadership, and it left in his place a man who by temperament and training was hopelessly disqualified for such a task. At the moment when the one thing needful was the soothing of vindictive tempers and the awakening of the spirit of forbearance and conciliation, it fanned the smouldering embers of resentment and distrust into a conflagration. In the day when the supreme need was such a handling of the business of emancipation as should enlist the interests of the southern people in their former slaves, and bind the two races together in friendship, the whole policy seemed to be directed toward the fomenting of antipathies between the races, and the employment of the blacks for the humiliation of the whites.

Social philosophers find the source of the social reforms which have characterized recent decades in a "great fund of altruistic feeling," which Christianity has been silently accumulating in the hearts of the people. But it is possible, by the indulgence of popular passion, to propagate and accumulate a great fund of hate and suspicion, which shall undermine the foundations of society and make the work of social reconstruction well-nigh impossible. Bitter indeed have been the fruits of that madness which was engendered in the popular mind during the last days of the war. For though we have the greatest reason for thankfulness that the sober second thought withheld the people of the North from those extremities of vengeance which, in those days, they were threatening, so that, in fact, not a single judicial victim was found needful to assuage the popular wrath, yet the seeds of distrust and ill-will were widely and deeply sown, and through the entire period of reconstruction the nation was gathering the harvest.

For myself, I must confess that if I had ever cherished any fond belief in the infallibility of the populace, that illusion was forever dispelled by the spectacle of those days. It became only too apparent that a whole people, swept by a flood of excitement, may go hopelessly wrong. Burke says that it is difficult to draw up an indictment against a whole nation. Difficult it may be, but it is sometimes necessary. That entire populations are subject to epidemics of unreason is historically true. And the only hope for this democracy is in the rise of a class of leaders who have the courage to resist the mob, and to speak the truth in the days when the truth is the last thing the people want to hear.

The danger in a democracy is on the side of the emotions. So long as the people can be encouraged to think, to use their reason, to govern their action by such intelligence and judgment as they are conscious of possessing, we are tolerably safe. Issues which are determined by free and fair discussion are generally well determined. But when passion is substituted for reason, and political action is guided mainly by prejudices and

THE END OF THE WAR

impulses and antipathies and resentments, the results are apt to be calamitous. If there is one thing that this nation has need to guard against, it is the prevalence of hysteria in politics. Such spectacles as those which we are witnessing in the great national conventions are not reassuring. The attempt to determine the choice of leaders and the destinies of the nation by such frantic demonstrations is essentially immoral. We have no right to submit the great interests of the state to the arbitrament of an unbridled emotionalism. Our business is "to make reason and the will of God prevail" in politics, and not to invoke and organize pandemonium in the assemblies which are called to settle the great affairs of the nation.

CHAPTER X

AMONG THE HILLS

> Early had he learned
> To reverence the volume that displays
> The mystery, the life which cannot die;
> But in the mountains did he *feel* his faith.
> All things, responsive to the working, there
> Breathed immortality, revolving life,
> And greatness still revolving; infinite;
> There littleness was not; the least of things
> Seemed infinite; and there his spirit shaped
> Her prospects, nor did he believe, — he saw.
> *William Wordsworth.*

IN the summer of 1865 many of the colleges gave to their Commencement exercises a commemorative character, and the Williams Society of Alumni arranged for an address and a poem celebrating the return of peace. For the latter service the choice fell upon me, and I had the honor of delivering, in the old church at Williamstown, on the day before Commencement, a poem entitled "After the War," which sought to rehearse, in descriptive lines, the march of events, and to reproduce in lyrical measures some of the more salient incidents of the great struggle. The verses were received with more favor than they deserved; but the most important consequence to myself was the presence in the audience of certain members of the Congregational church in the neighboring town of North Adams, by whose solicitation I was induced to spend the next Sunday with that church. Out of that acquaintance came, the next January, an invitation to its pastorate; and in the following March we bade farewell to our old home in Morrisania, and turned our faces toward the Berkshire Hills.

North Adams in 1866 was a smart factory village of eight or nine thousand people, situated at the junction of the two branches of the Hoosac River. South Adams, five miles distant, was perhaps half as large. Both these villages were included in the town of Adams, which boasted of being the largest "town" in Massachusetts. Within the territory of the town of Adams, which occupied the narrow valley between the Hoosac Mountain on the east and the Greylock group on the west, there must have been a population of perhaps fourteen thousand people, who were still governing themselves, after the manner of the primitive New England democracies, the business of the town being transacted in town-meetings, at which all legal voters were entitled to be present. The town-meetings were held sometimes in the North village and sometimes in the South; occasionally in a large schoolhouse midway between the two. They were called by a warrant issued by the "selectmen" of the town, in which the business to be transacted was definitely set forth in a number of "articles." These popular assemblies regulated by direct vote all the important public affairs of this large community: the bridges, the roads, the public buildings, the schools, the care of the poor, and all such matters were under their supervision; they appropriated the money which the selectmen might use in each of these departments. Like the Swiss *landsgemeinde*, the Adams town-meeting exhibited a free people in immediate control of their common interests. It was government of the people by the people, and, so far as I was able to discover, it was good government. There was no suspicion of jobbery or corruption; for although many of the details of administration had to be left to the discretion of the selectmen, they were too closely watched to leave room for any malversation. Not all the voters attended the town-meetings, but the numbers were often sufficient to crowd the largest hall in North Adams, and the discussions were keen and business-like. Anything savoring of what is commonly called oratory was at a discount; the assembly would tolerate no spread-eagleism; speeches must be short and to the point.

The time came when the affairs of this densely populated community became too complex to be regulated by the people in mass meeting, and when the pure democracy had to give place to a city charter with representative government, but during all my residence in North Adams the primitive form of local government prevailed, and I have always been grateful for the good fortune which permitted me to be for five years an interested participant in the business of an old-fashioned New England town.

North Adams was, indeed, a good sample of a New England democracy. All its traditions were of an uncompromising radicalism. If there were aristocratic elements in the population of many New England towns, Adams boasted none of these things. It was Sam Adams, and not John, whose name she had borrowed when her organization was set up. There were no old families who

AMONG THE HILLS

claimed homage on the score of birth or breeding. There were a few men to whom the war had brought large and rapid gains: the cotton and the woolen mills and the print works were in the high tide of prosperity, and several of these wealthy manufacturers were building for themselves fine houses; but nothing had yet occurred to disturb the sense of equality which characterized all social relations. These prosperous manufacturers were not disposed to put on airs, nor were their neighbors overmuch inclined to defer to them; they were addressed by their first names as they had always been; if one of them assumed too much in town-meeting, he was as likely to be called down as any other man.

Indeed, there was nothing resembling a social stratification in the society of North Adams at that day. I have attended an evening party in one of those new fine houses at which were present not only capitalists and merchants and professional people, but working mechanics and clerks and operatives in the mill of which the host was the owner. That class consciousness which some of our industrial leaders are so eager to cultivate would have been wholly inconceivable to the people of this New England town forty years ago.

I need hardly say that this change from Morrisania to North Adams was a most grateful experience. The conditions of life and work were far more stimulating in the new field. In the suburb of a great city there is so little social contact that there can be no common life; neighbors do not know one another; the cultivation of local interests and enthusiasms is almost impossible. Society is well-nigh inorganic. It is an aggregation of social atoms rather than a vital unity. In Morrisania I always found that any effort of mine to influence the community reached no farther than the few persons to whom my words were addressed; in North Adams I soon discovered that I was speaking to the whole community; that the neighbors were taking up and repeating and discussing anything which appealed to them. It might have seemed that in removing from a suburb of the metropolis to a New England town of ten thousand inhabitants I had narrowed my field of influence; on the contrary, it appeared to me that I had vastly extended it.

In truth, there is more or less of illusion in the supposed commanding influence of the metropolitan pulpit. The churches which exist in the great centres of population find it extremely hard to maintain among their members any vital social relations; attachment to the minister is the only tie that holds most of them to the church; and it is extremely difficult to relate the church, in any effective way, to the community round about it. A church in a small city is likely to be far more closely connected with the life of its own community, and thus to affect more directly and powerfully the life of the state and the nation. This is not saying that there is not need of churches in the great cities, nor denying that they have a great work to do; it is simply pointing out that in the performance of the work they are greatly handicapped by the social conditions; and that the minister who supposes that his influence is sure to be extended by removal to a bigger city does not quite comprehend the situation.

The mountains and the vales of northern Berkshire

came back into my life with great gifts of strength and peace. They had long been dear to me, and there was reassurance in their unchanging message. It was surely good for me to get away from the rush and roar of the metropolis and feed my soul for a little space upon the strength of these steadfast hills.

North Adams, in those days, was a wide-awake community, much less set in its ways than the average New England town, hospitable to fresh thinking, not afraid of the truth even if it was new truth. There was a Scotch deacon against whom I had been warned; he would be a permanent obstruction, they told me. Instead of that, he was my loyalest supporter from the beginning. "The young man has his ideas," he said. "He wants to lead. We want a leader. Let us follow him." That was the spirit in which the church took up the work. No young preacher could have asked for anything better. There were no financial problems; the people were sympathetic and enthusiastic; never before had the environment been so stimulating. There was time for reading, and the larger problems of theology began to lay hold on my thought. Fortunately or unfortunately, I had not been charged with the maintenance of any theological system, and the work of investigation must be done largely along independent lines; my theology had to be hammered out on the anvil for daily use in the pulpit. The pragmatic test was the only one that could be applied to it: "Will it work?"

An article or two contributed to the New York "Independent," during these early years in North Adams, brought me cordial words of recognition from editors and readers, and opened to me the possibility of service with my pen, — a possibility long coveted, but hitherto beyond my reach. From that time until the present my connection with periodical literature has been close and constant, and a large part of the work of my ministry has been done through the columns of the newspaper or the pages of the magazine. To those who are disposed to put the work of the press into a rank inferior to that of the oral ministry, it is sufficient to reply that the ministry of the greater apostles, Matthew and John and Paul, seems to have been mainly wrought with the pen. We can hardly put the work of St. Paul, which we possess, into a lower class than that of a traveling evangelist or a local pastor.

One of the first of the "Independent" articles was entitled "Are Dr. Bushnell's Views Heretical?" A young Congregational minister in Illinois had been refused ordination by an Ecclesiastical Council, because he had indicated his sympathy with the teachings of Dr. Bushnell on the Atonement. My own study of the subject had abundantly convinced me that in his main contention Dr. Bushnell was right; that there could be no such thing as a judicial transfer of blame or penalty from a guilty to an innocent person; that the entire transaction was within the ethical rather than the forensic realm. I knew that for me there could never be any other doctrine to preach than that which I had learned from this great teacher; and if men were to be denied the privilege of preaching it in the Congregational ministry, the sooner that fact was known the better it would be for me. Accordingly I set forth, as clearly as I could in a brief article, the substance of Dr. Bushnell's teaching, and expressly committed myself to it, declaring that if this was heresy I desired to be counted among the heretics, and offering the right hand of fellowship to the young man who had been rejected for teaching it.

I had never known Dr. Bushnell, but this article brought me a letter from him so cordial and grateful that it touched me deeply. He was living in Hartford, no longer in active service, with broken health; and although, in his disabled condition, no open warfare was made upon him, and he was still in good ecclesiastical standing in the Congregational body, yet "Bushnellism" was under the ban, and there were few Congregational ministers who were willing to confess their acceptance of it. So it was that this old hero, who had fought and won the battle for the moralization of theology, was not yet permitted to enjoy the fruits of his labors, in the full and grateful recognition of his brethren; and that this frank avowal of indebtedness to him, made by a person wholly obscure and unknown to him, was sufficient to bring forth from him this expression of his gratitude. It was evident that he needed, even then, such comfort as my poor letter could give him. It was good to know that a word from such a source had comforted him, but it was tragical to think that he could have needed it.

Thus began a friendship which, in its influence upon my life, was one of the most stimulating that I have known. Not many months after this, the question of my own installation over the North Adams church was raised. On coming to North Adams I had stipulated that there should be no formal settlement for the first year; if, at the end of that time, both parties were agreed to make it permanent, the installation might take place. At the end of the year the church signified its wish that I should remain, and a council was called. At once I wrote to Dr. Bushnell, asking him to come and preach the sermon. His health was infirm, but he occasionally preached, and I hoped that he might be willing to perform that service for me. His reply was characteristic. He thought it highly imprudent for me to take upon myself the odium which might be incurred in associating myself with one whose standing was questionable; it might make trouble for me; it would put the heresy-hunters on the scent; it would be far wiser for me to invite a safer man. My answer was that I wanted him and nobody else, and that I was prepared to accept the consequences. To this challenge his reply was prompt, and he came and spent nearly a week with me, before the installation.

Those were great days, driving over the Berkshire Hills, lying in the shade, talking of things visible and invisible, meditating upon the mysteries of the heavens above and the earth beneath. Horace Bushnell was one of the great talkers. There was something Carlylean in his rugged rhetoric and the raciness of his metaphors; and his homely speech was lit up with poetic touches which made it a delight to listen. He had a keen eye for natural beauty, and the glories of those Berkshire Hills filled him with rejoicing. He told me much about his life in California, and about his search for the site of the

AMONG THE HILLS

university; for it is to him that the Golden State owes the ideal location of the State University at Berkeley. It was the most natural thing in the world that he, an invalid, seeking health among the mountains and foothills of that new commonwealth, should have taken up and solved that vital question, convincing the Californians of the wisdom of his choice, and thus rendering to the state a gratuitous service of the highest value. Similar to this was his work for his own city of Hartford, whose beautiful park, that bears his name, was secured by his sagacity and persistence. While he was sojourning with me, in North Adams, he came in, one morning, from a walk which he had been taking before breakfast, saying: "I've found the place for your park. Now go to work and get it." It was the right location beyond a doubt; and if I had possessed his power of getting things done, I might have rendered a great service to that thriving Berkshire town.

Dr. Bushnell was, beyond a question, the greatest theological genius of the American church in the nineteenth century, but the facts which I have recited show that he was something more than a theorizer; his grasp of reality was very firm, and he had a statesman's vision of human needs and possibilities.

The council for the installation brought together the ministers and delegates of the Congregational churches of northern Berkshire, — among them President Hopkins, from the Williams College church, and his stalwart brother Albert, Dr. John Todd, of Pittsfield, and others. It was naturally an occasion of some solicitude to me; what might happen to me in view of my explicit avowals of heretical doctrine, I could not tell. Of one thing I felt pretty sure. The church was satisfied with my work, and the council would hesitate to forbid the work to go on. That proved to be the decisive consideration. Dr. Todd, who was the moderator of the council, was plainly unwilling that the council should explicitly tolerate my heresies, but he would not risk the wrath of the church by refusing me installation; so he skillfully conducted the examination over ground on which there was no chance of discussion, and, after about twenty minutes, brought it to an abrupt conclusion. It was a palpable evasion, but I was not responsible for it. "I thought," said Dr. Todd to me after the examination, "that you were a great heretic." "Perhaps I am," I answered; "but you did n't bore in the right place."

Dr. Bushnell's sermon on the occasion is included in his volume, "Sermons on Living Subjects," — "The Gospel of the Face" is the title. Delivered, as it was, in a voice somewhat impaired by illness, and with little of physical vigor, it was yet a most impressive utterance. One could see how perfectly his delivery had been adapted to his written style; one could catch even in those broken tones the ring of irresistible convictions. "Is not that the Gospel?" some one asked Dr. Hopkins, after the service. "Nothing else is the Gospel," was his prompt reply.

One episode of the North Adams ministry has a whimsical interest, as a revelation of the ascetic notions then almost universally prevailing respecting popular amusements. A Young Men's Christian Association had

AMONG THE HILLS

been organized, and in opening new rooms for the society, the question arose whether amusements of any kind should be admitted. The proposition was received with some disfavor, and a conference of ministers and leading laymen was called to advise the officers. All that was proposed was that a small room be set apart in which checkers, chess, and backgammon might be played by those who did not care to read. These were the only three games which were to be tolerated; cards were to be rigidly excluded; billiards were not to be allowed; but it was urged by some of the more daring spirits that it would be safe to permit the young men to play checkers and chess and backgammon. That view of the case commended itself to me; but I found myself, at the Conference, in a small minority. All my brethren in the ministry very positively disagreed with me; to them it seemed highly dangerous to allow worldly amusements of any kind to be practiced in a place for whose management the churches were responsible. Most of them, indeed, took the ground that amusement of any kind was to be deprecated, as withdrawing the thought from those serious concerns upon which it should be fixed; that a truly converted man needed no diversions; that the joys of religion alone should satisfy the soul. And I found myself subjected by my brethren in the ministry to a sharp cross-examination respecting my own views on various popular amusements, in the course of which I expressed opinions that to some of them appeared little short of scandalous. The proposition to have an amusement room in the hall of the Y. M. C. A. was incontinently voted down; to no such dangerous innovation as that could these good people be brought to consent. And the reports which went abroad from that conference respecting what the Congregational minister had said in it were of a character so inflammatory that I thought it best to set myself right by a sermon on "Amusements; their Uses and Abuses." The sermon was heard by a crowded audience, and was afterwards printed. As I read it to-day, it is difficult to believe that such an argument could have been needed in defense of a rational use of diversion. When one visits the rooms of the Christian Associations to-day, in all the cities, and observes the extent to which the play impulse is provided for, and the wide range that is given to innocent and healthy recreations, he is able to see that considerable change has taken place in public opinion. It was only the next summer after our controversy in North Adams that the same question was brought before the International Convention of Young Men's Christian Associations at Montreal; and there the proposition that amusements, carefully guarded, be offered to the young men of the Associations was blown out of the meeting by a whirlwind of popular wrath. The men who had ventured to stand for it were made to feel that they had deeply offended against the piety of their brethren, and had forfeited their right to leadership in the body. I have rarely witnessed an outbreak of intolerance more rank than that which triumphed in this Montreal Convention. Yet it was not many years before the policy so hotly disapproved was universally adopted by the Christian Associations.

AMONG THE HILLS

One reason why the ascetic view of the amusement question came to be discredited in North Adams may have been found in the fact that the minister who undertook the leadership of the crusade against amusements, and who preached several violent sermons, in which he maintained that all sport is sinful and that true piety has no place in it for any other enjoyments than those which are purely religious, was discovered a few weeks afterward to have eloped with a young woman of his congregation, and to have feigned suicide by drowning, in order to cover his flight to a distant state. His arguments did not need this kind of confutation, nevertheless there were, undoubtedly, those whose hold upon the bad logic was shaken by the conduct of the advocate.

I have spoken of the fact that the labor question had not made its appearance in North Adams, at the time when I made my home there. Before my departure it arrived, in a somewhat virulent form. In one of the largest shoe-factories a disagreement about wages resulted in a lock-out. The doors of the factory were closed for several weeks, during which time repeated attempts to fill the shop with workmen were foiled by concerted movements of the men out of work, who met the incoming strike-breakers at the railway station and persuaded them to return. No violence was used, but the picketing was effectual, and the employers were unable to start their machinery. After an ominous silence of a few weeks, word came that the superintendent of the factory was on his way from San Francisco with a force of Chinamen large enough to man the shop. The town was ablaze with excitement, and there were dire threats. When the train arrived, the streets between the railway station and the factory were lined with an excited crowd, but the police were out in force, and no violence was attempted. All kinds of noises and execrations assailed the ears of the slant-eyed Mongolians as they marched to their destination, and the poor creatures were terribly frightened, but they escaped with no injuries. In fact, the curiosity of the crowd was so acute that its brutality was held in check. These pig-tailed, calico-frocked, wooden-shod invaders made a spectacle which nobody wanted to miss even long enough to stoop for a brickbat. But all of us who looked on were profoundly grateful that the entrance had been effected without bloodshed.

A loft of the factory was fitted up with bunks for the Chinamen, and their own cooks provided their food within the walls, so that they had little occasion to be out on the streets. Few if any of them knew anything of the shoe-trade, and it became necessary to teach them all, even the simplest processes; it was several months before the output of the factory approximated to what it had been with white labor. But the Chinamen were fairly apt pupils, and at length it was reported that the experiment had justified itself, and that the profits were satisfactory. It had been necessary, however, to make a long contract with the men, to cover the losses sustained in the period of pupilage; and when the terms for which they were engaged had expired, most of them slipped away to other occupations, and the fear that the industries of New England were to be "ruined by Chinese cheap labor" was laid to rest.

On the whole, the venture can hardly be regarded as a success from any point of view. The social conditions under which these Chinamen were forced to live and work were not normal; industry which can be maintained only under such conditions might as well be abandoned.

The self-restraint of the working-people of North Adams, in the presence of this irritating spectacle, was a cause for gratitude. Although these Chinamen continued to live in the community for several years, there was very little disposition to interfere with them; they were permitted to go and come without insult or annoyance. The philanthropists of the community soon made these Orientals the object of their care, and various well-meant endeavors to teach them the English language and fit them for self-support and citizenship were promptly set in operation. In truth, the experience of North Adams with the Chinamen was an encouraging instance of the absorbent power of good sense and good will in an American community, in dealing with an acute case of social inflammation.

It was during the summer of 1868 that my first venture was made in the field of authorship. A series of Sunday evening lectures to young people had been condensed into weekly articles for the Springfield "Republican," and when the series was finished I collected them and sent them to Ticknor and Fields, under the title "Plain Thoughts on the Art of Living." Their prompt acceptance, as no writer of books needs to be told, was an experience wholly unique, never to be repeated. The first book and the first baby are in a class by themselves. It has always been quite impossible that any literary success should ever loom so large in my consciousness as this one did.

It was during my residence in North Adams that another literary enterprise was launched in which I was destined to have a large interest. Dr. Holland and Roswell Smith, with Charles Scribner, had organized a company for the publication of a new magazine, to be known as "Scribner's Monthly"; and Dr. Holland came to North Adams to arrange for an illustrated article upon the Hoosac Tunnel, then being cut through the Hoosac Mountain in the neighborhood of North Adams. The preparation of that article was assigned to me, and but for my illness, it would have appeared in the first number of the "Monthly." It went into the second number, and thus began a connection with the magazine, as contributor, which continued for many years, and proved of great profit and satisfaction to me. Dr. Holland and his associates, both in the "Scribner's Monthly" and in the "Century Magazine" (by which name the periodical has long been known), were always free to call on me for needed work, and the kind of service required was in the highest degree congenial. If one has a mind to use his pen in the service of the public, it is a great thing to have a medium of communication whose cleanness and integrity are unquestioned, and I have always esteemed it an honor to have been permitted to work with men whose journalistic aims were never below the highest. There was a touch of pathos, for me, in the fact that Dr. Holland's last work on earth was the reading of the proof of an editorial of mine, which he marked "O. K.," and locked within his desk as he went home in the evening. His death occurred that night. It was good to get from my dear old friend that final verdict. I wished that I might dare to give it a broader interpretation.

CHAPTER XI

THE FOOLISHNESS OF RECONSTRUCTION

> Gather you, gather you, angels of God,
>   Freedom and Mercy and Truth;
> Come, for the earth is grown coward and old,
>   Come down, and renew us her youth;
> Wisdom, self-sacrifice, daring and love,
> Haste to the battlefield, stoop from above,
>   To the Day of the Lord at hand.
>   *Charles Kingsley.*

DURING these quiet days in North Adams the great affairs of the nation were in a tumultuous state. The egotism and obstinacy of President Johnson were well matched by the vindictiveness of Thaddeus Stevens and the quixotic idealism of Charles Sumner, and amongst them they kept the witches' cauldron steaming. As I recall the moral attitude of the northern people in those days, it seems that they had but a dim apprehension of the nature of the forces with which they were dealing. Four years of war are certainly not a good school in which to learn the arts of peace. It could hardly be expected that the conquerors in such a fierce conflict would find themselves at the end of it prepared to be wholly just and magnanimous to those whose revolt against the national authority had caused them so much loss and suffering. And it cannot be denied that the average northern man found it difficult, in thinking of his southern fellow citizens, to rid himself of some rankling resentments.

FOOLISHNESS OF RECONSTRUCTION 177

One capital fact of the situation was scarcely apprehended by the northern people. They did not realize, as fully as they are now able to do, that the war was primarily a struggle between two conflicting theories of the nature of our government. The southern people generally believed that the United States *were* a confederacy of sovereign states; the northern people believed that the United States *was* a nation. The superior allegiance of the southern man was due to his state; the superior allegiance of the northern man was due to the United States. Robert E. Lee believed that Virginia had the supreme right to his loyal service; Ulysses S. Grant believed that the sovereignty belonged to the Government at Washington. This was an issue that had to be decided; the two theories were irreconcilable; one or the other must prevail. The theory of the North, the national theory, did prevail; this was the fundamental question settled by the war. But the people of the North needed to remember that the people of the South were brought up on the other theory; that they adhered to it with all honesty and good faith, and that there was much in the history of our national development to substantiate their claim.

When, therefore, we denounced them as rebels and traitors, and insisted on putting that moral stigma upon them, we were much less than just. Robert E. Lee, as I have said, believed that his first allegiance was due to Virginia; that the claim of the Union on him was a secondary claim. When Virginia seceded from the Union and summoned him to draw his sword in her defense, he would have been a conscious traitor if he had refused. Thus it was not true that the southern people deserved at the hands of the North the severe moral judgment which was visited upon them. They held a false and fatal theory of our political relations, but they held it honestly, and are not to be judged by a standard to which they had never consented.

The failure to make this distinction lent bitterness to the whole process of reconstruction. It was hard for the average northern man to believe that southern "rebels" and "traitors" could be honorable, loyal, trustworthy men; he was inclined to regard them as essentially treacherous. The leaders in Congress ought to have been able to take a larger view; some of them did, but unhappily the dominant spirits were men of narrow vision and vindictive temper, and there was enough bitterness in the popular mind to sustain them in the enactment of measures which made the speedy restoration of peace to the South a moral impossibility.

There was another strong reason why the northern people were inclined to make strenuous terms with the South — that was their determination to protect the negroes. Whatever arrangements were made for the restoration of the state governments in the South must include guaranties for the freedom and welfare of the emancipated slaves. How much the intelligence and good will of the former masters would be needed in securing this, they did not know; they had very little faith in any help from this source; and they had unlimited faith in the ability of the negro to take care of himself if the suffrage was given him. There was, therefore, an honest and laudable purpose behind these recon-

FOOLISHNESS OF RECONSTRUCTION 179

struction measures. The people of the North were responsible for having given the negro his freedom, and they were bound to see that it did not prove a curse to him. Nevertheless, it was a sad muddle they made of it. To imagine that it was possible, by any political device whatever, to invert the natural order of society, and give to the ignorance of the community the supremacy over its intelligence, was an infatuation to which rational legislators ought not to have been subject. Nor ought it to have required such costly tuition to convince an intelligent people that the ballot, in the hands of voters who are utterly unfitted to use it, has no magical power to transform them into useful citizens, but can only prove their own undoing.

The reconstruction measures, which were based on the disfranchisement of the people of intelligence and character, and the enthronement of the illiterate and degraded, and which were given efficacy by the complete prostration of the civil before the military power, thus sowed the South with dragon's teeth, whose crop will not be fully harvested, lo, these many years. Those of us who were living in Massachusetts then are able to recall with some satisfaction the attitude of our own great war governor, Andrew, to whom the futility of these methods was obvious. "Why not," he cried, "try the natural leaders of opinion in the South? They are the most hopeful subjects to deal with, in the very nature of the case. They have the brain and the experience and the education to enable them to understand the exigencies of the present situation. They have the courage, as well as the skill, to lead the people in the direction their judgments point, in spite of their own and the popular prejudice." There is no doubt that if these "natural leaders of opinion" had been taken into consultation, they would have agreed to the gradual enfranchisement of the negroes. Thus we should have been spared that hopeless separation of the races and that violent exacerbation of racial hostility which the attempt to establish negro supremacy inevitably provoked.

Another of the puerilities of our politics in this period was the attempt to impeach President Johnson. This was the culmination of Johnson's quarrel with Congress, a wrangle in which neither party was entitled to much sympathy. Congress had been seeking in every possible way to tie the President's hands; it had gone over the verge in interfering with prerogatives of his, hitherto unquestioned; it was ready on the smallest pretext to impeach him and remove him from office. As an illustration of the heated condition of popular opinion, I remember a double-leaded editorial of Theodore Tilton's in the New York "Independent," in which it was seriously urged that whether Johnson had violated the Constitution and the laws or not, he had certainly been guilty of disloyalty to the Republican Party, and that was good reason why a Republican Congress should impeach him. The technical basis on which the impeachment rested was weak; party animosity lent it all its force. It is humiliating to think that the Senate came within one vote of convicting the President, on a charge which few Republican partisans at this day would sustain; but there are reasons also for thankful-

FOOLISHNESS OF RECONSTRUCTION 181

ness. "The reflecting citizen," says Mr. Rhodes, "will like to recall the memory that the high state trial, taking place in the midst of great excitement, was conducted with gravity according to the forms of law. He will recall, too, that the verdict, which ran counter to an aggressive majority in the legislature and an intense popular sentiment, was accepted without any disturbance, indeed with entire submission. 'Few nations,' wrote Bagehot, 'perhaps scarcely any nation, could have borne such a trial so easily and so perfectly.'"[1]

And while we find much to deplore in the manner in which this entire business of reconstruction was managed, yet we must not fail to record the fact that there are no bloodstains on the legislative pages which tell its story. "The common sense of the American people," says the same authority, "saved them from crowning blunders. They confiscated (practically) none of the land of their prostrate foe; they hanged nobody for a political crime. These are grand results, furnishing a new chapter in the world's history. Never before, on the signal failure of so great an attempt at revolution, had a complete victory been attended with no proscriptions, no confiscation of land, no putting of men to death. Another Ireland would have been created in the southern states, had not our people been endowed in large measure with humanity and good sense."[2]

[1] *History of the United States*, vi, 155.
[2] *Ibid.*, vi, 49.

CHAPTER XII

FROM STUDY TO SANCTUM

Here shall the Press the People's right maintain,
Unawed by influence, and unbribed by gain;
Here patriot Truth her glorious precepts draw,
Pledged to Religion, Liberty and Law.

Joseph Story.

IN the early winter of 1871 a proposition reached me to become a member of the editorial staff of the New York "Independent." Mr. Theodore Tilton had been, until recently, the editor-in-chief of that newspaper, and his editorial policy had become so erratic and vagarious that the proprietor of the paper, Mr. Henry C. Bowen, had secured his resignation, and had commissioned Edward Eggleston to act as superintending editor, with William Hayes Ward as office editor. Through Eggleston the invitation came to me. The first offer was that of the literary editorship, lately vacated by Justin McCarthy, which I declined; it seemed rather aside from my chief aim. Then came the proposal to take the desk of religious editor, — to have under my survey the entire field of religious thought and action. This attracted me. Yet I did not find it easy to gain my own consent to turn from the work of the pastorate into this new field. There were misgivings as to the business side of the enterprise — fears lest the policy of the counting-room might embarrass the editorial management. On all these matters, however, the assurances were positive: the editors were to have an absolutely free hand. The "Independent" had been a great force in the nation; Mr. Tilton's wild notions had somewhat discredited it, but the determination to bring it back into safe ways was now declared, and it had still a very large constituency of intelligent readers. On the whole, it seemed to me that the opportunity offered me was far larger than any church could give me; and I took up the work with hope.

Nevertheless, it cost me a pang to separate myself from the associations and companionships of my Berkshire home. There is an old prophecy, — "the mountains shall bring peace," — the meaning of which I had verified. With all this region I had become very familiar. There were few heights to which I had not climbed; there were not many trout-brooks whose length I had not measured; and though it came to me late, something of the meaning of Nature which Wordsworth unfolds in "The Prelude," had been taking possession of me during those five memorable years. Nor had I ever before found so many loyal friends, or so many reasons for believing that my labor was not in vain.

It was in the early spring of 1871 that we turned our faces Babylon-ward, finding our home again in Brooklyn. The office of the "Independent" was in Park Place, New York, just west of the City Hall Park, and my desk in that office held me close for the next four years. But the work was in no sense drudgery; I have never found anything into which I was able to put more of vital interest and enthusiasm. It was my business to know what was going on in the religious world, among the churches; what was being said in the books and magazines; and to interpret and guide, as best I could, the movements which were bringing to earth the kingdom of heaven. There was never any lack of subjects to write about; there was never an hour when any number of significant things were not taking place. And I am bound to say that I did not shirk my job, or slight my work. I have a file of the "Independent" for the four years while I was on its staff, with my contributions marked, and the testimony is abundant that so far as quantity is concerned, I did my full share of the editorial work.

The editorial associates with whom I was at first most closely related were Edward Eggleston and William Hayes Ward. Eggleston was a versatile and breezy fellow, with high ideals and boundless enthusiasm; he was a most companionable workmate, and it was with much regret that I heard from him, only a few months after joining the staff, that he had accepted the editorship of another periodical. This left Ward the managing editor, and for the remainder of the four years the laboring oars were in his hands and mine. He had been in the service three or four years before I entered it, and he is still in it, — after Alden, I should think, the oldest of the active editors of the metropolis, — unless Richard Watson Gilder, of the "Century," may be his senior. Dr. Ward must have seen full forty years of continuous editorial service on the "Independent." Intelligent and capable service it has been; for light and leading the world's debt to him is much larger than it will ever know. Dr. Ward is by instinct and habit a scholar; with greatly impaired eye-

FROM STUDY TO SANCTUM

sight, he has been devoting all the leisure of his life to the study of the old languages of Babylon and Assyria; and there are few scholars in this country to whom the old cylinders and their inscriptions are more familiar. Yet his interest in these recondite concerns by no means obscures his judgment in practical affairs, or dims his interest in the problems of the present time. My association with him in the office of the "Independent" was always cordial and harmonious. If we did not always agree, we never failed to come to a good understanding, with entire respect for each other's opinions. I have rarely known a more just-minded man, nor one on whose practical sense I could more confidently rely.

The veteran of the staff was Dr. Joshua Leavitt, who had been connected with the paper from the beginning, and was now performing a nominal service, which brought him into the office for a part of every day. Dr. Leavitt was one of the war-horses of the Anti-Slavery Reform. When Garrison's war upon the church became bitter and relentless, Leavitt was the leader of those who separated from the Anti-Slavery Society and organized a society with which the churches could coöperate. The organ of that society, of which Dr. Leavitt became the editor, was "The Emancipator." When the "Independent" was projected, he was called to be its managing editor. He was a man of great dignity and kindness, — a magnificent figure, still erect in body and alert in mind, — with a deep voice and a fatherly demeanor. It was interesting to talk with him about the controversies of the early years, and to catch the enthusiasm which still glowed in his young heart. I have mentioned, on a former page, the prayer of thanksgiving with which he greeted the Emancipation Proclamation, eight years before.

One incident connected with Dr. Leavitt brings into clear light his strong personality. In those days the "Oneida Community" was laying considerable claim on the public attention. It assumed to be a religious commune, but its views of the relations of the sexes were astounding. It proposed to abolish monogamy, and to substitute for it a shameless promiscuity, and it based this cult on the teachings of Jesus Christ. The law had not yet interfered to break up this association, and the founder of it had recently been seeking to commend his system to the world through the organ of the community. It was about this time that he came one day to the "Independent" office, and presented himself, as good fortune would have it, to Dr. Leavitt, announcing his name and his address. Dr. Leavitt declined to take the proffered hand, but, rising slowly to his feet and looking his visitor full in the face, said in a voice like thunder: "Sir, I abhor you!" The man answered not a word, and paused not till he was on the other side of the door. Nobody else said anything. It did not appear that there was anything more to say.

Another associate of the early days in the "Independent" was Mr. Charles F. Briggs, whose pen name was "Harry Franco," a dear friend of Lowell's, and the man to whom "The Fable for Critics" was addressed. Many of Lowell's most intimate letters were written to Briggs. He was also a close friend of William Page, the painter, then a somewhat prominent figure in the world of art. Briggs was a genial and companionable gentleman. His taste, as might be supposed, was somewhat severe, and he was disposed to hold us to high standards in our work, but he was, withal, a most appreciative and generous critic, and his praise of work that pleased him was ungrudging.

The political editor of the "Independent," during these days, was the Reverend Samuel T. Spear, D. D., who had no desk in the office, but who contributed more or less matter every week to the editorial page. Dr. Spear had impressed himself upon Mr. Bowen as a man of great profundity; in the reaction against the Tiltonian radicalism he probably seemed to be a safe resource. Yet it must be admitted that he was neither an inspired nor an inspiring political leader; and when we came into the heats of political discussion, the narrowness of his partisanship was oftentimes intolerable.

Early in connection with the "Independent," the literary editorship was offered to a young man who had just graduated from Dartmouth, Mr. Charles F. Richardson. It was a large place for a mere boy, for the traditions of the "Independent" called for capable discussion of current literature. But our faith in the youth was justified. Without venturing beyond his depth, Mr. Richardson contrived to fill the literary department with fresh and entertaining matter, — illustrating, in the begininng of his career, the insight and discrimination which have made him an authority in American letters. When he first came into our office, Mr. Richardson was in the very freshness of youth. His college course had raised a multitude of questions in his mind and had settled very few; through art and sociology and theology his mind was ranging free; it would have been hard to find a more ingenious or a more persistent questioner. It is many years since I have seen him. I know of him now, through his work, as a man whose mind is pretty well made up on most of the subjects with which he has to deal; but I wonder if he remembers what a multitude of things there were, in the early seventies, about which he wanted to know. It was a perennial refreshment and delight to have him about the premises; at any moment he might come bounding in, to roost on the arm of your chair and plump at you some question about the supremacy of the Pope or the doctrine of the eucharist.

When Richardson went away, his place was taken by my college classmate, Dr. Titus Munson Coan, a skillful and accomplished writer, whose practice had begun with mine in the pages of the "Williams Quarterly." Dr. Coan's work as critic was intelligent and careful; he has since made for himself a good name in the world of letters.

Besides these names upon the regular staff, there were several who regularly contributed to different editorial departments, such as Science and Missions and Biblical Research. And there was a multitude of writers, male and female, with whom we were in constant correspondence, and whose faces we were likely to see, from time to time, in the office. The "Independent" had always made much of its list of contributors; it found great names a profitable asset, and sought to add as many of them as possible to the roll of its advertised writers. Our office therefore became a somewhat popular resort of literary people, and of public men and women who were then more or less conspicuous.

One of our frequent callers was Schuyler Colfax, then Vice-President of the United States, an exceedingly affable gentleman, who was frequently pleased to contribute to the "Independent," and with whom it was interesting to gossip about politics at Washington. Another was Senator Henry Wilson, of Massachusetts, who, a little later, succeeded to the Vice-Presidency. Senator Wilson was then engaged in writing his voluminous "History of the Slave Power in America," which was appearing serially in the "Independent"; this made his excuse for visits to the office whenever he came to the metropolis. Nor was he an unwelcome visitor. Wilson was not a brilliant writer, nor a man of culture, but he was an exceedingly shrewd, sagacious, well-informed politician, and a talk of an hour with him on what was going on at Washington would give a clearer idea of political conditions than it was possible to gain in any other way.

A fresh and piquant personality who often enkindled our spirits by his presence was the Reverend Gilbert Haven, afterward Bishop of the Methodist Episcopal Church, a man with whom it was delightful to disagree, and who had the happy faculty of stating with perspicuity the things which you knew you did not wish to believe. To few men do I owe a larger debt than to some who have put clearly before my mind the things which I knew to be untrue. It would be unfair to "Gil" Haven, as we then familiarly named him, to leave the matter here. I suppose that I agreed with him in ten matters where I disagreed in one; but there were various theological questions on which our differences were sharp, and his delightfully incisive and perfectly good-natured way of defining those differences was extremely serviceable.

Another frequent visitor of a somewhat similar mental habit was the Reverend Leonard Woolsey Bacon, who assumed the rôle of "General Suggester," and was always exercising his very fertile and ingenious mind upon our journalistic problems. We were indebted to him for some valuable hints, and always found him a helpful counselor as well as a welcome contributor. His nimble wit often enlivened our toil. When Ward came home from his college Commencement with the honorary degree of Doctor of Divinity, Bacon's greeting was: "I regret to hear that you have been removed from the small but select circle of untitled men into the indistinguishable herd of D. D.'s."

William Lloyd Garrison was also an occasional contributor, and his benignant countenance now and then looked in on us. It was interesting to note the atmosphere of quiet content by which he was always surrounded; he had fought the good fight and had entered into peace. I do not think that the reconstruction controversies troubled him greatly; not so much, perhaps, as they might reasonably have done. His faith in the efficacy of political emancipation was so strong, that he had no serious fear for the future of those emancipated. The last time I saw Mr. Garrison he was on his way home from a meeting of the Progressive Friends at Kenneth Square, Pennsylvania. That meeting was an

FROM STUDY TO SANCTUM   191

assemblage of reformers of all shades and stripes; the platform was free to every man or woman with a hobby, and Mr. Garrison was telling, with much amusement, of the queer people who had been ventilating their nostrums. One man, he said, after listening to the manifold indictment of society for innumerable great and growing evils, startled the assembly by declaring that nobody had yet struck at the root of the social malady; that all the ills society is heir to were due to one cause; one word with four letters told the whole story — s-a-l-t. The use of salt was the source of all our woes; abstinence from that would restore the lost paradise. Mr. Garrison had reached a point at which the queerness of reformers was diverting to him.[1]

Bret Harte was living in New York then, and I remember a call from him; Joaquin Miller visited us often, and Stedman and Stoddard now and then dropped in. Among the women writers, Mary Clemmer Ames, "Gail Hamilton" (Mary Abigail Dodge), "Susan Coolidge" (Sarah C. Woolsey), and Helen Hunt were occasional callers.

One's experience in meeting thus, in the flesh, large numbers of men and women whom he has hitherto known only through the printed page, is sometimes gratifying and sometimes not. There are those whose words always mean more to you after you have known them; and others whom you cordially wish that you had never seen. On the whole, however, I treasure, as a good

---

[1] Mr. Garrison's son, who has read these proofs, admonishes me that this sense of humor was not a late acquisition of his father's; that he was always able to see the ludicrous side of things.

part of my education, the extended acquaintance with the men and women of letters which I enjoyed in the office of the "Independent."

In 1871 the "Independent" was a blanket sheet of huge dimensions, with a page twenty-eight inches long by twenty-two in width; its regular issue contained eight pages, with nine long columns on a page; the first number of every month added four pages, and was somewhat crudely illustrated. It was a formidable sheet to handle, and there was a sense of relief to editors as well as readers when, at the end of 1872, the form was changed to that of a quarto, with thirty-two pages about half as long as the old ones, and four columns instead of nine to the page. We got rid of our pictures also, which was a deliverance. It was before the days of photographic half-tones, and such wood-engravings as we could command were far from being an unalloyed delight to all the members of the staff.

In national politics nothing inspiring was coming to light. The sordid and unsocial tempers bred by the war were bringing forth their corrupt fruitage. Grant was in the middle of his first term, and was beginning to exhibit the incapacity for civil leadership which might naturally have been expected of him. The reconstruction measures were working out their dubious results; much was made of "southern outrages," but it had become evident to many northern men that these were largely fictitious, invented or magnified to draw attention from the abuses with which the national administration was reeking, and to stifle the cry for reform of the Civil Service. Mr. Rhodes is certainly justified in his statement that "the Congressional leaders, who so powerfully influenced Grant, and who obviously rated the apparent and transitory interest in their party higher than the welfare of the country, found it easier to carry elections at the North by harping upon the 'rebellion,' and 'rebels,' than to undertake the real work of reform. The failures and scandals of Grant's two administrations were largely due to the easy pardon obtained, in accordance with Republican ethics, for any sort of rascality committed by one who was 'sound on the main question,' which meant being pledged to universal negro suffrage and the continued subjection of the southern states. . . . Patriotism in the ranks of the dominant party was now become almost synonymous with traducement and abuse of the South."[1]

It was a dark period in the life of the nation — such an era as might logically have been expected to follow a demoralizing war. The dubious financial policy which the nation had followed through the war had tended to unsettle the common notions of commercial morality; the irregularities in army and navy contracts, out of which great fortunes had been made, had helped to lower the tone of public opinion, and the worship of Mammon had begun to assume that ascendency over the mind of the nation which was destined to become so portentous in after years.

Nor was there, it must be confessed, much to counteract these evil influences in the administration of President Grant. That he was ever guilty of palpable dis-

[1] *History of the United States*, vi, 391.

honesty, few people believed; but he was singularly lacking in those delicacies of feeling by which men are preserved from offending against the larger proprieties of official station; his admiration for rich men was a symptom of weakness; he used his prerogative unblushingly in behalf of his relatives; and he not only permitted the members of his official family to accept presents freely, but he himself received them with no apparent sense of indecency. All this must be charged against his inexperience; he had had no training whatever in civil affairs; it was a cruel thing to thrust upon him these great responsibilities. His associates were largely men of doubtful record, from whom he could get neither guidance nor inspiration. Americans returning from Europe brought back tales of illiterate and uncouth characters traveling with letters of introduction from the President of the United States and conveying unhappy impressions of social conditions at the American capital.

It was true, however, that General Grant had called into his Cabinet three or four men of high character. Hamilton Fish, his Secretary of State, Jacob D. Cox, his Secretary of the Interior, and Ebenezer Rockwood Hoar, his Attorney-General, were men of the finest quality, and the most hopeful feature of the administration had been the loyalty of these men to the President and his apparent confidence in them. With what consternation, therefore, had the public witnessed the dismissal from the President's official family, first of Hoar, and then of Cox. The explanations given of the removal of these two upright and faithful men reflected no credit on the administration; it was quite too evident that influences of a pernicious character were gaining the ascendency at Washington.

These Cabinet changes had been made in the summer and autumn of 1870, and the disaffection of the country had shown itself at the fall elections in a decided reduction of the Republican majority in both houses of Congress. Another monitory symptom was the rising demand for a reform in the Civil Service. In January of this year, 1871, an article by General Cox had appeared in the "North American Review," in which the scandals of the spoils system were abundantly and strongly set forth. The people believed that General Cox knew whereof he spoke, and they were inclined to listen to what he had to say. When he testified that "by far the larger part of the time of the President and all the members of his Cabinet was occupied in dealing out the offices"; and when he said that "diplomacy, finance, military, naval, and internal administration are the minor affairs, which the settled policy of the country has relegated to such odds and ends of time as may be snatched from the greater cares of office," the country seemed to be listening to an authoritative word, which ought to require prompt attention and immediate action.

It was during the first months of my work upon the "Independent" that the demand for civil service reform began to make itself audible. General Grant, to do him justice, had already, in his last message, declared that such a reform was needed. Probably his convictions on the subject were sound; but the evil geniuses who were shaping his policy had less use for a purified service than the devil has for holy water. Nevertheless, a provision was smuggled into a sundry civil expense bill, approved March 3, 1871, which authorized the President to "prescribe such rules and regulations for the admissions of persons into the civil service of the United States as will best promote the efficiency thereof"; and empowering him to appoint a commission for the preparation of such regulations. President Grant showed his good faith by making George William Curtis the chairman of the Commission. Thus was launched the movement which was destined, in later years, to have large consequences. It was a matter that interested us keenly at the time; but our expectations of immediate results were not large. The appointment of the Commission was a sop to Cerberus; Mr. Curtis and his associates might formulate their plans, but ways would be found of making them of none effect. The politicians in power were of the same school as Ensign Stebbins, of Maine, who was "in favor of the prohibitory law, but agin its enforcement." Nevertheless, it was something to extort from the army of spoilsmen this hypocritical concession.

CHAPTER XIII

THE TWEED RING

> Only three instances I choose from all,
> And each enough to stir a pigeon's gall:
> Office a fund for ballot-brokers made
> To pay the drudges of their gainful trade;
> Our cities taught what conquered cities feel
> By ædiles chosen that they might safely steal;
> And gold, however got, a title fair
> To such respect as only gold can bear.
> *James Russell Lowell.*

IF the field of national politics was comparatively barren of incident in the first months of 1871, local politics were rapidly coming to a boil. The Tweed ring was now at the height of its power, and the storm was gathering which was destined to sweep it out of existence. It was my good fortune to arrive upon the scene in the months when this tremendous struggle was beginning. It would be difficult for the people of any American city at this day to conceive of the conditions which prevailed in New York in the spring of 1871. We have had a good deal of rotten municipal government in this country in the past ten years, but nothing comparable to the despotic brigandage of the Tweed régime. The Big Four of that combine, William Marcy Tweed, the President of the Board of Supervisors, Peter B. Sweeney, the Treasurer of the City, Richard B. Connolly, the Controller, and A. Oakey Hall, the Mayor, were despots, with power as absolute as any Babylonian satrap ever exercised. Through their control of the legislature of the state they had got the functions of the city government so parceled out among themselves that their control of its functions was complete, and they were proceeding without let or hindrance to rob the taxpayers of millions for their own enrichment. That such stupendous stealing was in progress was openly charged, and the persistent and cumulative attacks of the New York "Times" had given the people abundant reason to believe it. Nevertheless, the popular apathy was amazing. There were thousands of intelligent and respectable people who professed their belief that all was sweet and sound at the City Hall. There were tens of thousands more who knew better, but who were inclined to plead that nothing could be done about it, that the ring was so strongly intrenched that it was practically invincible. Just before the last election, in November, 1870, the gang had persuaded six of the rich men of New York — John Jacob Astor, Marshall O. Roberts, and Moses Taylor, among them — to look over the books in the controller's office, and to issue this certificate: "We have come to the conclusion and certify that the financial affairs of the city under the charge of the controller, are administered in a correct and faithful manner"! At that very moment those books, if thoroughly examined, would have shown the robbery of tens of millions of dollars. One ought not, I suppose, too curiously to inquire how it was that these six rich men were so easily convinced of the honesty of these colossal robbers.

On the week that I entered the "Independent" office,

THE TWEED RING

Tweed had before the legislature bills confirming the hold of the gang upon the finances of the city. The barefaced shamelessness of these schemes should have been apparent to everybody, and a feeble attempt was made to express the disapproval of the citizens. A mass meeting was called at Cooper Institute, at which William E. Dodge, William F. Havemeyer, Henry Ward Beecher, and William M. Evarts sought to rouse the citizens to resist the passage of Tweed's bills. But the effect was practically nil. The bills were passed without a grimace, and Tweed's defiant query was: "What are you going to do about it?"

There are a great many millions of American citizens who can sit still and look on while things of this kind are going on before their eyes; whose digestion is not impaired nor their temper ruffled by the most flagrant violation of public trusts; who are so intent upon private gain that they find no room in their lives for any concern about the commonwealth. They are represented by that New York citizen who told President Andrew D. White, in these very days, that he did not distress himself about politics, because he could make more money in the time that he should be required to give to public affairs than the thieves could steal from him in the same time. There are a great many millions, I fear, to whom that would appear to be an entirely reasonable exposition of the obligations of citizenship. The existence of these millions is the explanation and justification of Tweed rings and all such cancerous growths upon the body politic. For such citizens as these the Tweed ring is the right kind of government. If only the robberies of the rings could be confined to citizens of this class, all would be as it should be.

Not having been sufficiently disciplined in this school of indifference, I confess that the first months of my sojourn in the neighborhood of the City Hall and the County Court House were not a period of entire placidity. It seemed intolerable to live in the presence of such enormities; and yet there appeared to be little that could be done. The New York "Times" and "Harper's Weekly" were keeping up their bombardment of the ring; and there are few things in American history better worth remembering than the bulldog pertinacity of that warfare. To four men, Jones and Jennings of the "Times," Fletcher Harper and Thomas Nast of the "Weekly," the nation owes much for the unrelenting purpose with which they pursued these scoundrels. They did not wait to strike till the iron should be hot, they heated it by striking. It was their persistence which finally emboldened some of the minor officials of the ring to bring them the facts by which they were enabled to substantiate their charges, and to arouse this stupefied community to some sense of the iniquities with which it was infested.

It was a dramatic moment when "Jimmy" O'Brien, who had gained some standing with the ring and access to Connolly's books, and then had quarreled with the gang, walked into the office of the editor of the "Times" and threw down upon the desk transcripts of the city accounts which more than justified all the charges that the newspaper had been making. The fact that the "Times" had the evidence was soon known, and the

THE TWEED RING

desperation of the gang was not concealed. They had already offered Jones one million dollars if he would desist from his attacks; having failed in that, they supposed that the only thing needful was to raise the price. Mr. Rhodes tells the story: —

A lawyer, a tenant in the "Times" building, sent Jones word that he wished to see him on an important matter in his own office. Repairing thither and being ushered into a private room, Jones was confronted by Connolly. Jones turned to go, saying, "I don't want to see this man." "For God's sake," exclaimed Connolly, "let me say one word to you," and he then offered Jones five million dollars to forego the publication of the accounts. "I don't think," said Jones, "that the devil will ever make a higher bid for me than that." Connolly pleaded, argued, and pictured the delights of rest, travel, and luxurious living. "Why, with that sum," he declared, "you can go to Europe and live like a prince." "Yes," answered Jones, "but I should know that I was a rascal. I cannot consider your offer or any offer not to publish the facts in my possession." [1]

We are having, in these days, specious apologies for public men who yield to great temptation. It seems to be assumed that if the bribe is only big enough, and the pressure strong enough, almost any act of perfidy to public interests must be condoned. "They could n't help it; they had to do it," is the plea by which grafters of all stripes are sometimes justified. But the compulsion, in all these cases, is nothing other than the love of money. They had to do it because they could not resist

[1] *History of the United States*, vi, 405.

the temptation to get rich quick. That is all it means. It is to be feared that there are, indeed, multitudes who cannot conceive of any worthier or stronger motive. But this little story of George Jones introduces us to a higher realm of human conduct. "I should know that I was a rascal" is after all the testimony of the normal human consciousness. The thing that this man "had to do" was to keep his conscience free from that guilty knowledge.

It was on July 8, 1871, that the New York "Times" began the publication of these figures, giving, in facsimile, records of many of the more important transactions. What a revelation it was! It came like a thunderstorm in a sultry night. Destruction was in its path, but it cleared the air; and every lightning flash revealed a foe in ambush. Then Nast's tremendous cartoons came in to make the exposure vivid and convincing. Perhaps no speech from the rostrum or editorial in the newspaper ever had a more powerful effect in enlightening and inflaming public opinion than Nast's cartoon, "Who Stole the People's Money?" The members of the gang and their tools are standing in a ring, and each is pointing with his thumb to the one who stands next him, and saying, " 'T was him." No wonder Tweed was frantic to silence this accuser. "Let's stop these pictures," he cried. "I don't care so much what the papers write about me — my constituents can't read; but they can see pictures." Half a million dollars Mr. Nast might have had, if he would have taken a trip to Europe; but he, like George Jones, was not under the compulsion of cupidity; there was something else to live for besides money.

THE TWEED RING

It was refreshing to witness the confusion and consternation into which the gang was at once thrown by these exposures. They tried to reply through the newspapers, but the best they could say was so miserably inadequate that the public only laughed. Out of their own mouths they condemned themselves. Then they caught at the policy of silence. "Keep still a few weeks," they said, "and it will all blow over." Their faith in the indifference and irresponsibility of the average American was unlimited. Who shall say that it was not too well founded? But in this case they were at a loss in their reckoning. The storm showed no signs of abating. Every day the gale was higher and the lightning was more incessant. The facts which were daily coming to light sufficed to prevent the subsidence of the popular indignation. It began to be evident that a scheme of raising the accounts of all who had any transactions with the city had been for some years in operation, by which untold millions of money had passed into the hands of the ring. A man presenting to the city a bill of ten thousand dollars for work or supplies was told that that bill could not be paid, at present; but that if he could make it a hundred thousand, it would be attended to at once. Raising his bill to one hundred thousand dollars, and indorsing it over to Ingersoll, who was the stalking-horse of the gang, he received his ten thousand, and the other ninety thousand was drawn from the treasury and divided among the confederates. Tweed had twenty-four per cent, the others a fixed share. There was a Board of Special Audit which passed on all city and county claims; the members of the Board were

Hall, Connolly, and Tweed. The investigation showed that at one sitting this board had allowed claims for six million dollars, out of which the city got only six hundred thousand dollars. That County Court House which had been going up across the way, and whose marble façade invited our daily admiration, had cost the city already eleven million dollars, but the amount received by the builders had been only three million dollars. Such were instances of the kind of operation which had been going on for several years in the city and county of New York. What the total amount of these robberies may have been will never be known. A "joint committee," which went over the accounts, declared that the stealings for the past two years had been ten times as great as the actual expenses of the city. The amount of plunder captured by this gang has been variously estimated at from forty-five million dollars to two hundred million dollars. The lowest estimate is sufficiently astounding. It is evident from the amounts of hush money that they were ready to pay that their resources were princely.

It was on the eighth of July that the "Times" began to turn over the leaves of the book of doom, and by the end of the month the exposure had been so complete that no vestige of doubt was left in anybody's mind as to the guilt of the confederates. The only question was what steps should be taken to bring them to justice. On the first of August Dr. Ward went away for a month's vacation, leaving me in charge of the editorial pages. That seemed to be my opportunity, and the "Independent," for the next four weeks, trained all its guns on this citadel of corruption, seeking to guide public opinion toward an adequate handling of the business before the city. I am sure that the testimony was not lacking in point and conviction. The quotations from our editorials made every week by the daily newspapers seemed to indicate their sense of its seriousness. It was one of the times of my life when I have come across something that needed to be hit and have had a chance to strike hard. Such opportunities make life worth living.

I have found, in some of these old editorials, a breath of the gale that was blowing, just then, through the streets of Gotham: —

The gates of the Tombs have never opened to receive criminals of deeper dye than the men who compose the New York Ring. For it is not only against property, but against life and public virtue as well, that they have conspired. They pocket the money that ought to pay for cleansing the streets, and thus join hands with fever and pestilence to slaughter the innocent. They keep for their servitors the assassins of the purlieus, and murder and rapine own their fostering care. They make common cause with rumshops and brothels, and virtue and order cry out against their rule. If there are any criminals in the land to-day, these men are criminals. If it is worth while to punish any evil-doers whatsoever, it is worth while to punish them.

These men were still in power, and Tweed was defiantly demanding: "What are you going to do about it?" The next week an explicit answer to that question was ventured: —

We are going to turn you and all your creatures out of your offices. That we can do and shall do, please God, before the new year is a week old.

We are going to get back as much as we can of the booty you have stolen. We know the job will not be an easy one, but you may depend on us not to give it up without a fair trial.

We are going to use our best endeavors to send you to your own place, the penitentiary.

At any rate, we are going to make the city and the whole country too hot for you. There is some conscience in the land yet, and you will find it out before you die. Upon you shall rest, heavy and immovable, the weight of a nation's curse. You have perverted our laws. You have corrupted our young men. You have done what in you lay to destroy our Government. There are some sins that a nation may never forgive, and yours is among them. It is our solemn charge to hold you up while you live to the scorn and contempt of mankind. God may have mercy on you; but as for us, we promise you that your ill-gotten booty shall be but a poor compensation for the inheritance of shame which shall be yours forever.

That these hot words quite outran the hopes of most of those who were prosecuting the robbers is quite probable; but within three months they were substantially verified. It is often well to assume that what ought to be will be.

By the first of September the people of New York were ready to take up the matter in hand. A great mass meeting, which crowded Cooper Institute and overflowed into the street, registered the determination of the people to put an end to this monstrosity. A committee of seventy was appointed to take the necessary legal

THE TWEED RING

measures. And now these conspirators, with the chivalry of rats, began to plot against one another. Connolly was chosen the scapegoat of the other three, but he declined to be a "vicarious sacrifice," and the inquisition went on. Then Samuel J. Tilden and Charles O'Conor were called in; Connolly was induced to appoint as deputy controller Andrew H. Green, a man of high character; Tweed was arrested and held to bail in the sum of one million dollars; and Sweeney and Connolly both resigned their offices, making good, however, their escape to Europe, with booty enough to keep them in luxury for the rest of their lives. How Tweed was indicted, released on bail, convicted, imprisoned, released, and rearrested again and again, twice escaping from the country, and being brought back to end his life in 1878 in the Ludlow Street jail, is a story that I do not need to repeat. Suffice it to say that, before the end of 1871, the ring which at the beginning of the year was at the summit of its power, levying millions of tribute upon the tax-payers of New York, had been driven from office and scattered; one was under indictment as a felon, and two were in exile.

There were lessons in this overturning for all who were ready to learn. It presented a fearful example of the criminal neglect of duty of which the citizens of a municipality can be guilty, and of the extent to which they can be robbed and victimized, without resistance. It is a mere truism to say that people who live for any length of time under such a despotism as the Tweed ring prove, by that fact, that they are not fit for self-government. If they cannot find out what their servants in office are doing, they are too stupid to govern themselves; if they know about it but cannot stop it, they are too weak to govern themselves. The episode shows, however, how easy it is for an aroused and resolute community to put an end to municipal misrule. No other combination of selfish politicians in this country was ever so strongly intrenched as was the Tweed ring; they had the legislature of the state under absolute control; the judiciary of New York city were their tools; they had their plans laid to dictate the next nomination to the presidency of the United States; and yet, when the people of the city awoke and gave united thought to these iniquities, in a breath they shriveled and disappeared.

CHAPTER XIV

THE GREELEY CAMPAIGN AND THE CREDIT MOBILIER

> Was I too bitter? Who his phrase can choose
> That sees the life-blood of his dearest ooze?
> I loved my Country so as only they
> Who love a mother fit to die for may;
> I loved her old renown, her stainless fame, —
> What better proof than that I loathed her shame?
> . . . .
> This I know
> That man or race so prosperously low
> Sunk in success that wrath they cannot feel,
> Shall taste the spurn of parting Fortune's heel;
> For never land long lease of empire won
> Whose sons sate silent when base deeds were done.
> *James Russell Lowell.*

THE law of action and reaction in rotten politics was finding illustration in these days. It was because the energies of the party in power were so completely absorbed in the dubious reconstruction policies and in the maintenance of the spoils system, that an iniquity like the Tweed ring found room to flourish. And if anybody now threatened the party in power in the nation with political retribution, the question promptly asked was whether there would be any gain in turning the government over to a party of which Tweed was the shining light. Rascality in each party finds a strong bulwark in the rascality of the other party. And I have no doubt that the overthrow of the Tweed ring gave considerable impetus to the movement which began the next year for a renovation of the Republican Party. Originating in

Missouri under the leadership of Carl Schurz, and boldly attacking the southern policy of the party in power, this Liberal Republican movement soon found itself strongly supported by a number of the most influential newspapers of the country, and by several of the ablest Republican leaders, Senator Trumbull, Charles Francis Adams, General Cox, Governor Blair, of Michigan, Governor Palmer, of Illinois, Judge Noah Davis, and Judges Stanley Matthews and Hoadley, of Ohio, among them. It was a formidable uprising; and when a mass convention was called to meet in Cincinnati in May, with the purpose of making an independent nomination for the presidency, it appeared that something important in the way of political reform was about to take place.

That President Grant would be renominated was admitted by all; the machine was irresistible. But if an independent nomination could be made by these Liberal Republicans which the Democrats would accept, it seemed not improbable that it might carry the country. At this distance it appears that if the more sane influences of the movement could have prevailed, and a man like Trumbull or Charles Francis Adams could have been nominated, the result might have been different. But the nomination of Greeley reduced the movement to an absurdity. Greeley did not stand for the things which the serious men who were behind this revolt believed in. He had, indeed, come to sympathize with the demand for a more reasonable southern policy; but even here the columns of the "Tribune" bore witness to his support of the more drastic of the reconstruction measures. As for civil service reform, there was no evidence that

THE GREELEY CAMPAIGN 211

Greeley had any interest in it whatever; and as to the burning question round which the movement had gathered at the outset, the need of tariff reform, he was the one man in the country most strongly committed against it.

Mr. Greeley was a man of warm humanitarian impulses, and great enthusiasm for popular rights; he had done good service in arousing the anti-slavery sentiment of the North, and, in spite of certain petty eccentricities of dress and manner by which he called attention to himself and signalized his limitations, a kindly feeling toward him prevailed throughout the North. But many of those who had read the "Tribune" all their lives were far from being convinced that Mr. Greeley was the right man for the presidency of the United States; they could not help feeling that the man whose frantic cry, "On to Richmond!" had done much to precipitate the worst disaster of the war; whose demand for the resignation of the whole Cabinet after the battle of Bull Run had revealed a similar heated judgment, and whose impatience with Lincoln had again and again found almost hysterical expression, was a man of too emotional a habit to be a safe leader of the nation. And therefore many of those who had hailed the Liberal Republican movement with hope were constrained to fall back upon Grant as, on the whole, the more trustworthy executive.

The "Independent" supported Grant, as was expedient, but its method of supporting him was not at all to my mind. It was too narrowly partisan; its treatment of Greeley was often unfair. Those who depended upon it for information respecting the policy and purpose of the other party must have been seriously misled. In all this matter I found myself in sharp disagreement with those who controlled the political utterances of the paper, and I ventured to express my dissent. It appeared to me especially discreditable for a journal which sought to maintain a religious character to descend to misrepresentation and abuse of a political opponent. My protest had little effect upon the policy of the paper, and the result of the experience was to lessen, considerably, my sense of the value of my editorial opportunity. That the religious influence of the paper must be impaired by such political methods, I could not help seeing.

The campaign dragged on through the summer to its inevitable issue. It was by no means an inspiring contest. Mr. Greeley took the stump, and made, on the whole, an effective canvass. His plea for kindlier relations between the North and the South was urged with an eloquence that ought to have moved the people, but for the most part it was turned to ridicule. "The baleful fires of anger," kindled by the war, were still smouldering, and it was melancholy to see how ready the politicians were to fan them into flame for party purposes. The campaign descended, indeed, to a very low level. Nast's pencil, which had been used so effectively in the exposure of the Tweed ring, was employed in this political struggle in a manner which tended to lower the respect in which he had been held. It was a service to public morality to make contemptible and abhorrent such colossal criminals as Tweed and Sweeney and Connolly; it was quite another thing to treat in the same manner

THE GREELEY CAMPAIGN 213

men like Horace Greeley and Lyman Trumbull and Charles Sumner and Carl Schurz. The caricaturist needs a conscience and some moral perspective, else he may easily become a malefactor.

The sweeping Republican victory was a crushing blow to poor Greeley. He was far from being a sagacious political prognosticator; doubtless he had entertained hope of being President, though the October election must have greatly clouded that expectation. But he had come home from his speaking-tour to find his wife upon her death-bed, and she had passed away before the election day. For many days he had watched by her bedside, and the stress of the campaigning, and the burden of anxiety and sorrow, added to the bitter disappointment of his defeat, were more than he could bear. A little more than three weeks after the votes were counted, they carried him to his grave in Greenwood Cemetery. As the funeral cortège passed near my house to the place of the dead, I could not keep back my tears for the tragic fate of the man who had been from my childhood my political teacher, and who, in spite of many limitations and frailties, had done a good day's work for humanity. How needless, in that hour, seemed the brutal assaults upon his character with which the air had been resounding! In a letter to a friend in New Hampshire, shortly after the election, Mr. Greeley uncovered his grief: "I was the worst beaten man who ever ran for high office. And I have been assailed so bitterly that I hardly knew whether I was running for President or the Penitentiary. In the darkest hour my suffering wife left me, and none too soon, for she had suffered too deeply and too long.

I laid her in the ground with hard dry eyes. Well, I am used up. I cannot see before me. I have slept little for weeks, and my eyes are still hard to close, while they soon open again."

Some sense of the vast injustice which partisan passion had done this man seemed to take possession of the public mind when the grave offered him repose; and there was kindness and consideration in the words that were spoken everywhere concerning him. Grant and Colfax and Henry Wilson rode in the same carriage at his funeral. A small portion of the appreciation which was gladly given to him after his death would undoubtedly have saved his life. Thus we stone our prophets, and make amends for our cruelty by hanging garlands on their tombs.

During these four years of work on the "Independent" my house was in Brooklyn, and the renewal of the old associations with the religious circles of the city where my ministerial work began was grateful to me. Brooklyn was still, by right, "The City of Churches." Matters ecclesiastical held a leading interest. The popularity of Mr. Beecher was still undimmed; it was always difficult to gain admission to his church at any preaching service. Dr. Richard S. Storrs had taken on a new lease of preaching power, and his audiences, though less thronged, were enthralled by his majestic eloquence. Talmage was at the top of his fame; his great tabernacle was always crowded, and his unparalleled acrobatics, physical and rhetorical, were an astonishment to many. It was not possible for me to enjoy so much of this abundant provision for the needs of the spiritual man as I would gladly have done; for there were many vacant pulpits in the metropolis and its neighborhood, and nearly every Sunday found me occupying one of them. Thus my acquaintance was pleasantly extended, and the preaching habit was maintained by constant exercise.

One of the pleasant associations of those years was afforded by membership in a clerical club, known as Sigma Chi. It was an undenominational society, ministers of various communions being included in the membership. It met once in two weeks, on Saturday noon, for a luncheon, a paper, and a discussion. Dr. Howard Crosby, Dr. Thomas S. Hastings, Dr. Charles S. Robinson, of the Presbyterians; Dr. Foss (afterward bishop) and Dr. Bulkley, of the Methodists; Dr. William M. Taylor, of the Congregationalists; Dr. McVickar (now bishop), of the Episcopalians, and others, were in the membership. There were twenty-five or thirty men, most of them mentally alert and courageous, and the discussions were apt to be trenchant and enlightening. To Crosby and Hastings, who were among the seniors of the club, my memory goes back with especial gratitude for the many manifestations of their courtesy to those of us who were juniors. Crosby was a man of flashing wit; his repartee was instantaneous, and his goodfellowship was unfailing. The discussions of the club were mainly theological, but, as I recall them, they were kept within the lines of the traditional evangelical theology. As yet scarcely a ripple had appeared upon the placid surface of American orthodoxy. Matthew

Arnold's "Literature and Dogma" had excited some discussion, but Arnold was not taken seriously by many of those who read him. I cannot recall that any of the questions respecting the Bible and the future life, which were soon to agitate the church, were before the club during my membership in it.

"Too Much Success" is the title of a late essay by one of our most thoughtful writers. It is evident that the political party in power was suffering from this cause in 1872. The overwhelming victory had silenced the demand for reform. The political leaders accepted it as a mandate from the people to follow their own inclinations. The administration of the government had become loose and extravagant, and needed vigorous overhauling in many places, but there was little disposition on the part of the men at the head of affairs to take these matters in hand.

One of the politicians who had some sense of the seriousness of the situation was the newly elected Vice-President, Henry Wilson. Before the end of the year, on one of his periodical visits to the "Independent" office, he told us something of his anxiety. He had been to see the President, and had warned him that trouble was brewing; that the people were beginning to be critical in their judgment of the administration; that the only salvation for the party in power was in a prompt and energetic correction of abuses. To all this President Grant turned a deaf ear. "There is no occasion for anxiety," he said. "Look at the tremendous majority the people have given us. They are not worrying about matters

THE CREDIT MOBILIER

in Washington." Wilson shook his head gravely. He clearly saw that it was a case of too much success.

It was not many months before the most infatuated partisans were forced to see it. During the campaigns the astounding charge had been made by the New York "Sun" that a million dollars' worth of stock had been distributed in bribes to members of Congress by the Credit Mobilier, the construction company which was engaged in building the Union Pacific Railroad. The charge was treated by the dominant party as a mere campaign fabrication; but on the assembling of Congress in December, an investigating committee was appointed by the House of Representatives, and it soon began to appear that, while the matter had been grossly exaggerated, there was truth enough in the charge to give great concern to all honorable citizens. It is not needful here to rehearse the details of that disgraceful history, nor to mention the names of the men who were involved in it. The fact was that a great corporation, depending directly on Congress for favor and protection, had distributed considerable amounts of its stock among the members of Congress. The stock was sold in all cases for far less than market value; in some cases it seems to have been practically given away. Various grades and shades of corruption came to light in this investigation; in some instances the guilt was more flagrant than in others, but the whole revelation was a disturbing sign of the presence in our national legislation of dangerous influences, and of a deplorable lack, in many of our representatives, of that sense of personal honor which is the only safeguard of public morality. And the solemn words of the Committee of the House which investigated this business have been gaining force ever since they were written: —

This country is fast becoming filled with gigantic corporations, wielding and controlling immense aggregations of money and clearly commanding great influence and power. It is notorious in many state legislatures that these influences are often controlling, so that in effect they become the ruling power of the state. Within a few years Congress has to some extent been brought within similar influence, and the knowledge of the public on that subject has brought great discredit upon the body, far more, we believe, than there were facts to justify. But such is the tendency of the time, and the belief is far too general that all men can be ruled with money, and that the use of such means to carry public measures is legitimate and proper. No member of Congress ought to place himself in circumstances of suspicion, so that any discredit of the body shall arise on his account. It is of the highest importance that the national legislature should be free of all taint of corruption, and it is of almost equal necessity that the people should feel confident that it is so. In a free government like ours we cannot long expect the people will respect the laws, if they lose respect for the law-makers.

The light which has fallen upon these words out of the experience of the last thirty-six years makes them luminous and impressive. To what extent immense aggregations of money would seek to control the resources and the destinies of this people in the swiftly coming years Mr. Poland and his associates on the Committee could have had but a dim conception. Yet it must be said

THE CREDIT MOBILIER

that there probably have not been many attempts in the subsequent years to influence Congressional action by methods as direct as were those of the Credit Mobilier. The fate of those who were involved in this transaction has been a terrible warning to all their successors in office. The great combinations of wealth have found it inexpedient to influence legislation by the method of direct approach; it is safer, and probably more economical, to own legislators than to hire them. And ways have been found of guiding the choice of the people, in the primaries and at the polls, toward men who can be depended on to protect the interests of the moneyed classes. No one can know just how far this has gone; these methods are subterranean. But it has come to be believed by the people at large that the great corporations have long had trusty representatives in the national legislature. This much is surely true. During the last twenty years great aggregations of capital have been diligently inventing and improving methods by which they have been able to lay the industries of the land under tribute, and to build up enormous fortunes by the crippling or destruction of their weaker competitors. All this was done under cover of law, and could have been prevented by law. Yet the people who make the laws have shown but a languid interest in preventing and punishing these oppressions. It is only within the last few years, under the spur of a resolute executive, that any effective action in this direction has been taken.

The depressing effect of the Credit Mobilier scandals upon the public mind was not relieved by the progress of political events at the national capital. It soon became evident that the influences surrounding Grant were determined to kill the civil service reform, and Mr. Curtis, who had supported Grant, resigned the chairmanship of the Commission, because, as he expressly said, the things which were taking place showed "an abandonment both of the spirit and of the letter of the civil service regulations."

The "Salary Grab" which soon followed was another indication of the spirit which was ruling in the councils of the nation; it was engineered by Benjamin F. Butler, of Massachusetts, who had become the evil genius of the Grant administration. Nothing is so discreditable to the memory of Grant as the fact of the ascendency which this marplot succeeded in establishing over him.

The scandals connected with the New York and Boston Custom-Houses, the shocking revelations about the Whiskey Ring, the exposure of the villainy of Babcock, the President's confidential friend and private secretary, and the impeachment of Belknap, his Secretary of War, were all indications of the extent to which corruption was infesting the national administration. It is probable that no period in the history of the nation has witnessed such a carnival of graft and malfeasance as that of Grant's second administration.

And this was mainly due to the fact that the game of politics was being played in an insincere and fraudulent manner. The issues were largely false issues. The passions enkindled by the war were kept burning for political purposes; reconstruction measures were imposed upon the South which goaded the southern people to

THE CREDIT MOBILIER

madness, and when they undertook to free themselves from the oppression, the most harrowing tales were told of their lawlessness and brutality. Under cover of these southern outrages all sorts of rascality flourished in the national government. The eyes of the people of the North were kept fixed upon the disorders of the South so that they should not observe what was going on at Washington and in the Federal offices.

All this, I cannot help reiterating, was the natural fruit of the war. Just such *sequelae* as these are to be looked for at the end of any war, and especially of a civil war. War is hell, and it sets up continual pandemonium in any commonwealth. It inverts all moral relations; it undermines social obligations; it spreads its blight through every department of life. No nation can engage in a protracted war without suffering a serious loss of national probity and honor. The worst losses are outside of the army and after the war. We make much of the great military virtues of courage, and subordination, and readiness to sacrifice life for fatherland, and there are, beyond a question, moral gains of great value in war to those who meet these tests worthily. There is no terrible calamity out of which brave and faithful souls do not bring honor and virtue; but the total effect of war upon the nation is disastrous; inevitably it lowers the moral tone; it scatters the seeds of moral pestilence; it results in just such disorders and corruptions as those which disfigure the pages of our national history in the decade following the close of the Civil War. While we give full honor to the courage and consecration of the men who gave to their country on the battlefield the last full measure of devotion, we must not shut our eyes to the terrible moral effects of the enterprise in which they were thus summoned to lay down their lives.

The physical losses which a nation suffers in such a war — the loss of life, the destruction of property, the crippling of industry, the creation of an army of dependents — are appalling; but the moral losses, — the weakening of the social bond, the unbridling of greed, the letting loose of the plunderers, the fomenting of suspicion and distrust, the creation of enmities which make social reconstruction well-nigh impossible, — these are the deadly injuries of which, before entering upon war, we ought to make due account. It must be that the nations will soon find a better way of settling their disputes.

CHAPTER XV

THE SWING TRIAL

> O joy supreme! I know the Voice,
>   Like none beside on earth or sea;
> Yea, more, O soul of mine, rejoice,
>   By all that He requires of me,
>   I know what God himself must be.
>
> No picture to my aid I call,
>   I shape no image in my prayer;
> I only know in Him is all
>   Of life, light, beauty, everywhere,
>   Eternal Goodness here and there!
>
> I know He is, and what He is,
>   Whose one great purpose is the good
> Of all. I rest my soul on His
>   Immortal Love and Fatherhood;
>   And trust Him, as His children should.
>   *John Greenleaf Whittier.*

I HAVE said that the theological pool was still untroubled, when I took up my task upon the "Independent." But signs of disturbance began to appear after a year or two. I can hardly tell how it began; some indications of restiveness under the restraints of the traditional orthodoxy were audible in certain quarters. The "Independent" was interested in such phenomena, and began to take an active part in discussing them. Nothing very radical was contended for; the point mainly insisted on was that theology must be moral. Every doctrine must have an ethical foundation. Doctrines which fail to agree with the plain principles of morality cannot be true. Doctrines which represent God as acting unjustly must be false doctrines. The foundation of theology is in the statement that the Judge of all the earth will do right. And if God's government is a moral government, there must be between God and men a common measure of morality. The principles which govern the conduct of a righteous God must be principles which approve themselves to the consciences of righteous men. And when we are asked to believe doctrines which imply that God is unjust, we ought with indignation to reject them. Something like this was said somewhat frequently in the "Independent." I find in the number for July 3, 1873, an editorial entitled "Immoral Theology," from which I quote: —

To teach that God is a being who has a perfect right to bring into the world a creature with faculties impaired, with no power to resist temptation, utterly unable to do right, powerless even to repent of the wrong which he is fated to do, and then send to everlasting misery this helpless creature for the sin which he could not help committing, — to teach such a doctrine as this about God is to inflict upon religion a terrible injury and to subvert the very foundations of morality. To say that God may justly punish a man for the sins of his ancestors, that God does blame us for what happened long before we were born, is to blaspheme God, if there be any such thing as blasphemy. To say that any such thing is clearly taught in the Bible is to say that the Bible clearly teaches a monstrous lie. Yet such theology as this is taught in several of our theological seminaries and preached from many of our pulpits. It is idle to say that it is nothing but a philosophical refinement; that the men who come out

THE SWING TRIAL

of our theological seminaries with these notions in their heads never make any use of them in their pulpits. They do make use of them. They are scattering this atrocious stuff all over the land. They are making infidels faster than they are converting sinners. Men say, "If this is your God, worship him, if you want to, but do not ask us to bow down to your Moloch!" Who can blame them? For our own part we say, with all emphasis, that between such a theology as this and atheism we should promptly choose the latter.

The obviousness of these contentions does not need to be emphasized; it would seem that principles so elementary might have been taken for granted; but in maintaining them the "Independent" soon had a lively fight on its hands. The organs of several of the creeds came to the rescue of their traditions, and undertook to defend the dogmas which were thus impugned. The controversy extended in a more or less desultory manner through several months.

One of the newspapers which engaged most actively in this discussion was the "Interior," of Chicago, then edited by Professor Francis L. Patton, now of Princeton, who was then connected with the McCormick Seminary of Chicago. It was not long before Professor Patton found a heretic nearer home in the person of David Swing, pastor of a Presbyterian church in Chicago, who was preaching to great audiences every Sunday in McVickar's theatre, and profoundly influencing the thought of that city. Professor Swing was not a polemical preacher; he was not attacking the traditional theology, though the implications of much of his teaching may have contradicted it; he was a poet, and a seer, with a reverent insight into the deep things of the Spirit, a tender sympathy with everything human, a streaming humor, a radiant optimism, a keen delight in all things beautiful; and his preaching was attracting multitudes outside the ranks of the church-goers. Nor was there any just cause of complaint against him on the ground of heresy. He was not, indeed, preaching all the horrible doctrines of the Westminster Confession, nor were many of his brethren in the Presbyterian ministry; his divergence from the *ipsissima verba* of the creed was really no greater than that of thousands. The worst of his heresy was his determination to believe in a good and reasonable God, and to apply to all doctrines that ethical test for which the "Independent" had been contending. But the "Interior" found in him an enemy of the faith once for all delivered to the saints, and after a somewhat bitter newspaper warfare upon him, it was announced that charges of heresy had been preferred against him by Professor Patton. The trial took place in the spring of 1874, and created no little excitement in ecclesiastical circles. The Chicago dailies gave verbatim reports of it, the associated press devoted large space to it, the secular as well as the religious newspapers freely discussed it.

Professor Patton is a keen logician, and he is thoroughly grounded in the technicalities of the Calvinistic system. He presented a formidable array of extracts from Professor Swing's sermons, from which it was easily proved that he was failing to teach many things specified in the standards of the church. But there was no man among the judges in the Presbytery against whom this

THE SWING TRIAL

could not have been proved. Any attempt to force a strict construction upon the ministry of the Presbyterian church would result in driving a good share of its ministers from their pulpits. Nobody believed the horrible article which taught infant damnation, and which has since been expunged. All ministers of the church were taking more or less liberty in the interpretation of this obsolescent symbol. The only question was, how much liberty should be allowed. And while it was made to appear that Professor Swing had broadened, considerably, the interpretation of the standards, three fourths of the Presbytery were satisfied that he had held fast to the substance of the faith, and voted to acquit him.

But the Chicago Presbytery was made up of men of unusual breadth and intelligence; its leader, the Reverend Dr. Patterson, the grandfather of the young Socialist who is making things interesting nowadays in the western metropolis, was a benignant and liberal-minded man, and he put himself strongly on the side of Professor Swing; the ministers of Chicago who knew him were nearly all his friends. And the prosecutor judged that if the case were appealed to the Synod of Illinois, the local influence in favor of Swing would be overcome and the decision reversed. Notice was therefore immediately given of such appeal, and the announcement was promptly met by the resignation of Mr. Swing from the ministry of the Presbyterian church. That step the "Independent" greatly deplored. In an editorial entitled "A Good Fight Declined" it declared: —

Mr. Swing has made a great mistake. Through the whole of the trial before the Presbytery he has borne himself steadily and manfully; his good temper, his frankness, his courage have increased the respect in which his friends held him; but now, at the end of the first trial, when more than three to one of the members of his Presbytery, including every prominent pastor in Chicago, have voted to acquit him of the charges made against him, he has withdrawn from the Presbyterian church. His reason for this step is his unwillingness to continue the litigation which his prosecutor has forced upon him by appealing the case to the higher courts. . . . We have no doubt that Mr. Swing has done what seemed to him right. He is not a man of war; the excitements of the trial, though they must have been, for the most part, pleasurable rather than painful, have severely taxed his strength, and he is unwilling to encounter the fatigues and hardships which must attend the continuation of the case in the Synod and the General Assembly. Besides, it seems to him, doubtless, that the time and strength consumed in warfare of this sort are just so much subtracted from his proper work. . . . Nevertheless, we cannot help feeling sorry that he has not, at whatever cost to himself, accepted the challenge now addressed to him. . . . There is a set of literalists, like Professor Patton, who keep insisting that no man has any business in the Presbyterian church who does not accept, *ipsissimis verbis*, all the statements of the confession of faith. Everybody knows that this is absurd, but these people will keep up their clamor till their mouths are stopped by a decision of the General Assembly. Nearly everybody knows that an attempt to enforce a literal acceptance of the terms of the Confession would drive out of the Presbyterian church at least half of its ministers. The Confession was framed

THE SWING TRIAL

two hundred and thirty years ago, and it is ridiculous to suppose that the light which has been shed upon Biblical and theological science since that day has revealed no flaw in this old document, or that its phrases, many of which, when they were adopted, were shrewd compromises between conflicting opinions, are all in this year of grace the exact and scientific expression of the faith of the living Presbyterian church. Dr. Patterson was right, therefore, in saying the other day that the Confession ought to be revised, but it is doubtful whether this can be done. There is another alternative, and that is to let the Creed stand as a historical symbol, and to obtain from the highest tribunal in the church the decision that within certain limits there shall be liberty in the interpretation of it. Mr. Swing was the man above all others to secure this decision. His reputation is unblemished, his hearty acceptance of the vital truths of the Christian faith is manifest, his devotion to his work and his success in it are unquestionable, he is the best loved and the most influential Presbyterian minister in the Northwest. The Presbyterian church would not have ventured to expel such a man from its communion, and when the decision affirming his good standing had been proclaimed, there would have been light all round the sky, and thousands who are chafing in the bonds of old-time creeds would have rejoiced in the liberty wherewith Christ makes us free.

I have quoted these words as an expression of the principles by which I have sought to guide my own conduct in the difficult matters of creed subscription and denominational loyalty. There is an editorial here, written in one of the early months of my service on the "Independent," entitled "Come-outers and Stay-inners," —

based upon a saying of Governor Andrew: "I am not a Come-outer; I am a Stay-inner." The duty of liberal men to stay in the churches to which they belong — if they can be tolerated there — and, by kindness and patience and fidelity to the truth as they see it, to do what they can to enlighten and broaden the fellowship of those churches, has always appeared to me very plain. The question became, in subsequent years, a very practical one for me; these words will show that I had time enough to consider it.

Mr. Swing's subsequent career in Chicago was one of great honor and usefulness. The church which he organized, and to which he preached, for many years, in the great Music Hall, was a strong force in the life of that city; and, until the day of his death, this good man held, in an unusual degree, the respect and affection of the people. Nor was this due to any sensational or *ad captandum* methods. His art, as a preacher, was simplicity itself; there were no oratorical fireworks; he read his sermons, with no attempts at elocutionary effect; they bore the character of essays rather than of orations. What held the people was, partly, the beauty in which his thought was always clothed, but, more than all, the sincerity, the reality, the genuineness of it all. He was a pure-hearted, gentle, faithful soul; the words that he spoke, like his Master's, were words of spirit and life, and therefore the common people, and all the people, heard him gladly. The fact that by methods so quiet and unsensational a preacher could fill, Sunday after Sunday, so large an assembly room, in the heart of the business quarter of a great city, is reassuring to those who

THE SWING TRIAL

would like to believe in the effectiveness of simple truth.

The success of Mr. Swing as a teacher of religion was due also in part to the fact that he knew how to mediate between the church and the great outside multitude which has largely withdrawn from its influence. While he treated the dogmas of the church with great freedom, yet he sought to present the essential truths of religion in a manner so untechnical that they should commend themselves to the common sense of men. My belief is that great numbers of men who had been repelled from the traditional statements of religious truth, were led back to respect and reverence by the teachings of Mr. Swing.

CHAPTER XVI

NEWSPAPER ETHICS

> And they serve men austerely,
> After their own genius, clearly,
> Without a false humility;
> For this is Love's nobility, —
> Not to scatter bread and gold,
> Goods and raiment bought and sold;
> But to hold fast his simple sense,
> And speak the speech of innocence,
> And with hand and body and blood,
> To make his bosom-counsel good.
> For he that feeds men serveth few;
> He serves all who dares be true.
> *Ralph Waldo Emerson.*

TOWARD the end of my fourth year in the "Independent" office, certain matters which had been disturbing me more or less through the whole of my service there, took on a form so aggravated that it became evident to me that I must give up my work, and on November 3, 1874, I gave the stipulated three months' notice which terminated my engagement. It was not a grateful conclusion, for the labor in which I had been engaged was, in many ways, more congenial and inspiring than anything that I had ever tried to do; the compensation was the largest I had ever earned; the associations in the office, on the whole, were very pleasant.

What troubled me was the business management of the paper, especially in the matter of advertising. I do not think that the "Independent" was, in this matter, a sinner above all the weekly and daily journals of the period; most of them practiced, more or less continuously, the arts which appeared to me objectionable; many of them resorted, now and again, to methods which were never tolerated in our office. It was not uncommon to discover, in the editorial and news columns of some of these journals, matter which wore the garb of journalistic expression, but which the practiced eye discerned to be simply an advertisement. From this abuse our literary and editorial columns were absolutely free. Only once during my stay in the office was it attempted to insert an advertisement among our editorial notes, and the insurrection which that provoked brought a promise that it should never occur again. The methods of the "Independent" of which I was disposed to complain were confined to one or two departments in which advertising matter was more or less skillfully disguised. There was a department of "Publisher's Notices," adjoining the editorial page, in which the matter was printed in editorial type, and leaded to have the exact appearance of editorial matter. It was often written, also, in the editorial style, with the first person plural. There was an "Insurance Department," which purported to discuss insurance questions, and there was a "Financial Department," both of which, undoubtedly, were constructed in the same way. Now it is true that these departments were announced as advertising departments in every number of the "Independent"; and the public was informed that reading notices in them cost one dollar a line. Readers of intelligence were not deceived by this device. Of course it was not intended to deceive readers of intelligence. But a large percentage, perhaps a majority of the readers, even of a journal like the "Independent," are casual or careless readers, to whom these reading notices, in editorial form, would appear to be the opinions of the editor. It was in the expectation of deceiving these dull-witted readers that the advertisers were willing to pay twice as much for these reading notices as they paid for ordinary advertising space. And the journal, for the double rate, was willing to lend itself to this scheme of the advertisers, in deceiving the innocent and the unwary.

In a note to the publisher, written in May, 1873, I made this frank statement: —

I have never been satisfied that the Publisher's Notices are strictly honest. They appear to be what they are not. It may be said that very few persons consider them to be other than advertisements, but if this is so, why not put them under the head of advertisements? I suppose you get extra rates for them, and that these extra rates are paid because they appear to be the publisher's opinions, and because they may be quoted into other papers from the "Independent." That, as you know, is constantly done, and it gives the impression that the "Independent" is a monster puffing-machine.

Such was the scruple, in which I confess that I did not find much sympathy among newspaper men, but which kept growing more burdensome to me, until, in the fall of 1874, certain transactions transpired, concerning which it is not needful that I should go into particulars, but which made it clear to me that I could no longer share the editorial responsibility for this journal. In the note to the publisher in which I resigned my position I said: —

I cannot think as you do about those departments. They seem to me essentially evil, and a source of weakness to the paper. My scruple may be a foolish one, but I cannot overcome it. It is quite true that most of the other papers have something of the same sort, but if the thing is wrong, that is no excuse. You think that I am not responsible; but suppose that I was the pastor of a church in the basement of which the President of the Board of Trustees kept a policy shop; would n't my preaching be somewhat discounted? The analogy is not perfect, but it is close enough to indicate how difficult it is to separate two departments of a church or a newspaper in the popular mind, and count one clean and the other unclean. It seems to me that nothing will avail but a radical change in the management of the paper, by which these departments are abolished, and the business of advertising placed on a perfectly square and intelligent basis. . . . You act on what seem to you sound principles, — that I do not dispute, — but they do not seem so to me. Now that I have brought myself squarely to face the question which I have tried for three years to evade, my way seems very clear.

It ought to be said that the ideas of publishers in general were less clear, upon the matter, in those days than they are in these. Most reputable periodicals are careful, nowadays, to make a clear and bold distinction between reading-matter and advertisements. The "Independent," itself, so far as I can see, is scrupulously free, to-day, from all such devices.

Yet signs have not been wanting, within the past ten

years, of the existence of subterranean methods by means of which large portions of the press are subsidized for the misleading of the people. Beyond a question large quantities of what purports to be reading-matter are supplied to the journals of the country by interested parties, and paid for by the line. Certain great corporations pay large sums of money for influencing, in this manner, public opinion. It appeared, not long ago, in evidence before a court, that a certain magazine, which had no very obvious reason for existence, but which had been very friendly to corporate combinations, had been subsidized, for several years, by a large corporation. There are certain news agencies which supply country papers with news or New York or Washington letters, sometimes gratuitously and always at very low figures; the matter is well written, and is eagerly accepted by the lesser journals, but it is cooked to suit the taste of the "Interests" that stand behind the bureau and use it for the creation of a public opinion favorable to themselves. Many persons throughout the country have been surprised at receiving month after month a popular magazine for which they had not subscribed; few of them, perhaps, have observed the appearance in it of a series of articles, purporting to discuss the conditions of public service companies in various cities, and generally tending to cast discredit upon municipal ownership. It ought to be evident to the readers that somebody, who is not wholly disinterested, is trying to educate them on this subject, and is using this magazine for this purpose.

Such are some of the methods in which the press is

now being used by the money power to poison the springs of public opinion. Often when the innocent reader supposes himself to be instructed by some independent student of public affairs, he is reading matter which is furnished by some interested party, and which is paid for at advertising rates. Compared with these vast schemes for deceiving the people, the disguised advertising of the "Independent" in the olden time was a venial offense.

Any man has a right to use the press in defending his claims or promoting his interest, provided the thing is done openly and without deceit or concealment. But when a man or a corporation enters into a conspiracy with a newspaper to palm off upon the public its own special plea as the report or the judgment of a disinterested investigator — paying money for the insertion of such matter in the news or editorial columns of the newspaper — the man who pays the money is a swindler, and the newspaper that accepts it is a prostitute.

If Mr. Lawson wishes to issue his financial manifestoes in the form of advertisements, that is perfectly legitimate for him and for the newspapers which print them; his name is signed to his statement, and every reader knows what he is reading. But if some syndicate interested in public service properties buys space in the newspapers and fills it with its own statements artfully prepared for the promotion of its own interests, letting it appear that it is the work of some unprejudiced reporter or the judgment of some independent student, the deceit thus practiced on the reading public is one of the gravest offenses against modern civilization. The guilt of this offense is shared equally by the newspaper and the advertiser.

The press has come to be the principal agency for the creation of public opinion. The welfare of the commonwealth depends upon the intelligence and soundness of public opinion. The sacredness of the function of the press is therefore obvious. It is pledged, by all that is precious in our national life, to tell the truth; to help the people to see things as they are. When it suffers itself to become an instrument for misleading the people, it becomes the worst of our public enemies.

It was my own strong sense of the sacredness of the newspaper as a public teacher, and of the grave immorality of perverting its function for hire, that constrained me to give up my work upon the "Independent."

CHAPTER XVII

BACK TO NEW ENGLAND

Sing on! bring down, O lowland river,
   The joy of the hills to the waiting sea;
The wealth of the vales, the pomp of mountains,
   The breath of the woodlands, bear with thee.

Into thy dutiful life of uses
   Pour the music and weave the flowers;
With the song of birds and bloom of meadows
   Lighten and gladden thy heart and ours.

And well may we own thy hint and token
   Of fairer valleys and streams than these,
Where the rivers of God are full of water,
   And full of sap are His healing trees!
                John Greenleaf Whittier.

WHEN I turned my steps from the door of the "Independent" office, the world was all before me. There did not appear to be any promising opening in journalism, and the pulpit seemed to be my only refuge. Nor was the thought of returning to the active pastorate an unwelcome one; I had been preaching, most of the time, during my editorial service; two of the smaller churches in Brooklyn I had served for periods of nearly a year each, so that I had by no means lost contact with the life of the churches. Fortunately I was not left long in suspense. The North Congregational Church of Springfield was without a pastor; I had several friends in that church, and I was invited to supply its pulpit for four Sundays. The invitation was most welcome. Springfield had always been to me the most attractive of the New England cities; it was only a few miles from my father's old home; Mount Tom, over which I used to see the sun rise from my grandfather's house in Bedlam, was in full view; the lovely Connecticut valley had long held me by an enduring charm. My dear old friend Bowles, from my boyhood my critic and counselor, was there on the "Republican"; it would be good to be within hailing distance of him.

Of the church, too, I had known something. Dr. Holland had been one of its leading members; it was in the choir gallery of this church, leading its quartette in the Sunday worship, that I had caught my first glimpse of him. He was now living in New York. It had been a church of progressive temper, and its ministers had been, for the most part, men of light and leading. I had preached for the church, a few times, during my pastorate in North Adams, and did not come into its pulpit wholly a stranger. To add to the attraction was a new church edifice, one of the first and best of Henry H. Richardson's churches.

Before the four Sundays of my occasional engagement had passed, the church extended to me a call to become its pastor, so that, on the expiration of my three months' notice, on February 1, 1875, I found my home in Springfield. Thus begins nearly eight years of pastoral life, in the fairest of the lesser cities of the land, in the midst of fresh thought and stimulating movement, with delightful ministerial companionships, with plenty of congenial work to do, and with new roads opening every day into the great realities.

Springfield in 1875 had a population of about thirty thousand; it had five or six Congregational churches, among them the old First, founded in 1636 by William Pynchon and his brave pioneers, who pushed out to the Connecticut valley when the settlement about Massachusetts Bay was still very young. The name of Pynchon still survives in the locality, and the tradition of him has been cherished by lovers of free thought in all the generations. Like most educated laymen of his time, he was something of a theologian; and a book of his, "The Meritorious Price of our Redemption," made no small stir in those early days. It was printed in England, and some of the Puritan theologians there, falling foul of it before it was imported to this country, raised such a hue and cry about its heresies, that the "Great and General Court" in Boston commanded that the copies of it arriving by ship from England be seized and burned by the hangman on Boston Common. How many copies escaped the fire I do not know; only two or three are known to be in existence to-day. One of these it was once my pleasure to have in my custody for a few days, and the perusal of it was a revelation. The tradition had been that this book of Pynchon's, upon the Atonement, was a daring denial of all that is essential in substitutionary theology; instead of that, its orthodoxy is rock-ribbed and triple-plated; there is no Calvinistic stronghold in the land in which its doctrine would not to-day be deemed archaic. The head and front of Pynchon's offending seems to have been his denial that Christ as our substitute actually suffered the pains of hell in his soul, including the pangs of remorse. That he positively refused to believe; that refusal made him a heretic, and caused the burning of his book on Boston Common. There was a hot controversy about it on both sides of the sea. Pynchon was repeatedly cited to answer for his heresies before the ministers of Boston, but he appears to have disregarded the summons. So fierce, however, was the censure to which he was exposed that, in 1652, he returned to England, leaving to his children his estates and responsibilities in the Connecticut valley. It is a curious illustration of the manner in which the heresy of one day becomes the orthodoxy of the next. But the tradition of Pynchon, the founder of Springfield, as that of a man in advance of his day, who was unjustly persecuted by his contemporaries, may have had some tendency to moderate the theological climate and encourage toleration in that neighborhood.

Springfield was the natural capital of the four western counties of Massachusetts, and the cluster of large towns by which it was surrounded, Chicopee, Holyoke, Northampton, and Westfield, with Hartford, the capital of Connecticut, only half an hour distant on the south, made it a centre of considerable influence. What counted for much in this respect was the Springfield "Republican," a newspaper whose weight and force as an organ of public opinion has long been wholly out of proportion to the size of the community in which it circulates. It is doubtful whether the field of any newspaper was ever better cultivated than this of the Springfield "Republican." In every hamlet of these four western counties a correspondent gathered up the local news and forwarded it to Springfield, and these reports, generally

BACK TO NEW ENGLAND 243

crude, were skillfully edited and condensed in the office, so that a picture of the life of western Massachusetts, complete in its detail, was spread before the readers of the "Republican" every morning. By this means a community of interest and feeling was cultivated; in matters social and political the people could coöperate intelligently. Not that the lead of the "Republican" was always followed in such matters; often there was wide dissent from its positions, and loud complaint against the excesses of its independency; but the people had come to rely upon its truthfulness and its courage, and its influence was felt in every part of its field.

How pervasive and salutary this influence has been, the people of that community may not fully realize. Over all their affairs this guardian has always been watching sleeplessly; no conspiracy against the public welfare could escape its vigilance, and no corrupt consideration could muzzle its utterance. Municipal or political irregularities of all sorts were sure to be discovered and dragged into the light; graft and extravagance were held in check by its presence. I think that the municipalities of western Massachusetts will be found to be singularly free from civic and financial abuses. Springfield has expended money freely for public buildings and improvements, but its debt is small, its tax rate is low, and no scandals that I remember have appeared in its City Hall. The capitalization of its public service companies has always been very moderate — at least this was so until a recent day; what may have happened since the great New England railroad monopoly has been absorbing the electric lines of the cities, I do not know. But for all this social and civic health and vigor western Massachusetts is indebted, in no small degree, to the Springfield "Republican." It is not, of course, the only influence; other good newspapers and other moral agencies have been at work in this field, but there has been no other influence so salutary and so persistent as that of this leading newspaper. If newspapers of the type of the Springfield "Republican" could be planted all over this country at intervals of not more than one hundred miles, the foundation would be laid for a great improvement in social and political morality.

For all this large result the community was mainly indebted to Samuel Bowles. He was the second editor of the name. The "Weekly Republican" was founded by his father, in 1824; it was changed to a daily, in 1844, at the urgent instance of the younger Samuel, who was then but eighteen years old; the upbuilding and development of this paper had been his life-work. He had had good collaborators, chief of whom was Dr. Holland, whose wholesome and homely social essays had added greatly to the popularity of the journal. But the life and soul of the "Republican" had always been Samuel Bowles. For thirty years he had been pouring all his energies into it, and better than most men he had worked out his ideals. On the literary side they were distinct and sensible. He wanted no fine writing, but the news should be told and the comment presented in clear, crisp, idiomatic English, with no surplus verbiage. The paper must tell the truth; correspondents were encouraged to state the thing as it appeared to them; not

BACK TO NEW ENGLAND

seldom the editorial columns and the correspondence columns were openly at war. Readers were made sure that the facts would not be concealed from them, and that they were likely to get all sides of a controverted question. Over the staff of reporters and editors the influence of the chief was potent. "He was a man," says one of his old associates, "of notable presence, tall, spare, nervous, with keen cavalier face, full brown beard and dark brown hair that was neither of Indian stiffness nor of effeminate curl, but between the two; a rich brown-red complexion, a strong nose, and brilliant and divining eyes before which no falsehood could stand. . . . He was often severe, and sometimes the young apprentice would feel that he was cruel; but he was as generous in praise as stern in censure, and a word of approval from the chief coupled with one of his wonderful smiles was worth a hundred flatteries beside. The personal aura which surrounded him in social intercourse was nowhere more potent than among the young men in the office, when he criticised and inspired them."

When I first knew Mr. Bowles, during my college days, and afterward in North Adams, he was very modest about his ability as a writer. Of the management of a newspaper he knew that he was master, but he was diffident respecting his literary skill. Indeed, his earlier writing was by no means brilliant; it was clear, intelligent, businesslike, but it had little sparkle or color. All this came to him late in life. During the last ten years he developed a degree of skill as a writer which was a surprise to those who knew him in his earlier days. The blossoming of his art seems to have come on the occasion of his visit to California, in 1865; the letters which he wrote to the "Republican" on that journey, which are collected in his volume "Across the Continent," are full of piquant, fresh, poetical English. And the letters of all this period, which are gathered up in Mr. Merriam's admirable biography, are delightful examples of the epistolary art.

When I took up my home in Springfield in 1875, Mr. Bowles was fifty-one years of age, and ought to have had twenty-five years of good work ahead of him, but it was easy to see that his work was nearly done; the symptoms of nervous breakdown were manifest. I saw him not often; his strength was consumed by his daily duties, and he had not much left for social pleasures. He had been most cordial in his appreciation of my journalistic experience. "I hope," he had written me three months before, "you will not leave journalism. The harvest is large and the laborers are few. It is bigger than the pulpit. I won't be so conceited as to say that it is better." But when I became, so to speak, a member of his parish once more, he gave me a warm welcome, and showed a kindly interest in my work. Now and then I had the honor of a seat at his table, at those rather informal dinner parties which he sometimes gave to a few gentlemen, when guests of distinction were visiting him. Over all the questions of national politics we used to talk freely when we met; in the Hayes-Tilden campaign he was disposed to favor Tilden, but he asked me to give the "Republican" my reasons for the opposite preference, and printed it conspicuously, with a cordial word,

BACK TO NEW ENGLAND 247

on the editorial page. His fear was that Hayes was a man of putty, and could be manipulated by the worst elements of the Republican Party; he was sure, after Hayes was confirmed in his seat, that the Cabinet would be composed of rotten timber. About this he was quite pessimistic. On the day when the Cabinet was announced, I saw the bulletin, with the names of Evarts and Schurz and Sherman and Devens, — the strongest Cabinet for many years, and nobody representing the reactionary wing of the party,— and I climbed to the editorial rooms of the "Republican." "How now?" I demanded. "Well," he said, "it's too good to believe. I did n't think they would let him do it. The fact is, parson, there's one element these fellows never count on, and that is God." It was no irreverence; it was his way of saying that the machinations of the politicians had been divinely overruled. He was very chary of expressions like that, but I think that he meant it, that day.

Several years before his death they made him a Trustee of Amherst College. Free lance in theology as he notoriously was, his appointment as custodian of the interests of that very conservative institution was regarded as somewhat extraordinary. But he proved to be a most valuable member of the Board, nor were his religious views ever suffered to embarrass, in any way, the administration. One day I expressed to him my gratification at the appointment, and jocularly ventured the hope that he might do something to brace up the orthodoxy of the institution. "Well, no, parson," he said; "I don't go much on theology; but now and then a question of morals in the financial management comes up, and then I shine out!"

During the last year of his life he stirred up the people of Springfield to undertake a more efficient organization of their local charities. The "Republican," at his instigation, kept the matter before the public until a meeting was called and steps were taken to form an association for the care of the poor. It was my privilege to prepare the report and to draft the form of organization by which the Union Relief Association of Springfield was constituted, in which service I was brought into frequent conferences with Mr. Bowles. It was the last opportunity I had of talking much with him, and I gratefully treasure the memory of those interviews. As soon as the Association was organized, he himself took out a subscription paper, and raised the money necessary for putting the machinery into operation. It was almost his last public service.

Six months later came the fatal stroke which prostrated him, and left him but a few weeks of lingering suffering. I saw him once, after that; he asked for me. The great brown eyes were full of wistful friendliness; there were a few cheerful and courageous words. It was not many days later that we carried him away to his resting-place in the beautiful cemetery, near his home.

When my work began in Springfield, in the spring of 1875, the industries of the country had not yet recovered from the collapse of 1873. It was a season of industrial depression; large numbers of men were out of work, and

BACK TO NEW ENGLAND

the outlook for a multitude of industrious and capable men was gloomy. Meetings of the unemployed were held in the Police Court room at the City Hall, and various schemes were suggested by which the city might offer relief to those in want. Those who attended these meetings were not, as a rule, the soberest and most capable workingmen, but the more restless and turbulent of the laboring class. Their leader was an Irishman, of an impulsive and reckless temper, whose talk to the crowd had sometimes been of an inflammatory character. One day he came to me with an urgent request that I go down to the meeting that night, and speak to the multitude. I accepted the invitation, and found myself confronted with a company of laborers who were evidently not in a complacent mood. What I had to say to them did not fully harmonize with their ruling idea, for I expressed doubt as to whether it would be possible for the city to furnish work for them, and exhorted them to be ready to do any kind of work that might be offered, at merely nominal wages, rather than beg or be idle. It was not, as I am able now to recall it, a speech which was calculated to conciliate that audience; I fear it did not recognize so clearly as it ought to have done the responsibility of the community for the relief of such conditions. I am sure that I should put the case a little differently to-day, if I were speaking to such a company.

The men listened to me, however, respectfully, and at the close of my address I said to them: "I have told you what I think is the sensible thing for you to do; next Sunday night I am going to talk to your employers, to the people who are in the habit of hiring labor, and I wish you would come to the church and hear what I shall say to them." Quite a number of them accepted the invitation. In that sermon I urged upon my congregation the duty of furnishing work, wherever it was possible, to the unemployed; I suggested that building and repairing could be very cheaply done, in the existing conditions of the labor market; and that those who had any surplus funds could probably use them productively, just then, in the employment of labor. That sermon was one of the most effective I ever preached; it started two or three of my parishioners to building houses; it set quite a number of people to repairing and remodeling their premises; it resulted in organizing one or two small businesses which gave employment to several people. If one could only get such results as these quite frequently, preaching would seem to be better worth while.

Those of the workingmen who heard what I had to say to the employing class seemed to be satisfied that the pulpit was not prejudiced against them, and my friend, the Irish agitator, continued, after that time, regularly to attend my church, with which he afterward united, becoming one of my most loyal parishioners.

It was about this time that I began the series of lectures to "Workingmen and their Employers," which were published, in 1876, in a volume with that title. The field was one into which the pulpit had not often ventured, and my work had to be largely that of a pioneer. But it was becoming increasingly evident that a great social problem was thus forcing itself upon the thought

BACK TO NEW ENGLAND 251

of the world, — a problem in the solution of which the Christian church must have a large concern. Primarily it must be a question of conduct, a question concerning the relations of man to man, and it is the primary business of Christianity to define and regulate these relations. The application of the Christian law to industrial society would, it seemed to me, solve this problem, and the church ought to know how to apply it.

Against this assumption strenuous objection was raised in those days, and the protest is still heard. It was said that the minister has no business to bring questions of this kind into the pulpit; that his concern is with spiritual interests, and not with secular; that his function is the saving of souls and not the regulation of business. It was urged that if men are only "saved," all questions of this nature will solve themselves; that right relations will necessarily be established between social classes.

In dealing with this objection, it was only too apparent that the facts did not support it. It was by no means true that those who, in the judgment of charity, were "saved" were establishing right relations between themselves and those with whom they were associated in industry. Many of them were practicing injustice and cruelty, without any sense of the evil of their conduct. They were nearly all assuming that the Christian rule of life had no application to business; that the law of supply and demand was the only law which, in the world of exchanges, they were bound to respect. If a man was converted and joined the church, it did not occur to him that that fact had any relation to the management of his mill or his factory. Business was business and religion was religion; the two areas were not coterminous, they might be mutually exclusive. Nothing was more needed in the church than the enforcement upon the consciences of men of the truth that the Christian law covers every relation of life, and the distinct and thoroughgoing application of that law to the common affairs of men.

There were those who urged the materialistic doctrine that all these economic questions are outside the realm of morals; that economic forces are beyond the reach of moral causes; that nothing can be done by human agency to mitigate their severities or to modify their action. All this appeared to me profoundly and mischievously untrue; it seemed to involve a philosophy of history which was openly at war with the facts of history, and it was the denial of all that is heroic and inspiring in human endeavor.

The most common objection to the discussion of such topics in the pulpit was, however, the assertion that the minister was not competent to deal with them. Concerning economic questions and business questions he was not apt to have any adequate knowledge, and therefore he had better let them alone. That objection largely prevails, until this hour. A good proportion of our ministers avoid all reference to the matters in dispute between workingmen and their employers, and all the great issues arising in industrial society, because, they say, they have not the necessary information and technical skill to handle them satisfactorily.

It is worth while candidly to scrutinize this plea.

BACK TO NEW ENGLAND 253

Doubtless, for many of us, it is the easiest way to dispose of the matter. If we can get a dispensation from our consciences to evade this subject, we shall keep out of a thorny road. Doubtless, too, we may be aware that there are powerful influences which join to urge upon us this policy of evasion. But it is a fair question whether this is a subject which we can afford to ignore.

Let us say that our business is saving souls. Souls are men. How to save men, their manhood, their character, — that is our chief problem. Is there any other realm in which character, manhood, is more rapidly and more inevitably made or lost, than this realm of industry? Is the man saved, who, in his dealings with his employee, or his employer, can habitually seek his own aggrandizement at the cost of the other? Is not the selfishness which is expected to rule in all this department of life the exact antithesis of Christian morality? Is there anything else from which men need more to be saved than from the habits of thought and action which prevail in the places where "business is business"? Are we really "saving souls," when we permit men like the packing-house proprietors and the insurance wreckers to sit comfortably in our pews and enjoy our ministrations? I fear that some of these men may have grave accusations to bring against us, one of these days, for having failed to tell them the truth about their own conduct.

In fact, there is reason for the belief that in these very questions respecting the regulation of our industries, the Christian church is facing to-day its crucial test. If it can meet these questions frankly and bravely, if it can solve them successfully, its future is secure: it will have won its right to the moral leadership of society. If it fails in this, — if this tremendous problem is worked out without its aid, — the world is likely to have very little use for it in the generations to come. The church is in the world to save the world; if it lacks the power to do this, and industrial society plunges into chaos, are there any ecclesiastics infatuated enough to believe that the church can save itself out of that wreck? No; it must save society, or go to ruin with it.

The plea of the religious teachers that they are incompetent to deal with social questions is, t'.erefore, a fearful self-accusation. They have no right to be incompetent. Whatever else they are ignorant of, they must not be ignorant respecting matters which concern the very life of the organization they represent. If there are any subjects on which they are bound to have clear ideas and sound convictions, they are these subjects which concern the relations of men in industrial society. Here is the field on which the battle of Gog and Magog is being fought out to-day. Shall the teacher of religion confess that in the arena where character is mainly won or lost, where the life of the church is at stake, where the destiny of the nation is trembling in the balance, he is unfit for any efficient service? It is as if a physician should declare that he would only prescribe for nettle rash and chicken-pox and like disorders, but that he declined to deal with typhoid or diphtheria or tuberculosis or any of the deadly diseases. The services of such a physician would not be in great demand.

The fact is that the application of the Christian law to

social questions is not a recondite matter. Many of the abstruse questions of metaphysical theology with which all ministers are expected to be familiar are mastered with much more difficulty. The divinity schools have no business on their hands so urgent as the instruction of their students in the first principles of the Christian social order. It is far more important that young ministers should understand how men ought to live together in this generation than it is that they should be familiar with the Gnostic philosophy of the second century, or the Supralapsarian theories. To some extent the divinity schools are now seeking to meet this demand. But those ministers who had no such advantages during their professional studies may easily inform themselves upon all the more important aspects of the social question. And the plea of incompetency is one which no minister, with a due sense of the position he holds, and of the responsibility resting on him, ought to think of making.

It was a conviction of the truth which I have been trying to express which prompted me, in the autumn of 1875, to prepare that course of Sunday evening lectures to "Workingmen and their Employers," of which I have spoken. It has been many years since I looked into that old volume, and I have found some interest in glancing through it. It is not a profound discussion; in fact, it did not aim at profundity; it was meant for the average mechanic. It is by no means a radical utterance. I remember that some positions were called in question by some of my parishioners, but it is difficult to-day to understand how they could have found fault with ideas so obvious. The attitude of the discussion toward labor unions is not quite so sympathetic as it ought to have been. The right of the men to organize for their own protection is, indeed, maintained. "They have a perfect right to deliberate together concerning the wages they are receiving, and to unite in refusing to work unless their wages are increased. The law gives to capital an immense advantage in permitting its consolidation in great centralized corporations; and neither law nor justice can forbid laborers to combine, in order to protect themselves against the encroachments of capital, so long as they abstain from the use of violence, and rely upon reason and moral influence." I am glad to find that statement. Probably that was one of the positions to which my parishioners objected. On the whole, however, the treatment of the unions is critical rather than cordial; the evils which they harbor are magnified; the higher purposes they serve are imperfectly recognized. "I have no doubt" — thus it is written — "that such combinations of laborers are often unwise and unprofitable; that, as a general thing, they result in more loss than gain to the laboring classes." That was a narrow estimate; it rested on imperfect knowledge. In various ways I find these old lectures somewhat lacking in comprehension.

The principal suggestion in the way of social reconstruction is that of coöperation, which is urged, with much confidence, as a method of putting an end to industrial strife. What John Stuart Mill and John Eliot Cairnes had written about this was quoted, and the large success of the Rochdale Experiment in England

BACK TO NEW ENGLAND 257

was appealed to; it was also suggested that a steppingstone to coöperation might be found in industrial partnership, "by which the work-people in a manufacturing establishment are given an interest in the business; and, in addition to their wages, a stipulated portion of the profits is divided among them at the close of every year, in proportion to the amount of their earnings." But the fact was insisted on that all these methods must draw their force from Christian motives. "Let no one fail to see that coöperation is nothing more than the arrangement of the essential factors of industry according to the Christian rule — 'we being many are one body in Christ, and every one members one of another.' It is capital and labor adjusting themselves to the form of Christianity; and, like every other outward symbol, is a false, deceitful show, a dead form, unless filled with the living spirit of Christianity itself."

"Workingmen and their Employers" is not an important book; I have been quite resigned, for many years, to the fact that it is out of print; but it was a serious attempt, made at an early day, to apply Christian principles to the solution of the social question. I am not proud of the achievement, but I am not sorry that I made the endeavor.

Another little book was published in this Centennial year, — six short chapters of counsel to those contemplating the religious life, under the title "Being a Christian: What it Means, and How to Begin." I have explained on earlier pages of this story how I came to write this book. It was an attempt to make plain the way of Christian discipleship, which, before my own feet, had been made so obscure and difficult; and the favor with which it was received was very gratifying. It has had a larger circulation than any other of my books, with one exception; and I have been comforted in knowing that out of the perplexities of my boyhood, help has come to many who were seeking the way of life.

CHAPTER XVIII

HERESY HUNTING

> Opinion, let me alone; I am not thine.
> Prim Creed, with categoric point, forbear
> To feature me my Lord by rule and line.
> Thou canst not measure Mistress Nature's law,
>   Not one sweet inch: nay, if thy sight is sharp,
>   Wouldst count the strings upon an angel's harp?
>   Forbear, forbear.
>
> I would thou leftst me free, to live with love,
> And faith, that through the love of love doth find
>   My Lord's dear presence in the stars above,
> The clods below, the flesh without, the mind
>   Within, the bread, the tear, the smile.
>   Opinion, damned Intriguer, gray with guile,
>   Let me alone.
>   *Sidney Lanier.*

It was during the earlier years of my Springfield pastorate that the question respecting the inerrancy of the Bible began to trouble the mind of the churches. It was known, to begin with, that a company of learned men were meeting monthly in the Jerusalem Chamber of Westminster Abbey in London, for the revision of the received version of the Bible, and that certain eminent American scholars were coöperating in this revision. This was, in itself, to many, a disturbing suggestion. Revision implied change, and change, whether of word or phrase, in the language of the Bible, could be nothing less than sacrilege. It was known to some that considerable critical study had been bestowed upon the Bible, of late years, by German scholars, but, up to this time, very little was known in the churches, or even in the theological seminaries of this country, of the results of this study. Theodore Parker translated, in the forties, De Wette's monumental "Introduction to the Old Testament," but very few copies were sold; Parker's name on the title-page was the red signal of infection; not many of those who regarded their reputations would buy a book about the Bible for which he stood sponsor. Now and then one might hear from the pulpits sharp monitory words about the "German neologists," but just what their innovations might be, there was no way of finding out.

Gradually, however, the light that was shining all about us found its way through our shutters. In newspapers and magazines, and in an occasional heretical book, statements of fact appeared which arrested the attention of thoughtful men. There were even Biblical commentaries which ventured to call attention to interpolated verses and doubtful passages. It began to be evident to some that the doctrine of inerrancy had been overworked; that there was need of the application of critical study to the sacred Scriptures. Yet after this fact began to be plain to students and teachers, there was still great timidity in admitting so much in the hearing of the public. I remember sitting at table, at the Massasoit House in Springfield, in 1875, with a score of intelligent Congregational clergymen, when the question arose whether it would be judicious to tell the people of our congregations that 1 John v, 7 — a verse not found in the Revised Version — was an interpolation; and not

HERESY HUNTING

one of the twenty agreed with me in thinking that the fact could be safely stated. They all admitted that the verse was spurious, but feared the effect of letting the people know a truth so disturbing. About the same time I ventured to remark from the pulpit in reading the eighth chapter of the Acts of the Apostles, that the thirty-seventh verse was not in the original manuscript, and the next day I received an indignant letter calling my attention to the fate reserved for those who "take away from the words of the book of this prophecy." Such was the prevailing attitude of English-speaking Protestants upon questions of Biblical criticism, through the first three quarters of the nineteenth century.

Early in the seventies, a copy of the New Testament in English was published, containing the received version, with footnotes indicating the variations from this version of the three oldest and best manuscripts in existence, — the Vatican, the Alexandrian, and the Sinaitic Bibles. It was stated that none of these manuscripts had been known to the men who made the King James translation; and it was held by scholars to be almost axiomatic that where these three oldest manuscripts agreed, their reading must be accepted, and that where they unitedly disagreed with the received version, that version must be erroneous. This edition of the New Testament put within the reach of all intelligent readers the means of judging to what extent our English version needed revision, and made it plain that the task undertaken by the men at work in the Jerusalem Chamber was one of serious importance.

Such a concession, however reluctantly it might be

made, involved considerable relaxation of the rigidity of theological dogmatism, and opened the way for the examination of many traditional beliefs. There was "the sound of a going in the tops of the trees," — the spirit of inquiry was abroad.

In the autumn of 1877 the Reverend James F. Merriam, a son of Deacon George Merriam, of Springfield, was invited to the pastorate of the Congregational church in Indian Orchard, one of the Springfield suburbs. It was a factory village, and Mr. Merriam had already, by a year of service, greatly endeared himself to the community. He was a man of a most unselfish and consecrated temper; he had sought this field because of the opportunity it gave him to come into close contact with the working-people.

Before the council called to install him, Mr. Merriam indicated some slight variations from the traditional orthodoxy. The only one to which any importance was attached concerned the doctrine of future punishment. Mr. Merriam was unwilling to assert that all who die impenitent suffer everlasting conscious torment; he was inclined to believe that those who were incorrigible might suffer extinction. Over this heresy the council wrestled long and painfully; Mr. Merriam was called back once or twice and labored with to make him revise his statement, but he would not; and finally, after the hour for the evening service had arrived, a majority of the council voted to refuse him installation. The debate was a warm one, and there was great excitement in the community, where Mr. Merriam and his family were well known and greatly honored. The local newspapers

HERESY HUNTING 263

gave the matter large attention, and the press of the whole country, secular as well as religious, took it up; it became a matter of national interest.

Those of us who were in the minority in this controversy were naturally called on to give account of ourselves, and the whole question of the conditions of fellowship and of the obligations of denominational loyalty was up for wide discussion. In several sermons preached about this time, I tried to defend the action of the minority of the council, and to show that no interest of Congregationalism or of Christianity could be imperiled by including such men as Mr. Merriam in our fellowship; while their rejection was an act of narrowness for which we ought to suffer. The next Sunday after the council I reviewed its action, pointing out the precise doctrinal ground on which fellowship was refused to Mr. Merriam, insisting that such a divergence as his from the traditional beliefs was not a good ground for excluding him from the ministry, and concluding by saying: —

"As many as are led by the Spirit of God, they are the sons of God." Whomsoever we exclude, them we want to include, surely, in all our choicest fellowship. And how shall we find out who are led by the Spirit of God? We can only find out by looking at their lives. By their fruits we know them. "And the fruit of the Spirit is love, joy, peace, long-suffering, gentleness, goodness, faith, meekness, temperance — against such there is no law." No; there is not in God's Kingdom, and there never shall be by my help or consent in any human organization that tries to represent God's Kingdom. The man who believes in Christ, who has the spirit of Christ in him, who shows in his life the fruits of that spirit, who, denying himself and taking up his cross, is following Christ in toilsome but loving labor for the salvation of men — he is my brother, and nothing shall hinder me from offering him the right hand of fellowship. I do not care what name they call him by, whether he is Churchman or Quaker, Universalist or Roman Catholic, he who is united to my Master shall not be divided from me. And when such a man has found a company of people who love him, not because of any brilliancy of wit that has dazzled them, nor because of any tricks of sensationalism that have amused them, but just because of the Christ life that is in him, — and want him to live among them and show them how to serve and follow Christ, — and when he asks me to come and help to join him in loving bonds as pastor to this people, I shall go, every time! My blessing is not worth much, but, such as it is, God forbid that I should withhold it! And if anybody bids me be cautious, I answer, Yes, I will be very cautious lest I hinder in his work a true servant of Jesus Christ! I will take great care always lest I exalt the letter above the spirit, the dogma above the life. For I would rather make two mistakes on the side of charity than one on the side of bigotry.

Mr. Merriam's people insisted that he remain with them, in spite of the adverse decision of the council; and for this reason some other disagreeable things were done, in the ecclesiastical assemblies of the neighborhood, with the purpose of excluding the church from Congregational fellowship. Through the whole matter Mr. Merriam bore himself with exemplary gentleness and forbearance, refusing to engage in any controversy, and quietly going forward with his work, until broken health compelled him to lay down his charge.

HERESY HUNTING 265

It was only a few weeks after the Indian Orchard Council that another council was called at North Adams for the installation of the Reverend Theodore T. Munger over my old church. Of that council also I was a member. Mr. Munger was known to hold liberal views on many questions, and the issue of this council was awaited with much interest. The council was a more representative body than that at Indian Orchard; it included President Noah Porter, of Yale, and President Hopkins, of Williams. Mr. Munger's statement of his theological views was presented skillfully, but without evasion; on one or two points which Mr. Merriam had not touched he diverged from the traditional statements, and on the subject of future punishment he was even more emphatic in his rejection of the orthodox view than Mr. Merriam had been. He was somewhat sharply criticised, but he defended himself, and when the discussion was ended, the council voted to proceed with his installation. It was pleasant to be in the majority again, and to carry back to Springfield the testimony that there were other views of the conditions of Congregational fellowship than those which had prevailed at Indian Orchard.

These two councils created no small stir in our Congregational communion. Everywhere the ecclesiastical bees were buzzing. What were the conditions of fellowship? How much must one believe to be a Congregational minister in good standing? It was known, of course, that there was no national Congregational creed, and no ecclesiastical body which had the power to frame or impose such a creed upon the denomination; the only creeds were those of local churches, and these were by no means uniform, and were binding only upon those who belonged to the local church. It was argued, however, that there was a *consensus of doctrine*, which was sufficiently well understood by Congregationalists; and that those who did not, *ex animo*, accept that consensus of doctrine had no right to remain in the Congregational ministry. To this it was easy to reply that this *consensus* had been continually changing; that one doctrine after another once universally accepted had been modified or dropped, and that there must be room at the present, within the fellowship, for varieties of belief.

In default of any definite denominational standards to which ministers could be held, some of the defenders of the faith undertook to enforce the idea of self-discipline. Every man, they argued, knows whether he is an orthodox Congregationalist or not; if he knows that he is not, he is bound to take himself out of the fellowship; and if he fails to do so, he is acting a dishonorable and unmanly part. The "Congregational Quarterly," which assumed to represent the denomination, urged, with considerable acerbity, this method of eliminating heretics. Naming certain doctrines as not included in the Congregational system, — among them the moral theory of the Atonement, — it declared that the only way in which men holding those doctrines could "evince a noble manhood" was by promptly withdrawing from that ministry. To that challenge I ventured a reply in the columns of the "Congregationalist." After explaining that I held and taught some of the doctrines denounced by this censor, I said: —

To be told that I am not acting a manly part in remaining in this fellowship, is an impertinence which I heartily resent. I am here in the Congregational denomination; I suppose that I have a right to be here, and here I propose to stay. If, holding the opinions that I do, I have not a right to be recognized as a Congregational minister, I want to know that. I do not wish to be "tolerated." I do not care to be in a ministry in which I have not equal rights with every other minister. Such rights I suppose myself to possess, and I shall continue to exercise them until I am advised by some competent tribunal that they have been abrogated.

The editor of the "Quarterly" says that the moral theory of the atonement "does not belong to our orthodox system." Perhaps it does not belong to his, but it does to mine. . . . "There is no logical stopping-place," he goes on, "between the moral theory of the atonement and infidelity." An older if not a better pope has declared that there is no logical stopping-place between Protestantism and infidelity. The one saying is just as true as the other. I take the liberty of deciding for myself what logic requires of me.

I speak for nobody but myself; but I happen to know that I am not alone in my opinions, nor in my determination to stand by them. There are quite a number of us who have no wish for controversy, but who do believe to some extent in the manly art of self-defense, and we shall not be posted as sneaks in the "Congregational Quarterly" without mildly protesting. If, by refusing to go straight over to infidelity, we must lose the respect of the editor of the "Quarterly," so be it; we shall try not to lose our self-respect.

The response to this was surprising. Letters and postal cards came pouring in for a week or two with the heartiest approval of this declaration of independence. Yet those who were standing for the new measure of liberty in the denomination were still in a small minority, and many ways were found of making their position quite uncomfortable. There is always a denominational "machine," more or less political in its methods, by which ecclesiastical affairs are managed, and those who incur the displeasure of this machine are apt to find their paths to promotion obstructed, and their opportunities of service limited. A young man sometimes finds himself branded as a suspect, and avoided by those whose confidence he wishes to deserve. For several years I was passing through this experience. It did not greatly distress me, for I knew that it would not endure, and my own church never wavered in its loyalty. Sometimes, the manifestations of this suspicion, on the part of those who knew me only by name, were quite amusing. Yet I confess that this method of dealing with those who are supposed to differ, in certain matters of doctrine, from the majority of their brethren, often filled me with indignation.

Following the lead of the "Congregational Quarterly," the Vermont State Convention of Congregationalists, shortly after this, passed a resolution declaring that men who rejected "any substantial part" of the doctrines "commonly called evangelical" ought to take themselves out of the Congregational fellowship. And when an amendment was proposed, providing that the resolution involved no imputation against the character of a man who "neither in his own mind, nor by the decision of a competent ecclesiastical tribunal" was

HERESY HUNTING

unworthy of fellowship, it was overwhelmingly voted down. Thus it was sought to raise a hue and cry by means of which heretics should be scared out of the denomination. The comment on this procedure which I ventured to make in a letter to the "Republican" was this: —

It would seem that so long as a Congregational minister regards himself as being in substantial accord with the Congregational churches, and so long as no church and no council of his brethren has ventured to call his standing in question, he ought to be regarded as in good standing. I have never before heard of any device by which his standing could be impaired, without any action of church or council. But this resolution, as interpreted by the action upon the amendment, provides a way whereby any minister's standing can be impaired without any action of church or of council. What is that way? It is the way of private accusation. That is precisely what is authorized by the Vermont convention. By slurs and insinuations and mischievous reports a minister's standing can be badly damaged. The action of the majority in the Vermont convention is calculated to encourage this kind of practice. It permits every man to judge of the orthodoxy of every other man, and to pronounce those who do not come up to his standard unworthy of fellowship. It denies to every man who may be suspected of heresy the right of private judgment respecting himself, and gives to every one who may choose to accuse him the right of private judgment upon him.

This matter of the relation of a minister whose mind is moving, and whose beliefs are necessarily changing, to the church with which he is identified is one of considerable interest, not only to the clergy, but to the laity as well. Upon the cases of ministers who are not in entire harmony with the ecclesiastical organization to which they belong the secular newspapers are apt to comment freely. It is generally assumed that if a minister has ceased to agree in all respects with the majority of his brethren, he ought to leave them. But there are several considerations which ought to be carefully weighed before censuring him for the failure to depart.

In the first place, this fellowship may be very dear to him. He may have grown up in it; its associations and friendships are the best part of his life; to bid him begone and leave it is a harsh demand.

In the second place, while recognizing that he has come to differ, in some matters, from his brethren, he may not feel that these are essential matters. In the main concerns he still remains at one with them; there are a hundred agreements where there is one difference.

In the third place, he feels that he needs, for himself, this association; it furnishes to him not only stimulus but restraint, and it tempers the individualism of isolated thought with historic usages and social judgments.

In the fourth place, it may be very absurd in him, but he cannot help thinking that in some, at least, of the things concerning which he disagrees with his brethren, he is right and his brethren are wrong. He believes that the truth which God has given to him is truth which his brethren need. Fidelity to his Master and love for his brethren constrain him to continue in the fellowship. He will differ with them as kindly as he can; he will not emphasize his difference in divisive and unseemly ways,

HERESY HUNTING

but he will be faithful to the truth as he sees it, in order that those with whom he walks may be led to see it also.

In short, he is not a "Come-outer," he is a "Stay-inner." If such a relation as this is intolerable to his brethren, and they will proceed, in orderly ways, to acquaint him with that fact, he will go away and leave his blessing with them; until then he will remain in their fellowship.

Such have been the principles by which I have sought to guide my own conduct, and as I review my relations to the Christian communion with which, through all my life, I have been identified, I am satisfied that they are sound principles. I was invited, in former years, a great many times, and not always too politely, by those who "seemed to be somewhat," to take myself off, but I could not see that they had authority, and I declined to go. I am glad that I did not go. I know that it has been better for me to remain. The differences which were once emphasized have disappeared, and the fellowship has grown increasingly dear.

I should not leave the impression that in those years of controversy I was an ecclesiastical outcast. There were good friends in many of the strong pulpits of New England, — in Hartford and New Haven, in Worcester and Providence and Norwich and Boston; and my people frequently enjoyed the privilege of listening to the best preachers of the eastern states, who offered to exchange pulpits with me. After the first flurry over the Indian Orchard Council, most of my Springfield brethren were very cordial and neighborly, and all that

I suffered as a heretic is of small account. A little good fighting had to be done, which was not, on the whole, a hardship, and the loss of favor in ecclesiastical circles was quite made up by gains in other quarters.

There was a Connecticut Valley Theological Club, into which I was admitted soon after arriving in Springfield, and with which I continued in delightful comradeship until I left Massachusetts. It was made up of various denominations, who met, monthly, at the Massasoit House in Springfield and spent the best part of a day together. In the forenoon we heard three or four papers, on different aspects of a single theme which had been assigned for study; after dinner we discussed the papers and the topic. It was not a frolic; thorough and splendid work was done, both in the written and in the oral discussions. There was entire freedom and fearlessness of criticism, every man spoke his mind with few reserves, and the educational value of these meetings was to me not inconsiderable.

In January, 1878, there was issued, in Springfield, the first number of "Sunday Afternoon, a Magazine for the Household," of which I had undertaken to be the editor. It was a well-printed monthly of ninety-six pages, with a physiognomy not unlike that of the "Atlantic Monthly." The first editorial explained its purpose. It would furnish Sunday reading for the family, of a character at once wholesome and entertaining. The contents would not be wholly of a devotional or meditative character; a large portion of each number would be devoted to stories, of sound moral tendency; questions of social life and national well-being would be discussed, but always in

HERESY HUNTING

their relations to the Kingdom of God. "Questions of practical philanthropy will, however," — so the prospectus runs, — "occupy the largest space in 'Sunday Afternoon.' How to mix Christianity with human affairs; how to bring salvation to the people who need it most; how to make peace between the employer and the workman; how to help the poor without pauperizing them; how to remove the curse of drunkenness; how to get the church into closer relations with the people to whom Christ preached the Gospel; how to keep our religion from degenerating into art, or evaporating into ecstasy, or stiffening into dogmatism, and to make it a regenerating force in human society, — these are questions which our readers are likely to hear most frequently and most urgently asked."

For nearly two years I kept the entire editorial control of this magazine, conducting all the correspondence, reading and editing all the manuscripts, reading the proof, and writing about twelve pages in minion type of editorials and literary notices. After that, for a year or more I relinquished the management and wrote the editorial matter. Here came in play my practical training in the printing-office; without that technical knowledge I could not have managed all these details. For during these years the work of my church was not neglected, and it was steadily enlarging on my hands. It was hard work — more than I ought to have undertaken; but it was delightful work; the field of the magazine was one that I had chosen for myself; I was entirely free to cultivate it in my own way, and the journalistic instincts were again given free play. The magazine started well; we soon had a fair circulation and a generous recognition by the press, and we were able to call to our service a fine array of contributors. It seemed to be a promising venture, but the health of the publisher failed, and as there was no one to whom he was willing to relinquish his enterprise, it came to an untimely end.

Through the whole of my residence in Springfield my communications were open with the "Century Magazine." Dr. Holland called, now and then, for contributions to the body of the magazine, or to the editorial or literary departments; and after his death, in 1881, Mr. Roswell Smith, the president of the Century Company, seemed disposed to put considerable work upon me. He was a man of great fertility of suggestion, and, through his editors, he was always proposing topics for treatment in the magazine. Sometimes I found his suggestions practicable, and sometimes not; but there gradually grew up between us a close friendship, and I came to regard him as my most trusted counselor.

It was at his instance that I undertook what proved to be one of the most successful of my literary tasks, — the writing of "The Christian League of Connecticut." "I want you," he said, "to write a kind of a story showing how the people in some New England town got together and united their forces in practical Christian work." It was to have been a single article; but before I had gone far, I wrote to Mr. Gilder that I might want to extend it to two or three numbers, and after reading the first installment he gave me the right of way to fill as much space as I wished. The series of four articles

HERESY HUNTING 275

attracted more attention than any other magazine work of mine had done; not only church people, but all sorts of people, appeared to be interested in them. The practical question of Christian coöperation which they raised was one that appealed to many. To a large extent they were taken for veritable history; I received many curious letters both from this country and from England, where they were republished, asking for further information concerning the experiment. Quite a number of movements for coöperation among churches and for the consolidation of churches in over-churched communities were reported to me as having been directly suggested by these articles. After the series was concluded in the magazine, the articles were collected in a small volume. Toward the wide movement for the promotion of the unity of Christendom they furnished a contribution.

During the eight years of my life in Springfield, many notable things were happening in national affairs. Grant's second administration had come to an end, and the deplorable deadlock of the Hayes-Tilden contest, in the Centennial year, had ended in the seating of Hayes. Of his election I had been a hearty advocate; in the soundness and sanity of his mind I strongly believed; but the events connected with the settlement of the dispute were not such as to fill the hearts of thoughtful patriots with satisfaction. The last days of 1876, and the early months of 1877, were a critical period in American history. It is difficult, at this day, to determine who had the moral right to the presidency. In Louisiana, in

South Carolina, and in Florida, the elections were thoroughly vitiated by fraud and violence. The questions arising as to the method of ascertaining the result of the election were complicated and critical. Congress must decide, and the Senate was Republican while the House was Democratic. On the returns as presented, the President of the Senate was sure to declare Hayes elected, and the House of Representatives would decide that no election had taken place and would proceed to elect Tilden. There was imminent danger of collision and revolution. In almost any other country, such a result would have been inevitable. The sober sense of the Congress which finally determined to leave the whole matter to an Electoral Commission, composed of five Senators, five Representatives, and five Justices of the Supreme Court, registered a great victory for free government. It seemed at the first intolerable and shameful that a judicial tribunal like the Electoral Commission should divide upon the questions before it on party lines, every Republican deciding for Hayes and every Democrat for Tilden. Was there no man of the fifteen who was more of a judge than a politician? It was a humiliating spectacle. Yet the question had to be settled; Congress, which had all the power, had prescribed this way of settling it; and there was nothing to do, for a law-abiding people, but to acquiesce in the decision.

Too much praise is not likely to be given to Mr. Tilden and the Democratic leaders for their behavior in this exigency. Beyond a doubt they believed that the presidency rightfully belonged to them. They had agreed to the Electoral Commission with the understanding that

HERESY HUNTING

Justice Davis, of Illinois, an Independent, would be the fifteenth man. It turned out that he could not serve, and Justice Bradley, a Republican, was substituted for him. They believed that they had had something less than a fair show in the constitution of the tribunal. In any less law-abiding community they would have felt that they had good ground for refusing to accept the decision. But there was hardly a threat of resistance. The Democrats, realizing that they were wronged, submitted with perfect patience to a legal decision which deprived them of the fruits of victory, and of the control of the nation for four years. And those who had been identified with the Republican Party from its origin, and who had shared in the distrust of Democratic leaders and policies, felt bound, in those days, to confess that the patriotism of the nation was not confined to the Republican Party.

Aside from the dubious procedure with which it was introduced, the administration of President Hayes was one of great wisdom, purity, and efficiency. The removal of the troops from the South, the restoration of home rule, and the substantial pacification of that region brought relief to all parts of the land. This rational policy came too late to repair all the injury which had been wrought by the measures of coercion, but it was the only thing to do, and Mr. Hayes acted in the matter with great prudence and firmness. The resumption of specie payments, after a suspension of seventeen years, also occurred during this administration. Mr. Hayes greatly failed to please the politicians, but the people generally believed in him; the verdict of history is that few presidential careers have been more honorable and successful than his.

In subsequent years, after my removal to my present home, I had the privilege of meeting Mr. Hayes quite frequently. He was then living at his home in Fremont, Ohio, and finding constant employment in various uncompensated services of the commonwealth. "I thought," he said to me one day, "when I laid down my high office, that I was going to have plenty of leisure for the remainder of my life, but I am nearly as busy as ever I was." The question what to do with our ex-Presidents had not troubled him; he was active in our state charities, he was a trustee of our state university, he was always ready to help in any good work. It was a benignant ending of a faithful life.

The nomination of Garfield was, of course, highly gratifying to all Williams College men, and his triumphant election gave promise of a brilliant administration of the government. But the bitter political feuds in which he was soon involved were disheartening, and the terrible tragedy of his assassination was a blow that shook the nation to its centre. Well do I remember the shudder of horror that ran through our streets that July morning. One memory of my own gave the event a peculiar vividness. A few months before, there had come, one day, to my study, a rather unkempt person, with reddish hair and stubbly beard, who handed me a small placard on which he was named and described as "the brilliant and eloquent Chicago lawyer and orator." He was delivering lectures in reply to Robert Ingersoll, and he wished to speak in one of the churches of Springfield under the patronage of the ministers. I told him at once that I had no interest in his enterprise; that if the Christian people were living as they ought to live, what Robert Ingersoll said about them would not hurt them; that if they were not, the less said about it the better. He went away, but elsewhere succeeded in securing a church for his lecture, which was duly advertised. Before the hour appointed for it, however, an officer from a neighboring city appeared upon the scene with a warrant for the arrest of the lecturer for jumping a board bill. The brilliant and eloquent defender of the faith succeeded in making good his escape, and the dubious parcels left behind him in the house where he was lodging, which were supposed to contain his personal effects, were found to be filled with waste paper. The name of this personage was naturally impressed on my mind.

On the day of the assassination I called at the Massasoit House to pay my respects to Father Gavazzi, the distinguished Italian Protestant leader, who was then visiting Springfield. On the steps of the hotel I bought the latest extra, in which it was stated that the name of the assassin was "Charles J. Getto," his personal appearance was described, and the conjecture was ventured that he was an Italian. I read the dispatch to Father Gavazzi, and the venerable man threw up his hands with horror. "God forbid," he cried, "that he should be an Italian!" The name upon the handbill at once occurred to me, and I saw that this was a phonetic spelling. "No!" I said, "he is not an Italian. I know this man. His name is not 'Getto,' it is Charles J.

Guiteau, and his home is Chicago." The next extra had the name rightly spelled, and the assassin fully identified as our quondam defender of the faith.

The long agony of that summer, while the nation waited by the bedside of its dying chief, left its mark on the lives that passed through it. Most unadvisedly the recovery of the President was made a test of faith by many religious people. It was held, in many crowded and weeping assemblies, that if there were prayer enough, and if the prayer were the prayer of faith, he would surely be healed. And there were not a few who were ready to claim that they had the assurance of faith, and knew that his life would be spared. For those who had entertained this confidence the issue was a sore trial. There were many, doubtless, who came to doubt whether prayer has any efficacy; their faith was overthrown. Perhaps there were others who learned to take a more reasonable estimate of the relation of prayer to Providence. That is not prayer which assumes to dictate to the infinite Wisdom what He shall do in any given case; nor is that prayer which exalts a subjective assurance into a revelation of the divine will. There is no true prayer which is not summed up in the petition, "Thy will be done!" and which is not sure that whether the specific request be granted or denied, God's will is done.

One of the striking issues of this tragedy was the transformation which was wrought in the character of the man on whom the leadership of the nation fell. He had not been a man of high political ideals; it was with a great sinking of the heart that many of us saw the destinies of the nation committed to his hands. But the

HERESY HUNTING

sense of his high responsibilities roused him and braced his manhood. At once we saw him invested with a dignity and a discretion with which we had never credited him. Instead of being the leader of the "Stalwart" faction, he at once became the President of all the people; his policy was just and liberal; his administration called forth the praises of those who had distrusted him, and President Arthur laid down his office, at the end of his term, with the respect and confidence of the nation.

I remember a remark, made by President Hayes, some years later, shortly after the beginning of Cleveland's first term. Some good Republican had said, with an air of half-incredulous surprise, "I really believe that that man is trying to do right." "Of course he is," said Mr. Hayes. "What else can he do? That is the only way out. There is no position in this world in which the motives for doing right are so powerful as in the presidency of the United States. As long as a man sticks to that determination, he is safe; the moment he wavers in it, he is in infinite trouble."

It would seem that some sense of this truth has been apprehended by most of the men who have occupied this high station; for there are few of them in later years who have not come out of the presidency stronger and better men than they were when they entered upon its duties.

CHAPTER XIX

POSTMERIDIAN

> The day becomes more solemn and serene
> When noon is past; there is a harmony
> In autumn, and a lustre in its sky,
> Which through the summer is not heard or seen,
> As if it could not be, as if it had not been!
> Thus let thy power, which like the truth
> Of nature on my passive youth
> Descended, to my onward life supply
> Its calm, — to one who worships thee,
> And every form containing thee,
> Whom, Spirit fair, thy spells did bind
> To fear himself, and love all humankind.
> *Percy Bysshe Shelley.*

THE eight years of my life in Springfield, from December, 1874, to December, 1882, were busy and eventful years. I have told very little of what was most intimate and significant in my life; the relations of a pastor to his people cannot be reported in such a narrative. There were no surprising gains to be recounted; but the membership of the church and the congregation steadily increased, and the unity of the brotherhood was unbroken. Through all the days of controversy I never had a misgiving as to the support of my people; no words of dissent or criticism reached my ears. The work of the preacher had always been a welcome and inspiring labor, but in these eight years my sense of its importance had greatly deepened.

But the work of the pastor of a city congregation, in these inquisitive and strenuous times, is sure to grow harder every year. His congregation increases, his pastoral cares multiply; he is more and more enlisted in public interests; the calls upon him are more numerous, and the work of the pulpit is more exacting every day. There must be no sense of failure there, and unless he preaches a little better this year than he did last, there is apt to be a sense of failure. Any business man, any other professional man, as his success becomes more assured, is able to relieve himself of more and more of his load, but this is not the case with the minister; the more successful he is, the harder he has to work, and there is very little help for it. So it came about that the end of my eighth year found me considerably worn and jaded, and the need of some respite was apparent. I had not, however, mentioned this conviction to any one, when, one blue Monday morning, a letter arrived from Columbus, Ohio, inquiring whether I would consider a call to the First Congregational Church of that city. While I had the letter in my hand, a telegram was handed me, from my friend, Roswell Smith, of the "Century," to let me know that he was on his way to Springfield. The case was before me, and the counselor was coming. I went over the matter with him, and he was prompt and positive in the judgment that I must go. He had lived for several years in what we then used to call "the Middle West," and he was clear in his opinion that I should find profit in transplanting myself into that soil. The areas were larger, and so were the opportunities. I might want to come back to the East, some day, but for the next ten years, at least, that was the place for me.

His advice moved me to give a receptive answer to

the letter from Columbus, and the result was a call by telegraph, a visit to Columbus, and the removal to that city in Christmas week, 1882.

Columbus, in 1882, was a city of fifty-two or three thousand people. Commercially and industrially it has always been rather conservative; it has not much resorted to booms; its growth has been steady and solid; its enterprise has not been flighty. I have seen the city more than treble its population, but it has all been done soberly. Its first settlers came largely from Virginia and Kentucky; quite a perceptible southern flavor could be detected in its social life a quarter of a century ago. One sign of that was a hospitality rather more cordial than one would look for in a New England city, or in a typical western city.

Nothing was wanting to the welcome with which my new neighbors greeted me; they soon made me feel much at home. Yet the environment was, I confess, depressing. The hills to which I had been wont to lift up my eyes, and from which had often come my help, were nowhere in sight; the flatness and monotony of the landscape were a perpetual weariness. I put all this out of my thought as much as I could, but, at first, it was hard to bear. The time came when this craving ceased to give me pain, and I have learned to take great pleasure in the quieter beauty of these fertile plains and river-bottoms, and can now fully understand why the Hollanders find a keen delight in their own flat country, and why the artistic impulse has flourished there far more splendidly than in Switzerland; but nothing of this was credible to me in those first months in Columbus.

In those days Columbus, on the physical side, was rather crude; few of its streets were paved, its lighting was primitive, its domestic architecture was not, as a rule, a delight to the eyes. It presented no such trim and finished appearance as the best New England cities. Yet the streets were wide and well shaded, and there were large possibilities of beauty. It was not only the political capital of the state: it was also, in some sense, the educational and the philanthropic capital; for the state university was here, and state institutions for the blind, the deaf, the insane, and the feeble-minded, as well as the state penitentiary, were here located. This made Columbus the natural rallying centre for the philanthropic forces of the state. The state university was then in its feeble infancy, with twenty or twenty-five instructors and three hundred and fifty students. I have seen it grow to a roll of two hundred teachers and twenty-five hundred students. In this university, from the beginning, I have found many of the resources for my work; a large number of its faculty have always been connected with our church, and many of its students have been welcomed in our congregation.

Like every other capital city, Columbus has always been pervaded by the atmosphere of politics. Most of the state officials have their offices here; many conclaves of political workers are held here; it is the convention city, by eminence, of the state, and considerable numbers of those who have held political office make their homes here, after their terms of office have expired. Such influences as active partisan workers can set in motion are, therefore, likely to be encountered here.

It is perhaps needless to say that these influences are not always of the most salutary kind; one would not, naturally, resort to a capital city for the freshening of his political ideals. Yet I am bound to say that the people of Columbus have often, in recent years, manifested a strong disposition to think for themselves, and I doubt whether the "pernicious activity" of the politicians is much more influential here than in other Ohio cities.

Twenty-five years ago, partisanship in Ohio was far more intense than it is to-day. The lines were sharply drawn; every man was supposed to be a thick-and-thin adherent of one of the two political parties. To one who had been living in a community where nearly everybody reads the Springfield "Republican" at the breakfast-table, this kind of infatuation had a humorous aspect, and I did not easily adjust myself to it; often, I fear, my mugwumpery was a serious offense to some of my good neighbors; but as time went on, we came to a better understanding.

The church was an extremely plain structure, standing on Capitol Square, opposite the State House, and in the heart of the city; for a family church it was not well located, and as the city expanded, this disadvantage would be accentuated; but it was a good meeting-place for general purposes, being accessible to street-cars from all parts of the city, and there were people enough within reach if the church could attract them. The work began encouragingly, the church and the community seemed to be hospitable to such views of Christian truth as were presented, and there were early indications that the field of the church was wider than the city.

It was in the first year of my ministry in Columbus that what is known as "the Creed of 1883" was published. The history of this Creed throws light on Congregational ways, and some account of it may be interesting to those not Congregationalists.

During the days of our warm theological controversy, in 1877 and 1878, there was much discussion as to what were the Congregational doctrines. There is an old creed, called the Savoy Confession, which is substantially the same as the Westminster Confession of the Presbyterian Church, and which, in the early days of New England, had been recognized by the Congregational churches as the expression of their belief. But that creed had become utterly antiquated; few Congregationalists of any stripe were now willing to subscribe to it, and no other statement of doctrine had taken its place, except a brief confession of "the evangelical faith," adopted by a mass meeting on Burial Hill, in Plymouth. It had come to be recognized as Congregational doctrine that no ecclesiastical body existed, or could be created, with power to frame such a creed and impose it upon the churches, — each church, by the primary Congregational principle, having the right to make its own creed. Yet there were many who insisted that Congregationalists must have a creed; and that the National Council ought to formulate such a statement, representing the present belief of the churches. That demand found strong expression at the St. Louis Council of 1880, and was met by a determined opposition on the part of those who contended that the council had no power to adopt such a creed; that it would be an infringement of the liberty of the churches. The Gordian knot was cut by a decision to appoint a committee of twenty-five of our most competent theologians, with instruction to prepare such a statement of doctrine, at their leisure, and print it, when completed, in the newspapers. It was not to be reported back to the council, and the council was not to hold itself responsible for it; it would go forth as the judgment of twenty-five of our leading men respecting the essential Christian truths believed by Congregationalists. It would probably be accepted as a substantially true statement of what was generally believed among us.

This committee of twenty-five was made up, of course, mainly of very conservative men; they took plenty of time for their deliberations, and when they were ready to report, their creed was found to be a document of surprising breadth and liberality. All the distinctively Calvinistic dogmas, for which our conservatives had been contending, were eliminated; there was no formal doctrine of the Trinity — "three persons in one God"; election, in the Calvinistic sense, was not in it, nor was original sin, nor Biblical infallibility; and the sufferings of Christ on the cross were described as his "sacrifice of himself." Twenty-three of the twenty-five names were signed to this creed; two signatures were withheld, and it soon transpired that these were refused because the creed failed specifically to declare that all persons, dying impenitent, were forever lost, — that there was no possibility of repentance beyond the grave. The twenty-three had been unwilling to make this statement, because, as they maintained, there was no clear Scripture

POSTMERIDIAN

to support it; the two had insisted on it as essential to orthodoxy.

Thus began the discussion upon "second probation," or "probation after death," which made such a stir in our Congregational circles. One of the two dissentients was a secretary of our Board of Foreign Missions; and we speedily heard that the Board would be erected into a bulwark against this loose doctrine; that no missionary would be commissioned who was not sound on this question of future probation. For, it was argued, the admission that there was a possibility of repentance after death would "cut the nerve of missions"; there would be no adequate motive to work for the salvation of the heathen, if such a thing could be believed.

But presently there began to come from the mission fields themselves earnest protests against being compelled to teach this doctrine. Intelligent Hindus and Chinamen were crying out against the brutality of it. If no man can be saved who has not heard of Christ, and death is the limit of probation, then all their ancestors were in remediless misery. They positively declined to accept a "Gospel" of which this was a cardinal doctrine. It became evident, by the testimony of some of our strongest missionaries, that the "nerve of missions" was most effectually cut, not by omitting this doctrine, but by teaching it.

All this, however, availed nothing to such cocksure dogmatists as those who were pushing the propaganda. Some of these heretical missionaries were called home and put under the ban; the tests were rigidly applied to all missionary candidates; those who were not sure that death was the end of hope to all who died impenitent were refused appointment.

The controversy waxed hot. Theological seminaries were involved in it; every meeting of the Mission Board witnessed a great debate on the question of probation. The conservatives were, at first, in a large majority in the corporate membership of the Board; but the minority persisted in its protest, steadily increasing its force, until, in 1892, at Worcester, the whole propaganda collapsed; those who had been pushing it retired from the management of the Board, and the attempt to fasten this mediæval conception upon the Congregational faith was abandoned.

It was an enlightening controversy; the real nature of the Christian faith was better understood because of it. And it was an interesting fact that the strongest testimony against this benighted notion came from the missionaries. It is often supposed that missionaries are a narrow and bigoted class of men; the truth is that we are indebted to them for much sound thinking on the great problems of Christianity. The missionaries are helping us to-day to take a broader view of the relations of Christianity to the other religions, and to cultivate that sympathy of religions by which alone ours may vitalize and transfigure those with which it is brought into contact.

Thus my work in Columbus began just as this controversy was launched; the debate in the Mission Board and the Andover controversy were in full blast in the early years of it, and the public mind was awake to these theological issues. For, in truth, there is nothing that people of ordinary intelligence are so much interested in, as in these deep questions concerning the life that now is and that which is to come. I did not burden my congregation with discussions of these controverted questions, but I found them eager to hear what was said about them.

It was an interesting period in which to exercise the function of the Christian ministry. The spirit of inquiry was in the air. Very little change had been made in the statements of religious belief or in the forms of church administration, but some ancient traditions were challenged, and it was evident that the Christian world was getting ready for a forward movement.

What seemed to me of the greatest importance, however, was the solution of the social problems which had been rising into prominence since the war, and to which the industrial depression had given emphasis. That terrible strike of the railroad men in 1877, in Pittsburg; the telegraphers' strike in 1883, and a bitter struggle between the operators and the coal-miners in the Hocking Valley, which began in April, 1884, had brought very strongly before my own mind the critical character of the relations between the men who are doing the work of the world and the men who are organizing and directing it.

The Hocking Valley strike came very close to me; for the company which was engaged in it was largely represented in my congregation: the vice-president and general manager was one of my board of trustees; so was another vice-president, and the treasurer was also a member of my congregation. The struggle began with a demand for higher wages, but it was shortly merged in a conflict over the right of the miners to organize for their own protection. The company had had trouble with the Miners' Union, and had come to regard that as the chief source of the disturbances in the valley; it had now resolved to exterminate the union, no matter at what cost. I remember a conversation with the general manager, in his office, in which he expressed to me that determination in very emphatic terms. "We'll kill that union," he said, "if it costs us half a million dollars." Yet he was not a narrow nor an inhumane person; he was one of the kindest and fairest-minded of men. I had had frequent conversations with him on the relations beween employers and employed, in which he had expressed a strong wish to bring their interests into harmony. In this contest, however, it seemed to him that he was seeking the best good of the miners as well as of the operators in fighting the union to the death.

I had frequently expressed my conviction of the right and the necessity of labor organizations, and I did not hesitate to reaffirm the conviction during this dispute; but my judgment did not go far with these men who were in the thick of the battle. The struggle was protracted for many months, and it cost the company quite as much as my friend had indicated; it was ended by the ostensible surrender of the miners, who signed, on their return to the mines, an iron-clad agreement that they would never again join a miner's union. The futility of this compact might have been evident to the employers; for these starving men regarded it as a promise made under duress, and as a contract void by reason of its conflict with public morality; they felt no more bound by it than they would have been by a promise made to a highwayman at the point of a pistol. Within three months all the miners were fully organized, and the union, which half a million dollars had been spent to kill, was thoroughly alive again.

About a year later, another demand was made by the miners through the union for increased pay, and the demand was promptly submitted to arbitration, by consent of both parties. The arbitrator chosen was Senator Thurman, a man in whose justice everybody had confidence, and his decision was in favor of the miners. The operators submitted without complaint, and an agreement was then formed by which, every year, the rate of wages should be fixed by a convention of both parties. That agreement has been adhered to until the present day.

A year or two later, I inquired of my friend, the general manager, how matters were getting on in the valley. "All right," he said; "we are having no trouble. The fact is that it is far better to have an organized and disciplined force to deal with than to deal with a mob." It had become evident to him that a labor union, when wisely handled and dealt with in a just and friendly spirit, is not necessarily an evil thing.

CHAPTER XX

THE INDUSTRIAL REVOLUTION

These things shall be — a loftier race
    Than e'er the world hath known, shall rise,
With flame of freedom in their souls,
    And light of knowledge in their eyes.

Nation with nation, land with land,
    Unarmed shall live as comrades free;
In every heart and brain shall throb
    The pulse of one fraternity.

New arts shall bloom, of loftier mould,
    And mightier music thrill the skies,
And every life shall be a song,
    When all the earth is paradise.
                    John Addington Symonds.

I HAVE shown how it was that, at the beginning of my ministry in Columbus, the labor question in its most acute form was thrust upon me. I was not required to go in search of it: it was made my duty, as a Christian teacher, and as the moral counselor and guide of the men under my care, to grapple with it, and try and get at the rights of it. These men in my congregation who were employing labor were sure to be deeply affected in their characters by the manner in which they handled this difficult business. The men and women who worked for wages, inside the church and outside of it, would have their attitude towards the church determined by the way in which it dealt with this serious question. I knew these employers, many of them, to be men of

THE INDUSTRIAL REVOLUTION 295

humane and generous purposes; I knew many of the workingmen, and was in entire sympathy with their efforts to improve their condition; and I witnessed with sorrow and alarm the widening of the breach between these classes; the deepening tendency, in each of them, to erect its own social group into a separate principality, ignoring the solidarity of society, and pushing its own claims at the cost of all the rest.

To deal with this question, it was necessary to have some kind of social philosophy, some theory of the right relations of men in society. By what principles or laws ought men who are coöperating in industry to govern their conduct?

The prevailing social philosophy of the nineteenth century was grounded in the principle of *laissez faire*. From the excessive paternalism of earlier centuries the revolt in the direction of a let-alone policy was natural. But such reactions are likely to go too far. *Laissez faire* had come to mean not only "Let well enough alone," which is always a wise maxim, but also, "Let ill enough alone." Its contention was that ill enough, if let alone long enough, was sure to turn out well enough. About that there is question.

The maxim applied, primarily, to governmental interferences with industrial and commercial affairs. It was contended that the government had no call to meddle with trade or production; that its only function was to keep the peace, to prevent encroachments of the strong upon the weak, to establish and guarantee full liberty of contract and action, and then leave all other relations among men to settle themselves by natural law. The reasoning was plausible, but it was easy to show that governments had found it impossible to keep within these limits; that the freest of them were constantly exerting their power for other and higher purposes. The post-office, the public-school system, the public parks and museums and libraries and art galleries, are evidences that the kind of government which springs from the life of a free and intelligent people is sure to do a good many other things besides keeping the peace. But just how far it may interfere to regulate the industrial relations of men is still a question of great difficulty. It is notorious that many such attempts have been productive of more harm than good, and the advocates of non-interference are able to make out a strong case.

But there has been a tendency to extend the maxim to individual action; to make it mean that the whole industrial process is under the dominion of inexorable law, so that nothing can be done by intelligence and good will to change its issues; that we can only let it alone and permit it to work out its inevitable results. Some such philosophy as this lies at the bottom of many minds. It is the notion that "the great natural law of supply and demand" is supreme; that its hardships, whatever they may be, are part of the natural order of things; that it is futile to attempt to alleviate them. Many employers, confronted with discontent and even suffering among their employees, shelter themselves behind this theory of the inexorableness of the economic process.

The essential untruth of this philosophy, as I have

before indicated, was apparent to me; for, taught by such economists as Francis A. Walker and Cliff Leslie and Wilhelm Roscher and Adolf Wagner, I had been able to see that human intelligence and will do profoundly affect the course of economic development. Take such a capital fact as this, — that the rents of agricultural land in England had always been lower than in Ireland, for this plain reason: public opinion in England frowned on the rack-renting practiced across the Irish Channel. Here was a moral force essentially modifying the economic process. And there are multitudes of such instances. The inexorableness of economic law did not, then, forbid the attempt to bring the principles of justice and kindness to bear upon the solution of the labor problem. Reason and conscience must have much to do in finding the right solution.

To bring the reason and the conscience of the community, and especially of the Christian community, into close contact with this problem was a large part of my endeavor during the first years of my life in Columbus. In several Sunday evening addresses, more or less closely related to this theme, most of which were afterward printed in the "Century Magazine" and other periodicals, and which were finally included in a volume entitled "Applied Christianity," I sought to deal with this central question. The title of the volume indicates the gist of the discussions. I remember that when I submitted this volume to the publishers, Mr. Scudder, who was then the reader for the firm, hesitated over the title. He could not see the force of the adjective. I tried to show him that the whole significance of the book was in that adjective; that the thing which the world needed most was a direct application of the Christian law to the business of life. He accepted the explanation, and I fancy that whatever may have been the fate of the contents of the book, the title of it has served to call attention to an important fact.

That the sufficient remedy for the disorders of the industrial world is the application to them of the Christian rule of life is the conclusion to which my study brought me, and the entire progress of events since that day has confirmed the judgment. But it is necessary to understand what the Christian rule of life is. The form in which it is stated in Christ's compend of the moral law is, I believe, exact and adequate; but the full force of it is not always apprehended. "Thou shalt love thy neighbor as thyself" is sometimes taken as a maxim of sheer altruism. But the fundamental obligation is rational self-love. That is made the measure of our love for our neighbor. How much shall I love my neighbor? As much as I love myself. This implies that I regard myself as a being of essential worth. I am a child of God as truly as my neighbor is; and I am bound to honor and cherish the selfhood intrusted to me. I have no more right to neglect and despise myself than I have to neglect or despise my neighbor. I ought to have some sense of the value and sacredness of my neighbor's personality. I am not to degrade or destroy myself in ministering to him, nor am I to degrade and destroy him in ministering to myself; I am to identify his interest with mine, and we are to share together the good which the divine bounty distributes to all.

THE INDUSTRIAL REVOLUTION 299

This is the Christian law, as I understand it, and it gives ample room for that legitimate self-assertion which some moralists have failed to find in Christianity, as well as for that self-denial which restrains the excesses of self-love. In the first chapter of "Applied Christianity" this principle, as it relates to human society, is stated in words which I venture here to repeat.

Society results from a combination of egoism and altruism. Self-love and self-sacrifice are both essential; no society can exist if based on either of them to the exclusion of the other. Without the self-regarding virtues it would have no vigor: without the benevolent virtues it would not cohere. But the combination of capitalists and laborers in production is a form of society. These two elements ought to be combined in this form of society. The proportion of altruism may be less in the factory than in the home or the church, but it is essential to the peace and welfare of all of them. Yet the attempt of the present system is to base this form of society wholly on competition, which is pure egoism. It will not stand securely on this basis. The industrial system, as at present organized, is a social solecism. It is an attempt to hold society together upon an anti-social foundation. To bring capitalists and laborers together in an association, and set them over against each other and announce to them the principle of competition as the guide of their conduct, — bidding each party to get as much as it can out of the other and to give no more than it must — for that is precisely what competition means,— is simply to declare war, a war in which the strongest will win.

The Christian moralist is, therefore, bound to admonish the Christian employer that the wage-system, when it rests on competition as its sole basis, is anti-social and anti-Christian. "Thou shalt love thy neighbor as thyself" is the Christian law, and he must find some way of incorporating that law into the organization of labor. It must be something more than an ideal, it must find expression in the industrial scheme. God has not made men to be associated for any purpose on a purely egoistic basis, and we must learn God's laws and obey them. It must be possible to shape the organization of our industries in such a way that it shall be the daily habit of the workman to think of the interest of the employer, and of the employer to think of the interest of the workman. We have thought it very fine to *say* that the interests of both are identical, but it has been nothing more than a fine saying; the problem now is to *make* them identical.

The substance of what I have been trying to say on this subject, through all the years of my ministry, is included in this short extract. Nothing is plainer to me than that the existing system of industry, with rigid organization of employers on the one side and laborers upon the other, each determined to override and subjugate the other, is the essence of unreason. The entire attitude of both parties is anti-social. It is simply absurd to imagine men are made to live together on any such basis. They are putting themselves into deadly conflict with the primary laws of life.

In the spring of 1886, when a fierce strike had been raging in Cleveland, a philanthropist of that city conceived the idea of getting the employers and the employed to come together in a mass meeting to be addressed by some one who was supposed to be reasonably impartial in his attitude toward the contending parties. The choice fell on me, and I found myself confronted,

THE INDUSTRIAL REVOLUTION 301

in the Music Hall of that city, by an audience in which the laboring-class was mainly in evidence, though a sprinkling of the other class was visible. "Is it Peace or War?" was the question to which I addressed myself. The workingmen before me were evidently in a critical mood. They listened, through the first half of my address, with respect, but in silence. They had their doubts about parsons; they probably expected me to take sides with their employers. In due season they were reassured on that point; they saw that they were listening to one who was able to get their point of view, and it was pleasant to see the suspicion fade out of their eyes and the signs of appreciative interest appearing. This is part of what they heard: —

Since this is the day and age of combinations, since capital in a thousand ways is forming combinations for its own advantage, who will deny to labor the right to combine for the assertion of its just claims? Combination means war, I admit. Combinations, whether of capital or labor, are generally made in these days for fighting purposes. And war is a great evil — no doubt of that. But it is not the greatest of evils. The permanent degradation of the men who do the world's work would be a greater evil. And if, by combination, the wage-workers can resist the tendencies that are crowding them down, and can assert and maintain their right to a proportional share of the growing wealth, then let them combine, and let all the people say Amen.

The present state of the industrial world is a state of war. And if war is the word, then the efficient combination and organization must not all be on the side of capital. While the conflict is in progress, labor has the same right that capital has to prosecute the warfare in the most effective way. If war is the order of the day, we must grant to labor belligerent rights. The sooner this fact is recognized, the better for all concerned. The refusal to admit it has made the conflict, thus far, much more fierce and sanguinary than it would otherwise have been.

When the workingmen heard that, they were not silent; they gave me a rousing cheer. But they were compelled to listen to quite a number of things after that which did not make them cheer. For I did my best to bring home to them, and to the employers who sat among them, the foolishness of the enterprise in which both sides were enlisted. The utter stupidity and absurdity of an industrial system based on war; the enormous waste of the common resources which it involves; the far worse destruction of the moral wealth of the community, the good will and mutual trust in which all human welfare is grounded, — all this I tried to make plain to them. "Is not this business of war," I asked them, "a senseless, brutal, barbarous business, at best? Does either side expect to do itself any good by fighting the other? It is about as rational as it would be for the right hand and the left hand to smite each other with persistent and deadly enmity, or for the eyes and the ears to array themselves against each other in a remorseless feud. It is a sorry comment on our civilization that here, at the end of the nineteenth Christian century, sane and full-grown men, whose welfare depends wholly on the recognition of their mutual interests and on the coöperation of their efforts, should be ready to spend a good share of their time in trying to cripple or destroy

THE INDUSTRIAL REVOLUTION   303

one another. It is not only wicked, it is stupid: it is not simply monstrous, it is ridiculous."

Some very frank words were then spoken to both parties in this controversy. While I was laying down the law to the employers, the men cheered heartily; when I began to drive home to them their own blunders and sins, they were less demonstrative, but presently evinced their fairness by cheering the points that were scored against themselves. And, at the end, after a warm appeal for peace, the prolonged applause was a most grateful testimony that the hearts of fifteen hundred workingmen were in the right place.

The next week I had an engagement to lecture in Tremont Temple, Boston. The occasion was one of some importance: Governor Robinson, an old friend and neighbor of mine, was to preside, and the audience would be composed of some of the solid men of Boston. I determined to repeat this address, "Is it Peace or War?" Would these people, mainly of the employing class, warm up to it as the workingmen had done? I had my misgivings. But the event showed that this audience was quite as cordial as the other had been; and at the close of the address, the men on the platform, including the Governor, a member of Congress, who was also a leading manufacturer, and others, united in inviting me to return to Boston on the next Saturday night and repeat the address in the same place to the workingmen of the city, to whom the hall was to be made free. On that occasion I had with me on the platform several employers, and several labor leaders, among them the head organizer for Massachusetts of the Knights of Labor;

and at the close of the address, every one of these men indorsed, without qualification, my argument and appeal.

I have given the history of this address,[1] because it indicates the position which I have tried to maintain, and because it shows that, at that time, the chasm between the contending classes was not so wide but that it could be spanned by reason and good will.

Another opportunity of a similar sort came to me a little later. The Ohio State Association of Congregationalists made me chairman of a committee to investigate the labor conditions of the state; and this committee arranged for two conferences between employers and labor leaders, one at Columbus and the other at Toledo. To each of these conferences a number of the most intelligent and influential employers of the neighborhood were invited, and about an equal number of the leaders of organized labor. Most of the men invited responded to the invitation. In each of the cities a day was spent in the conferences, with two sessions, afternoon and evening. A short series of very simple questions had been prepared and printed on the letters of invitation, — questions calling out the opinions of the men invited upon existing conditions in the industrial world; upon the reasons for the present conflict; upon the practicability of industrial partnership and other possible methods of promoting peace and welfare. The conference was conducted by calling first on a labor leader, and then on an employer, to express his views of the situation. Some

[1] It was published, in May, 1886, in the *Century Magazine,* and is included in the volume *Applied Christianity.*

THE INDUSTRIAL REVOLUTION 305

questioning was permitted, but it was all civil and respectful; we all understood that it was not a dispute, but a fair opportunity for each one to speak his own mind. There was much frankness in the utterance of opinion, but very little acerbity; it did not seem impossible that such men as were facing each other in these discussions should be able to arbitrate their differences.

I fear that the relations between the contending parties have not improved since that day. So far as I can see, the breach is widening. The fierce strike in the anthracite coal regions was the worst of our labor disputes; and, although it was amicably settled, the conditions which followed were not reassuring. The workingmen, in that case, had the sympathy of the public, and they won a notable victory; I fear it must be said that they failed to make the best use of it. Their demands grew more exacting and unreasonable; in all parts of the country there were symptoms of a disposition to push their advantage to the discomfiture of their employers. The result of that has been a serious exacerbation of temper on the part of the employing class. Organizations of employers have arisen in late years, whose attitude toward organized labor is more hostile than anything which has been known in our history. And I fear that it will be found that there are thousands of employers in all parts of the country who, a few years ago, were disposed to be reasonable in their treatment of the labor unions, but who, to-day, are maintaining toward them an attitude of almost vindictive opposition.

The Civic Federation has done something to mitigate these antipathies, but in so doing it has gained for itself the warm dislike of the belligerent employers on the one hand, and of the fighting labor federations on the other.

What the outcome of this conflict is to be, I do not predict. The evident expectation of some of the employers that they will be able to kill or cripple the unions is hardly rational; the evident determination of some of the labor leaders to extend the use of the boycott and the sympathetic strike is not intelligent; such a conflict as both sides seem bound to invoke can result in nothing but disaster. Chronic warfare in the industrial world is intolerable, and the world is coming to understand it so. We are going to make an end of international wars very soon; the absurdity of that way of settling the disputes of nations is becoming apparent to all civilized peoples. And the foolishness of industrial strife is not less obvious. If the wage-system means perennial war, the wage-system must pass, and some less expensive method of organizing industry must take its place.

The alternative now constantly in sight is Socialism. Socialism proposes that the functions of the capitalist and the *entrepreneur* shall be merged in the commonwealth. That seems to abolish one party to the quarrel, and is indicated, in the Socialist diagnosis, as the way of peace. That it may come to this sometimes seems probable. Yet I have never been able to regard this possibility with enthusiasm. There is an old Latin proverb about making a solitude and calling it peace. The Socialistic solution, applied as a panacea, would not give us a solitude, but it might give us stagnation. It does not agree with that theory of human nature of which I have spoken; it gives no adequate play to the

THE INDUSTRIAL REVOLUTION 307

self-regarding motives. The present system overworks them; Socialism undervalues them. What we have to do is to coördinate them with the motives of good will and sympathy, and get the full force of both in our schemes of social construction. The gains of coöperation must not be purchased at the cost of the integrity of the individual.

We may be plunged into a Socialistic experiment at no distant day; toward that precipice our employers' associations and our labor federations seem to be driving us; but if, in our haste, we take that step, we shall find leisure to repent of it. This people is not yet, in its prevailing ideas and tempers, sufficiently socialized to work the machinery of Socialism. The testimony of one of the ablest of the Socialists is in point: "It is well to keep in mind the entire dependence of Socialism upon a high level of intelligence, education, and freedom. Socialist institutions, as I understand them, are only possible in a civilized state, in a state in which the whole population can read, write, discuss, participate, and, in a considerable sense, understand. Education must precede the Socialist state. Socialism, modern Socialism, that is to say, such as I am now concerned with, is essentially an exposition of and training in certain general ideas; it is impossible in an illiterate community, a basely selfish community, or in a community without the capacity to use the machinery and the apparatus of civilization. At the best, and it is a poor best, a stupid, illiterate population can but mock Socialism with a sort of bureaucratic tyranny; for a barbaric population, too large and various for the folk-meeting, there is nothing but monarchy and the ownership of the King; for a savage tribe, tradition and the undocumented will of the strongest males. Socialism, I will admit, presupposes intelligence, and demands as fundamental necessities, schools, organized science, literature, and a sense of the state." [1] It is impossible for us to persuade ourselves that "the whole population" of the United States of America, or of any state in the Union, has attained unto any such standard as is here prescribed. With the vast illiterate and unassimilated elements of our national life, with so many millions who are separated from the commonwealth and from one another by the barriers of race and language, it would be, indeed, a mock Socialism which we should succeed, at this juncture, in setting up.

It would be a great calamity, therefore, if the intolerable strife between organized capital and organized labor should precipitate an attempt to put all our industries upon the basis of collectivism. But though we could not wisely go all the way with the Socialists, we might, safely, go part way with them. Indeed, we are already moving in the direction in which they would lead us. The Post-Office is a socialistic institution; it would be wise to extend its service, and make it the universal carrier of small parcels. That the telegraph should be added to this branch of the public service is evident; and the relation of the railways to the industries of the country is so close and vital that they, too, must soon be brought under governmental control. Doubtless we shall keep on for several years trying to

[1] *New Worlds for Old*, by H. G. Wells, p. 113.

THE INDUSTRIAL REVOLUTION 309

regulate them, but doubtless we shall fail; the only solution of the problem is public ownership. This need not mean public management; the government may own the tracks, as most European cities own the tracks of their street railways, and may prescribe rates and regulations, and then lease them, for definite terms, to companies or syndicates to operate. The stock objection to government ownership is the danger of adding such an enormous number of employees to the civil service; but that is not a necessary condition. The power of oppression which resides in the private ownership of the means of transportation is so tremendous, and so impossible of regulation, that the people will be compelled, at no distant day, to take the business into their hands. I think that it will also be necessary for them to own the mines, and to establish a rigid supervision over the watercourses. And, in the cities, not only the water-supply, but the lighting and the transportation and the telephone service, will soon be brought under public control.

All these are steps in the direction of Socialism which we are likely to take at no distant day. All the industries which I have named are virtual monopolies, and the people must own all the monopolies. That is the essence of democracy, on the economic side. There must be no monopolies of goods or services necessary to the life of the people which the people do not themselves control. If democracy is to endure, it must assert and maintain this prerogative.

But, after this principle has been fully established, there will still remain wide areas in which private property may be recognized and private enterprise liberated, — in which individual initiative may have free play. That industrial society in the future will have large features of collective ownership and control, and alongside of them extensive and varied enterprises in which men are employing their own capital and managing their own affairs, seems to me highly probable. The main problem of statesmanship will be to draw the line between these two industrial methods, to know what industries can best be taken over by the commonwealth and what can best be left in private hands. We shall coöperate, more and more, through the state, for common purposes, and we shall make vast gains by that coöperation; but we shall still cultivate the virtues of self-direction and self-reliance, we shall still keep the privilege of choosing our own careers, and of expressing ourselves freely in our industries.

But in this coming industrial society, where freedom of occupation is protected and cherished, there will still be need of a guiding law for industry, and there can be no other law than that of the Christ. In those days as in these, the law of human association must be the law of Good Will. The good of life is not found by those who prey upon one another or plunder one another; it is found only by those who in friendship serve one another.

The existing industrial order virtually rests upon the assumption that it is every man's business in this world to get for himself — and, of course, to get away from his neighbors — as much as he legally and prudently and safely can. That principle of life, no matter how artfully disguised, nor how cautiously practiced, is sure to bring strife and poverty and wretchedness. Any organization of society which is founded on selfishness will come to grief. That is the bottom trouble with the industrial world to-day; and the only radical cure for it is a change in the ruling principle of life. The stable and fruitful social order will be that which rests on the assumption that it is every man's business to give as much as he can, prudently and safely, and with due regard to his own integrity, to all with whom he deals. This does not mean that he is to cripple or impoverish himself in his giving, for his own well-being should be precious to him, and he must not give in such a way as to destroy his power to give. Cases may, indeed, arise, in which the sacrifice of all may be demanded; but the ordinary regimen of life will require him to husband his power of service.

This, as I understand it, is the meaning of Christ's law of life. It is not his law because he originated it; it is his because he most clearly taught it, and most consistently lived by it; because he made it central in morality. It rests on no man's word; it is as truly a natural law as is the law of gravitation or the laws of chemical affinity; it is an induction from the facts of human nature. Experience, if men will only pay attention to it, will prove to them that this way of living together makes for universal welfare and happiness; that the way of living which keeps self central and supreme is the way to destruction. The fundamental objection to the world's way is that it is unnatural and unscientific; it is an inversion of life; it is like an attempt to make plants grow with their roots in the air and their branches on the earth.

This is the truth which the world is beginning to see. It is only as in a blurred mirror, dimly, that most men see it yet, but never before was it visible to so many. The conviction is steadily strengthening that the one thing needful is a change in the direction of the ruling motive from self-aggrandizement to service. And to all who will carefully study the prevailing tendencies it will be clear that this is the way the world is going. "One perceives," says Mr. Wells, "something that goes on, that is constantly working to make order out of casualty, beauty out of confusion, justice, kindliness, mercy out of cruelty and inconsiderate pressure. For our present purpose it will be sufficient to speak of this force that struggles and tends to make and do, as Good Will. More and more evident it is, as one reviews the ages, that there is much more than lust, hunger, avarice, vanity, and more or less intelligent fear, among the motives of mankind. The Good Will of our race, however arising, however trivial, however subordinated to individual ends, however comically inadequate a thing it may be in this individual case or that, is in the aggregate an operating will. In spite of all the confusions and thwartings of life, the halts and resiliences and the counter strokes of fate, it is manifest that, in the long run, human life becomes broader than it was, gentler than it was, finer and deeper. On the whole — and nowadays almost steadily — things *get better*. There is a secular amelioration of life, and it is brought about by Good Will working through the efforts of men."

Good Will is at work, and it is making things better. In spite of the prevailing social philosophy, it is gaining ground. Even now, with such partial, halting, half-hearted recognition as we give it, Good Will is making things better. How much faster things would grow better, if all the people who call themselves Christians would accept what St. James calls "The Royal Law," and would give their lives to making Good Will regnant among men!

No matter what the form of the social organization may be, it is to this principle of Good Will, ruling the lives of individuals, that we shall owe all our social peace and welfare. Our collectivism will be confusion and a curse, where it is wanting; where it is present, our individual initiative will be beneficence and bounty.

Is it not a Utopian dream that the principle of Good Will will supplant the principle of *Laissez faire* in industrial society? Can we rationally expect that such an ingrained tendency of human nature as that which is represented by the maxim "Every man for himself," will yield to the other-regarding motive so that men will learn to identify their interests with those of their neighbors? The answer is that when men see that Good Will is the law, they will learn to obey it. Most of them have never yet clearly seen it. The maxims of business have all made self-interest supreme. The whole industrial structure has rested on that philosophy. The world is beginning to see that Good Will makes things better. That, so far as the business world is concerned, is a new revelation. It is easy enough to see that a good deal more Good Will would make things a great deal better.

That is a fact which the logic of events will force upon the convictions of men. And in the light and warmth of that knowledge the ingrained egoism of human nature will slowly melt away.

Such, then, is the substance of the social faith which I have been trying to inculcate.

I believe that monopolies, actual or virtual, which supply the primary wants of human beings, must be owned and controlled by the commonwealth.

I believe that in this way, collective ownership and control will be and should be greatly extended; that many of the industries which are now in private hands will become departments of the public service. I believe that such coöperation of all the people through the state will result in great economies, and will put an end to some of the worst oppressions.

I believe that when we have gone as far as we can safely go in this direction, there will remain large room for private enterprise which will offer a free field for the cultivation of virtues quite essential to the social welfare.

I believe that all this activity, whether organized by the state, or conducted by independent enterprise, must have as its ruling motive the principle of Good Will, the spirit of service; that the church by its ministry, and the school by its training, and the state by its legislation must inculcate and enforce the doctrine that the primary business of every man in this world is service; that the man who is here to be ministered unto, and to levy tribute on his neighbors for his own aggrandizement, is living a life of sin and shame.

THE INDUSTRIAL REVOLUTION 315

When this principle of Good Will becomes regnant, shall we see wealth increasing as it has been increasing during the last four or five decades? Certainly not in the same way. In a society in which the Christian law was recognized as the practical rule, there could be no such enormous accumulations in the hands of individuals as those which have been heaped up in the last twenty-five years. Such swollen fortunes are the symptoms of social disease; they have the same relation to social health that hydrocephalus or elephantiasis has to the health of the individual, and to all sound moral vision they are not less repulsive. It is profoundly to be hoped that the day of their prevalence may quickly pass. But it is probable that the social good created under the impulse of Good Will would be far more widely diffused; that in the greatly enlarged possessions and advantages held in common, all would share; that the slums would disappear; that family life would be more secure and permanent; that the crushing burden of toil would be lifted from the shoulders of little children; that there would be leisure and comfort and happiness among men, in which faith could find root and hope get some anchorage, and in which it would not be incredible that love is indeed the greatest thing in the world.

CHAPTER XXI

A WIDENING VOCATION

> That low man seeks a little thing to do,
>   Sees it and does it:
> This high man, with a great thing to pursue,
>   Dies ere he knows it.
> That low man goes on adding one to one,
>   His hundred's soon hit:
> This high man, aiming at a million,
>   Misses an unit.
> That, has the world here — should he need the next,
>   Let the world mind him!
> This, throws himself on God, and unperplexed
>   Seeking shall find Him.
>   *Robert Browning.*

THE presidential campaign of 1884 was waged with ardor in Ohio, and I found great interest in watching the political operations on this field. The intensity of the partisanship was noteworthy; it was difficult for many worthy people to have any respect for a man who was not on one side or the other. Mr. Blaine came to Ohio and made a sensational canvass, but it was impossible for me to vote for him; over Mr. Cleveland I hesitated, on the ground of the moral delinquencies charged against him. His perfect manliness in the treatment of those charges ought to have reassured me, and I have always regretted that I did not give him my vote; for I came to honor and trust him as one of our bravest and most conscientious chief magistrates.

We had two elections, in Ohio, in 1884, — a state

A WIDENING VOCATION

election for governor and state officers, in October, and the presidential election in November. Ohio was thus regarded as one of the "pivotal states," and the machinery of both the national parties was set in operation early in every presidential year to carry the state at the October election. This gave us more than enough of politics for that year; it kept the people in a state of excitement from June to November, it deranged business, it brought into the state a great deal of money for the use of the politicians, and it invited the colonization of voters from the surrounding states. Admittedly it was a great source of injury to the state, economically and morally.

With this conviction I undertook to get the constitution amended, so that the state election should be held in November. Believing that the movement would best succeed if quietly started, I wrote a petition for such a change, and secured the signatures to it of the governor of the state, George Hoadley, all the ex-governors living but one, all the judges of the Supreme Court, the two United States senators, and a few other leading men. Among these signatures both parties were about equally represented. The petition thus signed was then printed in the newspapers, and with such a backing the project readily commanded the attention of the people. I then printed copies of the petition, and with my own hand mailed them to representative men in every county. The matter was taken up everywhere promptly and enthusiastically; petitions with thousands of names poured in, and by the time the legislature met, in January, the sentiment in the state was so strong that a joint resolution was easily passed submitting the amendment to the people, to be voted for at the next election.

In preparing the ballots for the election, the Democrats and the Prohibitionists readily agreed to print only the affirmative vote, so that those who did not scratch their tickets would be counted as voting in favor of the amendment. The Republican committee refused to do this, though I earnestly besought them. The grist which would come to the mill of the politicians by keeping Ohio an October state quite outweighed, in their minds, the moral injury which the state thus suffered. There were, however, enough Republicans who took pains to mark their ballots to carry the amendment by a decisive majority. Thus a rather important change in the government of the state was very simply effected. No eloquence nor influence was called for. The people all knew what they wanted; they did not require to be convinced or persuaded; all that was necessary was to give them a chance to express their minds, and that required a little painstaking effort. It was all done without holding a single public meeting, or making a speech, or appointing a committee; it cost me a few dollars for postage and printing, and it cost nobody else, so far as I know, one cent.

I have alluded to the fact that the disturbing question of what is known as the Higher Criticism had hardly been raised in New England at the beginning of my Springfield ministry. Before my work in Columbus began, the air was full of it. The epoch-making book of

A WIDENING VOCATION 319

Professor Robertson Smith, "The Old Testament in the Jewish Church," had brought it before intelligent men with a clearness which made it impossible to ignore it. The traditional conception of the Bible as verbally and scientifically inerrant was made, by this investigation, untenable.

My work in Columbus brought me into contact with many young men. The students of the university and of the medical colleges were well represented in my congregations; of the evening audiences it was often true that two thirds were men, and the majority of them young men. My acquaintance with them revealed the fact that many of them were skeptical concerning the Bible. They had read or heard the popular lectures of Robert Ingersoll; and they could not help knowing that many of the statements he made about the Bible were true; they had looked for themselves, and had found the discrepancies and contradictions all there. When, therefore, they were told by their pastors and teachers that the admission of a single error in the Bible rendered it worthless, they saw no other way than to cast it aside, and this they were doing by scores and hundreds.

As one who was convinced that the Bible, after all the truth had been told about it, would still remain the most precious and inspiring book in the world, — more precious and inspiring when the truth had been told about it than it could be as an object of superstition, — I could not help being deeply pained by the growing contempt for the Bible which I could not help observing, and which, as I perfectly well knew, was due to the persistent attempt to force upon the acceptance of men a theory of its origin to which its own pages gave overwhelming contradiction. I knew very well, however, that this was a very sensitive question in the minds of many excellent people. The infallibility of the Bible seemed to them the foundation of religion; if that were gone, nothing would be secure. It is not a comfortable business to raise such questionings in honest minds, and one is powerfully moved to accept Tennyson's counsel: —

> Leave thou thy sister when she prays,
> Her early Heaven, her happy views;
> Nor thou with shadow'd hint confuse
> A life that leads melodious days.

But there are others, besides that sister praying, to whom the truth is due, and who can be saved only by knowing it; we have to consider the needs of all classes, and we must not doubt, as religious teachers, that on the whole, and in the long run, the safest thing to tell the people is the truth. What would happen to me, as the consequence of telling the truth about the Bible, I did not know; there were grave doubts whether it would not end my ministry in Columbus; but the duty was before me, and I could not evade it without cowardice and infidelity.

The series of Sunday evening lectures which were afterward published in a volume entitled "Who Wrote the Bible?" attracted larger audiences than any course I had previously given. I asked my auditors to reserve their judgment upon the argument until they had heard it all. They seemed to think that a reasonable request, and they graciously acceded to it, and there was no excitement or controversy in the congregation while the

A WIDENING VOCATION

lectures were in progress. At first I saw many troubled and anxious faces, but as I tried to tell the people nothing which I could not abundantly make good on the authority of the Bible itself, they were soon listening with increasing interest and sympathy. At the close I felt that I had the nearly undivided assent of my congregation to the truth and wisdom of the exposition; those from whom I had expected opposition were most cordial in their expressions of gratitude for the service rendered them; there was not a ripple of controversy over the matter in the church. We are sometimes quite too apprehensive, brother ministers, about the risks we run in telling the truth. If we speak it kindly and considerately, with due regard for the convictions of those who differ from us, truth-speaking is not ordinarily a dangerous venture.

"Who Wrote the Bible?" has had the largest circulation of all my books. It has been widely used as a manual of instruction in Bible classes, and in Young Men's Christian Associations. It is now properly regarded as a very conservative book; such careful scholarship as that represented in Hastings's "Dictionary of the Bible " leaves many of its positions far in the rear. It ought to be revised and brought up to date, but I fear that I shall never have the time or strength for that; it will have to stand as it is; there are still multitudes in the morass of traditional infallibilism to whom it may furnish a bridge to a more intelligent understanding of the Bible.

The anxiety about a fixed standard of belief with which many minds are troubled is natural enough, but a little careful thought would help to dispel it. To many minds "foundations of belief" seem to be indispensable. But it is well to remember that some things need no foundations. The old cosmogonists were put to it to find foundations for the earth. Under each of the four corners of it they put a colossal elephant, and under the elephant a tortoise, and under the tortoise a serpent, and under the serpent — but what was the use of exploring further? The problem had to be given up. By and by Copernicus helped them to see that the earth needed no foundation; that it was moving through space nineteen miles a second, sustaining itself by its own motion. Our present conception of its relation to space is certainly far more sublime, and far more satisfying to the mind, than was the conception of the old cosmogonists. We have not lost respect for the earth, nor confidence in it, since we have found out the truth about it. The foundations on which it once rested are gone, and we do not wish to restore them.

Is not something like this coming true with respect to our religious beliefs? We have clung to the notion that the body of truth must have a fixed and stable foundation, and we have had much dispute over the foundation, some putting the church in that place and some the Bible. It is now beginning to be evident that the orb of sacred truth needs no such supports; that it is moving with resistless power through the eternities; that our task is not to bolster it up or anchor it, but to move on with it, and keep our eyes open for the new constellations always swimming into view. The ground of our faith is not the church nor the Bible, but the living God, who as Inspirer and Leader of men is as near to

A WIDENING VOCATION 323

us as He has ever been to the men of any generation, and who, if we will trust Him, will enable us to draw from the messages of the past the truth that we need for the life of to-day. Great need have we of the Book which has been for so many generations our guide and counselor. It contains the record of that continuous revelation which God has been making to our fathers in the flesh and in the spirit; it is the only Book that tells us of Him from whose life and words comes all that makes this age significant. But we need to read this Book in the light of this day, and under the guidance of the same Spirit who spake by the prophets, and who speaks to-day to all who have ears to hear.

Few experiences of the last twenty-five years are more gratefully recalled than those which have brought me into contact with the life of a number of the colleges and universities of the country. It has been my happiness to visit many of them, and I find nowhere audiences so keenly receptive and sympathetic. Several of my books owe their existence to demands made upon me by these audiences. In 1886 a series of lectures to the students of our own Ohio State University, on fundamental religious truths, was reported by one of the professors for the "Christian Union," now the "Outlook," and reprinted in the "Christian World" of London. The publishers of the latter journal proposed to gather them into a volume, and "Burning Questions" was thus originally published in London, and republished, on this side, by the Century Company. In 1893 I was invited to deliver the lectures of the course on the Lyman

Beecher Foundation in the Divinity School of Yale University. Those lectures, part of which were afterward delivered at Cornell University, and at Mansfield College in Oxford University, in England, and all of them at Meadville Theological Seminary, make the volume entitled "Tools and the Man; Property and Industry under the Christian Law." A series of lectures on "Social Facts and Forces" was given first at Chautauqua, then at Iowa College in Grinnell, and afterward on the Ryder Foundation in Chicago; these were published under this title. "Witnesses of the Light" is a course of lectures delivered before the students of Harvard University; "Social Salvation" is a second course on the Lyman Beecher Foundation at Yale; and "Christianity and Socialism" consists of lectures given before the students of Drew Theological Seminary. The weeks that I have spent in these great institutions, in pleasant companionship with instructors and students, are among my most delightful recollections.

In 1893 I was invited to become one of the staff of preachers to Harvard University. This staff consists of six men, who share among themselves the spiritual oversight of the students of the University. Each man is expected to spend about six weeks of the year in residence at the University, dividing his time into two terms, one before and one after Christmas. He takes up his residence in the minister's rooms in the old Wadsworth House in the College Yard; he conducts prayers in Appleton Chapel every morning, leads a vesper service on Thursday afternoon, and preaches in the Chapel on Sunday evening. Every week-day he is expected to

A WIDENING VOCATION 325

be in his room in the Wadsworth House for two or three hours, to meet any students who may wish to call upon him, and he is permitted to make himself useful, in such ways as he may choose, in the University community. I have had the happiness of serving three years in this capacity, and the experience is memorable. The public service has always been grateful and rewarding. I have never conducted worship in any place where the decorum was more perfect or the attention more reverent than at morning prayers in Appleton Chapel. I have never seen a sign of a book or a newspaper during the services. In the responsive reading and in the singing the students join heartily. Attendance is, of course, voluntary; no one is there who does not wish to be.

The best part of the preacher's work, however, is his personal contact with the students. All this, too, on their part, is voluntary; he meets only those who wish to meet him. They come, as Phillips Brooks said, with all sorts of questions; "some are inquiring the way to the bursar's office, and some to the kingdom of heaven." Not a few of them have theological tangles which they want straightened out. "I want to know," said one young fellow, "how you reconcile the first chapters of Genesis with what they teach us here about geology." "They cannot be reconciled," I replied. "That story in Genesis is not science; it is a beautiful hymn of the creation, full of the noblest religious truth, but not a scientific account of how the world came to be." "I think," he said slowly, "that if my father should hear you say that, he would tell you that you are an infidel." The father, as the boy told me, was a high officer in a leading

Protestant church in one of our great cities. But the son had never heard, from his father, nor from his Sunday-school teachers, nor from his minister, one word about the subject which was now disturbing his thought, and he went away from me, I know, full of misgivings as to whether he had not done wrong in listening to what I tried to tell him. In such a benighted state of mind as this our youth are still often left by those whose business it is to teach them the rudiments of religion. I found among the students of Harvard not a few whose religious ideas were astonishingly crude. A tragedy it is when a boy who has had his eyes bandaged from his infancy is led into the noonday blaze of a modern university. Are those pastors and Sunday-school teachers of this country, who are feeding their young people upon traditions which modern science has outlawed, aware that these young people are soon going out into the world?

It was not, however, for theological instruction that most of these young men came to the minister. There were serious problems of personal conduct on which some of them wanted counsel; I began to understand the value of the confessional. They came to me on such errands much more freely than the young men of my own city and congregation have been wont to come, — partly, perhaps, because I was more nearly a stranger; partly because they were away from home and felt the need of friendship. But the largest class of my visitors was composed of those who sought counsel about their life-work. There were many who had not yet determined what calling to follow; there were many others who had chosen their work and wanted to talk about the best way of preparing for it.

A WIDENING VOCATION

One fact deeply impressed me, — that was the extent to which the idea of service appeared to be the controlling idea in the minds of these young men. The note of personal ambition was sometimes struck, but it was not the prevailing note; the emphasis was put upon the desire to find something to do which would be worth something to the world. No doubt it will be said that men of this spirit would be the only ones likely to come and see a minister; but I am not quite sure of this; my experience in other places does not justify that judgment; I have found people of all ages quite ready to come to me for counsel and help in pushing their selfish ambitions. But the seeming drift of the young fellows whom I met in Harvard toward altruistic aims was a phenomenon in which I have found much encouragement. And all my experience with college students, which has been considerable, strengthens my belief that the generation of educated men and women now coming upon the scene possesses a more sensitive social conscience than the generation which is disappearing.

This privilege of service in Harvard University I recall as one of the best things that has ever come to me. It was with much regret that I was constrained to decline a reëlection to this service. The distance from home was great, and the absence from my pastoral work for six weeks of the year was a matter so serious that I felt obliged to relinquish the delightful task. It is only fair to my own people, however, to say that their behavior in the matter was most generous; twice they overruled my own decision and bade me go, when I was not so minded.

CHAPTER XXII

THE MUNICIPAL PROBLEM

> Even here do I behold
> Thy steps, Almighty! — here amidst the crowd
> Through that great city rolled,
> With everlasting murmur deep and loud —
> Choking the ways that wind
> 'Mongst the proud piles, the work of human kind.
>
> Thy Spirit is around
> Quickening the restless mass that sweeps along;
> And this eternal sound —
> Voices and footfalls of the numberless throng —
> Like the resounding sea,
> Or like the rainy tempest, speaks of Thee.
> *William Cullen Bryant.*

THE problems of municipal reform began to engage my interest at an early day. The city government of Columbus, in the first year of my residence here, was in a very chaotic condition; its parts did not cohere, and there was no concentration of responsibility; the mayor served as the police justice, but he had little executive power. The need of a better organization was palpable, and the people were beginning to agitate for a new charter, but the matter drifted from bad to worse for several years. The formation of a Board of Trade, which was intended to promote the general welfare of the municipality, encouraged the hope of better things, and I sought the opportunity of reading before that body of business men a short paper urging the appointment

THE MUNICIPAL PROBLEM 329

of a strong committee to study the problem, and draft a new charter. Such a committee was appointed, and spent some years in the investigation, but there was no practical outcome.

At this time Seth Low was mayor of Brooklyn, and that city had adopted a reformed charter, which concentrated executive responsibility and seemed to be resulting in efficient administration. At my suggestion the Columbus University Club invited Mr. Low to speak upon Municipal Problems, and he accepted the invitation, giving an admirable address in the First Congregational church to an interested audience.

About this time the general looseness and inefficiency of our municipal governments began to excite much attention, and organizations were formed in some of the cities for the agitation of this question. Believing that the time was ripe for a full discussion of the matter, the editor of the "Century Magazine" authorized me to take it up in a treatment similar to that of the Christian League of Connecticut, and the story of "The Cosmopolis City Club" ran through three numbers of that magazine. It was an imaginary tale, showing how a group of men in an American city organized a club for the study of municipal conditions; how they investigated and exposed abuses, and how they threshed out among themselves the whole problem of municipal organization. The papers were published in a small volume, in 1893.

That this discussion came in at the nick of time is evident from the reports of movements in all parts of the country during these years, looking toward improvement of municipal conditions. A manual of such organizations, published in 1895, gives the names of five municipal leagues formed in 1892, nine in 1893, and twenty-six in 1894. One of the societies formed in the last-named year was the National Municipal League, which aimed to federate the local leagues, and unite their studies and efforts for better city government. This organization grew out of a conference held in Philadelphia in January of that year, in which I participated. I also had the honor to be invited to take part in the organization of the City Club of New York; and at the meeting in which the Civic Federation of Chicago was formed, it was stated that the story of the "Cosmopolis City Club" had been influential in awakening the interest which had resulted in that meeting.

While Mr. Roosevelt was at the head of the Police Commission in New York city, I made his acquaintance, through a letter which he wrote me; and at my request he came to Columbus and gave an address, reciting his experience in that difficult situation, and discussing, with the lucidity and force which are characteristic of his utterances, the problems of municipal administration.

The problems of municipal organization to which most of the leagues and clubs have given much of their time are of great perplexity. We are far from having solved it yet; I sometimes doubt whether we have made much progress toward the solution. The rapid growth of our cities has been one main cause of the difficulty. The municipal machinery which answered well in a semi-rural community of four or five thousand people became

THE MUNICIPAL PROBLEM 331

utterly inadequate for the management of a population of fifty or one hundred thousand. The methods have not changed so rapidly as the needs have developed.

There has been a great deal of experimentation with executive boards and commissions, by which responsibility is divided and scattered. Nothing of that kind is risked in business affairs; three or five heads of a department in a railway or an iron mill would never be thought of. A single head of an executive department is the rule of efficient business administration. It is only in municipal business that this tangle is tolerated. Bipartisan boards and commissions have also been a frequent resort of those who feared the spoilsmen, but they are a lame device; usually they spend a good share of their time wrangling over the patronage. Worst of all are the attempts to rob the cities of the right to govern themselves, by erecting state commissions for the control of municipal business.

The Brooklyn plan, of which **Mayor Low** was an able advocate and an admirable exponent, contemplated the concentration in the mayor of executive responsibility, giving him the right to appoint and remove the heads of city departments. Thus the police department, the fire department, the water-works, the streets and sewers, the health department, each was under a single head who was directly responsible to the mayor, and who was required not only to report to him, but to consult statedly with him and with the other heads of departments about the work of the city. The power of the purse still was left with the city council, chosen by the people; and two or three other officers — a clerk, an auditor, and a treasurer, perhaps — were elected in the same way.

This plan, which has been styled, not very felicitously, the Federal plan, seems to me in its general features far better than the scheme of parceling out the executive power among hydra-headed boards and commissions. When it has been permitted to stand long enough to test its operation, it has given reasonably good results. It is not a panacea. It is entirely possible to have very bad government under this or any other form of municipal organization. The people may be so careless or so infatuated as to choose an incompetent or a malign person for mayor; this system gives him the power to do vast injury. In fact, any system which enables a good officer to be efficient, necessarily enables a bad officer to do great mischief. The best when perverted always becomes the worst. Unfortunately our governmental methods have been largely contrived with the possible mischief always in sight, and with the main purpose to avoid that. In preventing that, they have necessarily crippled the efficiency of the good officer. The question is whether, on the whole, it is not better to calculate on having good officers, and to arrange our governmental machinery with this contingency in view. In that case we may have good and efficient government; in the other case we never can. And when the people have had a chance to become thoroughly familiar with the fact that everything depends on their choice of a competent and upright chief magistrate, they are likely to take pains to select such an one, and to keep him in power.

What is known as the Galveston or Des Moines plan of municipal government is now exciting much discussion, and it is possible that in this device we are approaching a more satisfactory solution of this difficult problem. Doubtless this seems a drastic method. To sweep away the entire fabric of municipal organization, and commit the whole legislative and executive business of the city to five men chosen by the people — giving them the power to frame all the laws and ordinances, to raise and expend revenues, to appoint all the subordinate officials, and to manage and control all the business of the city — is a reform so radical that it takes away one's breath. But it is not impossible that it may prove to be the way out of the wilderness. The experiments which a few of our cities are trying with this plan will be watched with keen interest.

The choice of a quintuple instead of a single head for the city government may seem to contradict what has just been said about boards and commissions, but this is not really the case, for the five men are by law commanded to divide the administration among themselves, one of them being made chief executive, and each one being placed at the head of a department of the city, for the conduct of which he is held responsible. It is for legislative purposes, mainly, that the five act together.

Between such a plan as this and that by which all English cities are governed, — where the supreme power is vested in a council of from thirty to one hundred and forty members, chosen by the people, and where each department is controlled by a committee of the council, — the contrast is striking. The English plan works well in England, but all American experience indicates that it would be a failure here. What makes it efficient there is the fact that under each council committee is an executive officer whose tenure is practically permanent, by whom the committee is advised and through whom its work is carried on. There is thus in practical charge of each city department a skilled and trained executive, who is never changed for political reasons, who holds his position as long as he proves his efficiency. Such a state of things as that would never, of course, be tolerated in any American community, where the principle of rotation in office generally overrides all considerations of efficient administration. What we Americans are most concerned about is not how we shall secure good government, but how we shall give the largest possible number of people a chance to take a hand in the government, and secure the emoluments thereof. That appears to be the American idea; and while it prevails we shall never, of course, have good municipal government.

What would the people of an American city say, for instance, to the proposition to choose sixty or eighty or one hundred of their leading business and professional men to seats in the city council, — with the understanding that many of these men would continue to serve the city in this capacity without compensation for ten, twenty, thirty years? And what would these leading business and professional men of the American cities themselves have to say to such a proposition? Is it not obvious that a scheme of this sort would be

THE MUNICIPAL PROBLEM 335

utterly "un-American"? We cannot therefore consider the British plan of municipal government. We shall have to invent a system more in accordance with American ideas of the obligations of citizenship. Perhaps the Des Moines plan will prove to be more practicable.

One or two advantages it will certainly possess. In the first place, it will narrow, somewhat, the field of responsibility. Even under what is called the Federal plan, where executive responsibility is concentrated in the mayor, there is apt to be a lack of harmony between the mayor and the council, and legislation and administration are often obstructed by such conflicts. In the Des Moines plan, deadlocks of this kind would be avoided. At any rate, the field of observation for the people would be so small that they could easily keep their eyes on the whole of it. If anything went wrong, it would not be difficult to find out who was to blame for it.

Another obvious advantage is in the fact that the people would have to choose but five men to govern them, instead of the score or more whom they are now usually called upon to select as their representatives. There would be some chance that they could gain some intelligent opinions about the qualifications of the men for whom they were voting. I have never yet met a man who would maintain, when narrowly questioned, that he had ever voted intelligently in any municipal election; that there had ever been an occasion in which he had had full and satisfactory information respecting the character and the capacity of every candidate for whom he voted. We often know three or four of them fairly well, but most of them are names which represent nothing; we take them on the recommendation of the political machine. In this matter the British voter has an immense advantage over us. Each man votes for his own member of council, — the member who represents the district in which he lives; this is all he has to do. He may, without much difficulty, become instructed respecting the qualifications of this one man. It is evident that voting, in British municipalities, is a far more intelligent business than in most of ours. But under the Des Moines plan, where there were only five men to be voted for, it is natural to suppose that the merits of these men would be canvassed, and that the choice of them would represent more knowledge and judgment than usually finds expression in municipal elections under present conditions.

It will be found, however, that no plan can be devised which will give us good city government, so long as the great majority of our citizens are unwilling to take any responsibility for the government of our cities. It is not the fashion, in America, for men of substance and standing to take any active part in the administration of city affairs. Many of them seem to think it bad form to interest themselves in such matters; more of them feel that they cannot afford the sacrifice of their business interests which such a service would require of them. So long as anything resembling this is true, we shall, of course, have bad government in our cities. We are shirking the primary obligations of our democracy, and we shall get our deserts.

Some sense of these obligations constrained me, in the

THE MUNICIPAL PROBLEM 337

spring of 1900, to take upon myself a task for which I could claim no special fitness, and which might have been far better performed by some of my neighbors. In conversation with the editor of one of our daily papers, I was told that a ring had been formed among the members of the city council whose terms were then expiring, to reëlect themselves and to levy tribute, in the coming council, upon those public-service corporations which would be applying to that council for an extension of their franchises. My informant seemed to believe that a corrupt understanding had been or was likely to be reached between these corporations, and a combination by means of which the interests and rights of the people would be sacrificed. It was also represented that the member of the council from my ward was in the ring. How much truth there was in this report I never have known; probably it represented the imaginations of some who wished to have it come true. But there seemed to be reason for fear, under the circumstances, that corrupt considerations would be employed in the business of the council at its next session. Without taking counsel with any one, I announced the next day, over my own signature, in all the daily papers, that if the people of the Seventh Ward desired to have me serve them the next term in the city council, I would endeavor to do so. This was all that I found it necessary to do. My neighbors took up the matter and elected me; not only did I make no canvass for the place, I scarcely mentioned the matter in conversation to any one.

In April, 1900, I took up the duties of this office, and served in it for two years. This involved attendance upon the regular meetings of the council on Monday evenings, and upon the meetings of the committees on Friday evenings — two evenings of every week. It involved, also, of course, the devotion of much time to the business of the city outside of the meetings; for I was made chairman of one important committee and a member of three others. It precluded absence from the city for more than a few days at a time; my usual summer vacation had to be foregone. Altogether it added much to the burden of one whose life was already pretty heavily encumbered.

I did not, however, find the service in any sense a hardship. From the beginning it was extremely interesting to me. There were three young lawyers, one physician, three or four small business men, — grocers, retail coal-dealers, and so forth; five or six clerks or bookkeepers, and two or three saloon-keepers. We could hardly claim for ourselves that we represented the intelligence, the business sagacity, or the administrative experience of the community. There were very few of us who had ever given any study or thought to the problems of municipal organization. There were one or two of us who were often forced to cry out in wonder that a city of more than one hundred thousand people should be willing to intrust its great concerns to such a body of men as we were.

For great matters were coming before us for our decision. The street-railway franchises were expiring, and it was necessary for us to make a new contract with that company. The same was true of the company which supplied us with natural gas. The city had a

THE MUNICIPAL PROBLEM 339

small electric lighting plant, and the time had come to determine whether it should be enlarged or abandoned. Several interurban electric railways were seeking entrance to the city, and charters must be granted them. The water-supply of the city was lamentably inadequate, and steps must be taken to replenish it. The sewage was defiling the river, and the towns below were crying to us for protection. Here were interests of tremendous importance committed to us for our care and furtherance; did we know enough to deal with them intelligently and efficiently? I am sure that there were quite a number of us who had not the slightest misgiving about their entire competency to handle such matters, but there were a few of us, at least, who could not help being appalled by the magnitude and intricacy of the tasks before us.

My associates in the council were disposed, on the whole, to treat me courteously. At first there was apparent shyness and suspicion in certain quarters, but that soon disappeared, and the tinge of sarcasm which once or twice in the early days was heard in some allusion to my calling, was dropped when it became clear that no notice would be taken of it. It seemed to be expected, when I entered the council, that I would be a speech-maker; but I did not find it necessary to consume much of the time of the sessions in this way; it was better to depend on personal conference with members in carrying any measures in which I was interested. On the whole, my relations with my colleagues were altogether cordial. Good order prevailed at our meetings, and there were few occasions upon which the decorum of the council was marred by any unseemly conduct.

The first important business on our hands was the legislation called for by four or five electric trolley-lines seeking entrance to the city and terminal privileges; that was disposed of with reasonable expedition and upon terms advantageous to the city. Next came our local street-railway company with a demand for the extension of its franchises. It was a strong company, with a capitalization of about ten million dollars, and the interests which it represented were, of course, very powerful. Such companies are not, so far as I have observed, in the philanthropic line; they wish to make as good a bargain as they can for themselves. The proposition which the company submitted involved but a slight concession in the way of reduced fares; and the counsel of the company prepared an elaborate statement, showing, by statistics gathered from many sources, that it was impossible to make any reduction. The inaccuracy of this statement was easily exposed; my studies of the street-railway problem had put me in possession of the facts; and, in a letter, printed the next day in all the newspapers, I made it plain to the people that there was a mass of experience accessible to all of them, showing that the company could well afford materially to reduce its fares. The demonstration was not called in question, and from that time it was pretty well settled that the people would not accept any contract with the company which did not greatly reduce the cost of street transportation. A long and sharp struggle ensued, the result of which was the adoption

THE MUNICIPAL PROBLEM

of a contract which, although it is less favorable in some features than some of us desired, is yet, on the whole, the best that I know of in any American city. Our people buy for twenty-five cents seven tickets, which permit transfers in any direction; and after the gross receipts have reached a certain sum, which is not far off, the number will be increased to eight.

The saving of a cent and a half or two cents on a street-railway fare seems a small matter to contend for; but it is such small matters that make a difference, with people of small incomes, between health and feebleness, between decency and squalor, between hope and despondency. Take the case of a laboring-man with a family of five, living at some distance from work and market and school. It is a safe calculation that a difference between a five-cent fare and a three-cent fare may make a difference to this family of fifteen cents a day, one dollar and five cents a week, fifty-four dollars and sixty cents a year. That may mean quite a substantial addition to the amount of nourishing food; it may mean a Sunday suit for the man and a decent gown for the woman, and clothes and shoes for the children, — items which have a great deal to do with self-respect and contentment. It is out of these minute exactions that great fortunes are built up; a street-railway company which is carrying fifty million passengers in a year adds to its gains half a million dollars by adding one cent to its passenger fares. And it is equally true, on the other side, that it is by these small exactions that the comfort and welfare of the laboring-class is greatly reduced. When these exactions are multiplied, — when a few cents a day are added to the cost of living by very slight unnecessary additions to the price of carfare, or gas, or electricity, or oil, or water, and by slight enhancements of the cost of food or fuel which come through the increase of freights, — the burdens of the poor are aggravated that the revenues of the rich may be enlarged. The gravest injustices and oppressions of our modern life are of this nature, and out of them spring our worst inequalities of condition. So long as the private ownership of public-service industries is permitted, the regulation of these businesses must rest with the legislative bodies of the state or the city. That is, as any one may see, a tremendously intricate and difficult problem. It calls for the most expert knowledge of business and of finance, but it demands men who can look beyond the immediate financial results and estimate the effect of municipal policies upon the health, the intelligence, the contentment, and the self-respect of the people. There are no questions of administration requiring a higher order of statesmanship than those which are now before the councils of our American cities. To deal justly with all parties in interest requires a grasp of affairs which few of us can claim to possess. So long as public-service industries are privately owned, we must not deprive their owners of a just reward for their services and sacrifices; but neither must we permit them, by shifty financiering and corrupt bargaining with politicians, to bind heavy burdens on the necks of the producing classes. To deal wisely and justly with these great interests, we must have the services of the ablest and purest men in the community.

THE MUNICIPAL PROBLEM 343

In dealing with the franchise of the natural gas company, the council struck a problem of exceptional difficulty. The city had had a very favorable contract with that company; and the benefits of this most convenient and serviceable fuel were enjoyed by the majority of householders in the city. In asking for a renewal of the franchise, the company strongly represented that, owing to the lessening supply, and the increasing cost of production, the price must be raised. The truth of the representation it was almost impossible for us to verify. The cost of producing artificial gas we could fairly estimate; of the sources of supply of the natural gas we could not judge. When, therefore, the company laid before us a proposition, as an ultimatum, and told us that unless we would permit them to charge a certain rate, they would sell their gas in another market, we were confronted with a serious dilemma. The loss of this fuel would be a great public injury; should we make sure of keeping the gas by acceding to the company's demand, or should we risk the loss of it by insisting on the lower rate? Many shrewd people refused to believe that the company would execute its threat; others took the word of the officers and urged that the offered terms be accepted. For myself, I hesitated to take the responsibility, and determined to throw it upon my constituents. Accordingly I called for instructions from the consumers of my ward, promising to vote as the majority directed. The response was general, and the verdict was in favor of accepting the company's offer. For that, therefore, I was constrained to vote. But I did so with some reluctance, being quite inclined, at the last, to agree with the majority of my colleagues, who did not believe that the company would make good its threat, and who insisted on the lower rate. The event proved that they were right; the gas was not taken away, and the people enjoyed the cheaper fuel.

Out of this transaction I learned one or two lessons. The first was that a corporation, in dealing with a city, need not be expected to tell the truth. The men who gave me positive assurance respecting the purposes of the company were men on whose word I could have relied explicitly in any transaction between man and man; as representatives of a corporation dealing with a city, a different rule of morality seemed to obtain.

The second lesson I learned was that a representative had better, as a rule, rely on his own judgment and not seek instructions from his constituents. The elements of the problem were better known to me, at the moment when I was called to act, than they were to my constituents; I should have decided more wisely for them than they decided for themselves. That, I believe, is often the case with a representative of fair intelligence and conscientiousness. It is better for him to assume that he has been chosen to exercise his own judgment; in that way he is more likely to serve the interests of those who have chosen him.

The question respecting the maintenance and extension of our municipal electric plant was one of considerable perplexity. It was only a fragment of a plant, supplying the city with less than a third of its street lights; the rest were furnished by a private company at contract rates. There was much dispute as to whether

THE MUNICIPAL PROBLEM 345

the city lights were cheaper than the contract lights; but a careful investigation made it clear to me that, although the city plant had been poorly handled, it was effecting a real economy. When the private company came to put in its bids for the new contract, its prices were so high that a strong public sentiment demanded the extension of the municipal plant. In furtherance of this demand, I succeeded in bringing to Columbus the superintendent of the municipal lighting of Chicago, whose testimony respecting the success of the experiment in that city convinced the majority of my colleagues, and led to the decision that the city should provide its own street lights. We have now a well-equipped municipal plant, and the cost of the lights, when all legitimate expenses are reckoned, is lower than any contract lighting that has ever been offered to the city.

I am not at all sorry that I had a chance to serve the city in the day when this important matter was decided, and that I was able to contribute toward the formation of the public opinion which resulted in the adoption, to this extent, of the principle of municipal ownership. For I am as sure as I can be of anything that the municipal ownership and control of public-service industries is the right policy, — the only policy under which there is any hope of preventing corruption and oppression. As I have already tried to show, the public-service industries are necessarily monopolies; they are monopolies which furnish us with the necessaries of life; and monopolies of that nature must belong to the people. It would be just as rational to give a private corporation the right of levying taxes, as it is to give it the exclusive control of an industry by which the welfare of all the people is affected. No such control as this over the public welfare can rationally be delegated by the people to any private agency. If this does not belong to the rudiments of democracy, it would be hard to think of anything that does.

To say that the people cannot be trusted to manage such matters is simply to say that the people cannot govern themselves. Even, therefore, if it could be shown that municipal ownership resulted, for a time, in increasing the cost of the service, that would be no reason why it should not be chosen. If the people thus, by their carelessness and neglect, bring suffering upon themselves, that is just as it should be; they will know that they have brought it upon themselves, and will know how to avoid it. Nothing is safe in a democracy but the method which brings directly home to the people themselves the consequences of their own misdoing. That is the only way in which they can be educated.

The peril of private ownership of public-service industries arises from the enormous power which, as a vast experience shows, they possess to corrupt the government of the cities. If in any city there are ten or twenty or two hundred millions of dollars invested by private persons or corporations in public-service industries, these millions, as human nature goes, are directly interested in having bad government in that city. Good government, government by thoroughly intelligent and efficient men, would not play into the hands of the owners of these millions, and could not be controlled by

THE MUNICIPAL PROBLEM 347

them for their purposes. Good government would not give them the kind of concessions and franchises which they seek. Good government would not permit them to levy tribute on the public for the payment of dividends on vast issues of fictitious capital. With corrupt or inefficient government, all these things are possible. Dishonest men can be bought — most of them at a very low price; weak and ignorant men can be easily manipulated. This is the kind of government which private capital invested in public-service industries naturally feels that it must have. It is simply rehearsing the long and dark record which has been abundantly spread before the reading public, to say that private capital invested in public-service industries has been and is to-day the one overshadowing and all-pervading influence by which municipal government in America has been debauched. In many cases its plans are deeply laid to secure the election of men who can be used; in other cases it finds that it is safe enough to trust the people to provide officials who will serve its purposes. Unhappily that confidence is not often misplaced. It must be true that there are public-service corporations that deal fairly with the public, and that do not seek to corrupt the officials; but I am saying what every intelligent man knows to be true when I affirm that, as a rule, the capital invested in such industries is well aware of the fact that its interest lies in promoting bad government.

It is not reasonable to expect that such a power will refrain from pushing its interest. It will continue to do just what it has done in Philadelphia, in New York, in St. Louis, in San Francisco, in Minneapolis, — and, in a smaller and more cautious way, in scores of other cities.

I do not think that the people of any city can afford to have ten or twenty or two hundred millions of dollars directly and consciously interested in promoting bad government. It is a foolhardy thing to permit such a makeweight to be thrown into the scale on the side of political immorality. It is a crime to allow such a mighty organized force to be used for the destruction of free government. Free government will never be secure until that force is eliminated from the body politic.

I am aware that the municipal ownership of public-service industries would not entirely abolish corruption and temptation. There would still be opportunities of graft, and room for all sorts of corrupt combinations; there would still be no possibility of good government unless intelligent and competent men were willing to take office and the people were vigilant and sensible enough to choose them; the spoilsman would still be in the field plying his trade with diligence; but whatever dishonesties and infidelities prevailed would be in plain sight of the people; and no such stupendous aggregations of material power would be insidiously assailing the foundations of government.

Nor is it necessary to say that the success of this kind of administration, as of every other, must depend on the elimination from our city business of every vestige of the spoils system, and in the adoption of the same principles of efficiency and economy which prevail in all other kinds of business. So long as our city offices are

THE MUNICIPAL PROBLEM

vacated and refilled at every election, and so long as they are regarded as stalls in which faithful party workers are fed from the public crib, the public business will be done in a slovenly and extravagant way. But, as has been said already, if the people were managing their own business, the consequences of their management would be brought directly home to them; and the millions of private capital would be directly interested in having good and economical government. That makeweight would be thrown into the scales on the side of political morality. Instead of having a large part of the wealth of the city enlisted in the promotion of weak and dishonest administration, we should have the most of it enlisted in securing honesty and competency. That this would have a powerful influence in reforming the methods of municipal administration, I cannot doubt.

It has been, therefore, a satisfaction to me that I had the privilege of doing something, during my short period of public service, toward bringing municipal monopolies under public control. That the evolution of democracy must result in this is entirely clear to me. The ownership and control of all monopolies is the goal ahead of us, toward which we must move with no faltering.

Our two great problems of water and drainage gave us also some interesting experience. A good share of the members of our city government felt quite competent to solve them, off-hand, and a picturesque variety of suggestions was soon before us. We were so fortunate, however, as to have an intelligent city engineer, who had some sense of the magnitude of the problems; and by his advice the best authorities on these two subjects were summoned, to give us their counsel. It was not easy for some of our number to consent to the appropriation of several thousand dollars for such advice; the idea of employing experts to tell us what we should do in matters of this nature appeared to some of them quite preposterous; the word "expert" was flung about the council chamber with much contempt. The engineer's proposition was, however adopted; the preliminary studies and surveys were made, and the first steps were taken toward the provision for our city of an abundant supply of filtered and softened water and the purification and disposal of our sewage. It was a great and costly undertaking, and years have been occupied in accomplishing it, but, as I write these words, in the summer of 1909, we are rejoicing in an abundance of filtered and softened water, and the work for the cleansing of our river from the pestilence-breeding germs is also quite complete.

The observation of these great public utilities and the study of the needs to which they minister deepens one's sense of the tremendous interests that are involved in the growth of our cities, and of the extent to which it is necessary for us to work together for the common good. To supply a city of two hundred thousand people with pure water is a colossal undertaking; but working together, we accomplish it with comparative ease, and enjoy, at a nominal cost, a blessing of incalculable value. It is a signal instance of the beneficence of coöperation.

One part of our experience in pushing this enterprise was disenchanting. As soon as our source of water-supply was determined, all owners of land along the river-

THE MUNICIPAL PROBLEM 351

bank rose up to obstruct the city. For rights of way for our mains, and for alleged riparian damages of one sort or another, the most extravagant demands were made. If the city instituted condemnation proceedings and a jury of the vicinage was summoned to assess damages, we found the natives standing together to extort two or three times the value of their property. It was a pitiful revelation of human nature, and it is, I am told, the common experience of cities. They are generally compelled to pay enormous tribute to land-owners for access to sources of water-supply. This is a species of brigandage for which some remedy ought to be provided. It is akin to the extortion which demands of a famishing man a king's ransom for a cup of cold water. Our Christianity has not much vigor if it cannot make men ashamed of such unneighborly conduct.

I took my leave of the Columbus city council in April, 1902, with a sincere regret. I had no consciousness of having achieved great things; but I had come into close contact with the vital needs of my city, and I had had some part in solving some of its most pressing problems. I laid the burden down because it was not possible for me to bear it any longer. The work of my church was heavy and exacting, it could not be delegated, I must resign either my charge or my office. The results of my experience were a deepened sense of the seriousness of the business of municipal government and a more vivid realization of the lack of knowledge and skill on the part of those who are handling it. This is the crying evil — incompetency. There were not many occasions on which I suspected the presence of corrupting influences in the council; I do not think that money was often used; but the lack of the adequate knowledge and experience for the tasks in hand was often painfully apparent. I believe that this is true of city governments as a rule, — perhaps of state governments also. They are generally in the hands of men who have no fitness to deal with them; and this is mainly because the men who have the necessary equipment for such work almost uniformly refuse to undertake it.

CHAPTER XXIII

BOUQUETS AND BRICKBATS

While the manners, while the arts
   That mould a nation's soul,
Still cling around our hearts,
   Between let ocean roll,
Our joint communion breaking with the sun:
   Yet still, from either beach,
   The voice of blood shall reach,
   More audible than speech,
     "We are One."
                 Washington Allston.

Not Thine the bigot's partial plea,
   Not Thine the zealot's ban;
Thou well canst spare a love of Thee
   Which ends in hate of man.
           John Greenleaf Whittier.

THESE Recollections would be altogether incomplete without some mention of the journeys overseas, in which I have found so large a fund of stimulating experience. It was in the spring of 1888 that I first saw the green shores of Ireland, and the may blooming in the English hedgerows. Memorable are those first days in the sweet English landscapes, wandering about the winding streets of old Chester, following the banks of the Avon from Warwick to Stratford, resting in the gardens of Oxford, or upon the soft slopes and the willow banks that border the Cam, wondering and worshiping in the minsters of York and Lincoln and Canterbury and Ely and Winchester. To one whose mind has been nursed on English letters, no other land can offer anything akin to that which is constantly spread before him in the country of Chaucer and Shakespeare and Wordsworth and Scott and Burns and Ruskin and Tennyson and Browning. The Alps and the Rhine and quaint little Holland and sunny France had charms of their own, but when we recrossed the Channel, we knew that we were coming home. "Are you a foreign delegate?" asked one of the reception committee of the World's Missionary Conference in Exeter Hall, London. "No," I answered, rather indignantly, "I am an American." Five weeks in London were enough to go round about her and tell some of the towers thereof and consider a few of her palaces, and lay by a store of memories that would need refreshing at no distant day.

I heard Archdeacon Farrar preaching in Westminster Abbey to a crowd of delegates — bishops and priests — then in attendance upon the Pan-Anglican Council. It was brave and strong truth that he told them, too, about the inclusiveness of Christ's church, and the meaning of Christian fellowship. I had my only glimpse of Gladstone on that visit, and the occasion was not altogether an engaging one. It was at the Sydenham Palace, at the Haendel Festival. Mr. and Mrs. Gladstone were there to hear the "Israel in Egypt," and they occupied the Queen's box in the transept, opposite the choir. Their presence had not been noted, apparently; but when, in the middle of the performance, an intermission of half an hour was taken, the audience, rising to move about, saw the great Commoner and his companion sitting there, and immediately there was an indescribable uproar. Hisses and hoots came first, but these were met and sub-

BOUQUETS AND BRICKBATS

merged by cheers. The voice of scorn has less volume, happily, than the voice of acclamation. But there was plenty of hot breath behind these hisses, and of spite in the eyes that glared defiance at the venerable statesman. Answering the applause, he bowed and withdrew; but on the reassembling of the audience, when he came back to his seat, the same tumult was repeated. A woman, not of the lower class, who sat near me, turned her face toward the Queen's box and hissed like a snake. "What does it mean?" I asked a well-dressed man who was joining in the hubbub. "He is ruining his country!" was the hot reply. There was not, at that time, any political crisis, and Mr. Gladstone had done nothing recently to challenge criticism; it was simply an outburst of partisanship, and I confess that I had never seen, in the heated political atmosphere of my native land, anything quite so unlovely. It seemed an unspeakable outrage that a man like Gladstone could not attend a musical festival in the capital of his own country without exposing himself to insult.

One evening in London got itself underscored on the tablets of memory. By invitation of my venerable friend, the Reverend Henry Allon, D. D., of Islington, I went with him to a meeting of what I think was called the Christian Union. It was a company of men of all ecclesiastical sorts and conditions, — Churchmen and Dissenters, — who met, statedly or occasionally, in the Jerusalem Chamber of Westminster Abbey, to discuss the possibilities of fellowship and coöperation among Christians. I think that the movement had been started by Dean Stanley. We arrived at the Abbey early in the evening, and passing through the close to the deanery, first paid our respects to Dean Bradley, the successor of Dean Stanley, and then returned to the refectory in the Abbey, where tea was served. Then, led by Dean Bradley, the company, consisting of fifty or sixty men, marched through the nave, in the solemn twilight, to the choir, where, seated in the stalls, we joined with the Dean in a prayer which he read by the light of a single flaring gas-jet; after which we walked softly back to the west end, and entered the historic Jerusalem Chamber. One need not blush to admit some tingling of the nerves as he seats himself within the venerable walls where the Assembly of Divines fashioned a good part of the Westminster Confession, and where two companies of Biblical scholars, one in King James's time and one in Queen Victoria's, spent months and years of labor upon the translation and revision of our English Bible. Hither, too, Shakespeare brings King Henry IV, for his last breath. He had meant to die in Jerusalem, and whimsically deemed it the next best thing to die in the Chamber that bore that name.

> It hath been prophesied to me many years,
> I should not die but in Jerusalem;
> Which vainly I supposed the Holy Land:
> But bear me to that chamber; there I'll lie;
> In that Jerusalem shall Harry die.

The ancient carvings and tapestries bring back the memories of those old days. And here is a silent and attentive company ready to hear reasons why men of differing creeds should dwell together in unity, with some misgivings, alas! lest they may not be able to do so.

What was said was not so memorable; but it was good that men were moved to come together in this place to say it. It was in this company that I saw, for the only time, the benignant face of James Martineau, and that I first grasped the kindly hand of my gracious friend Dean Fremantle, of Ripon, — then Canon of Canterbury.

Other visits to England and the Continent bring back each its sheaf of memories, which I must not now unbind. In 1891, as delegate to the International Council of Congregationalists, I revisited the old country; and again in 1894 renewed associations and friendships there, which had been multiplying. In the summer of 1898, during the Spanish War, my English publishers, Messrs. James Clarke and Company, of London, announced, through the "Christian World," that I would speak within the Kingdom, wherever desired, on the "Causes of the War, and the Reasons for Friendship between England and America." This was not a lecturing tour; it was distinctly understood that I would pay my own traveling expenses and receive no compensation for my addresses; hospitality I would gladly accept, if that were proffered. On these terms I found no difficulty in filling a number of engagements, in various parts of the Kingdom, and a more delightful summer I have not often spent. The meetings were generally held in some public hall, — sometimes in a church; the mayor of the city, a member of Parliament, or some honorable citizen would take the chair, and the welcome of the town would be cordially extended. Almost everywhere the "Star-Spangled Banner" was sung, — rather better sung than by most American audiences. What I had to say about our national affairs, and especially about the reasons for friendship between the two countries, was received with the heartiest favor. I never have spoken to audiences in which the signs of enthusiasm were so marked. An English assembly, when it agrees with you, is an inspiring audience. It has its own ways of going along with you, and — to use the Parliamentary phrase — "associating itself" with you, which are very reassuring to a speaker.

All this experience was memorable. The reasons for friendship between England and America multiplied with every meeting. The throngs of men and women who filed past me, at the close of the meeting, grasping my hand, were all the while saying: "I've got a son, or a daughter, or a brother, or a sister, over there!" That there could be any other than the most friendly relation between the two countries was to most of these men and women inconceivable. One Englishman told me of the shock which was given to his countrymen when Cleveland's message upon the Venezuelan business suggested the possibility of war. He said that men met one another in the street, holding up their hands in horror and exclaiming: "War! War with America! It is monstrous! It is preposterous!" That, beyond a question, is the attitude of the average middle-class Englishman. There could hardly be a more unnatural or horrible offense against civilization than any attempt to promote hostilities between this country and England.

It will be observed that these Recollections are not attempting to follow a strict chronological order; it

BOUQUETS AND BRICKBATS 359

seemed better to bring together related topics without strict adherence to the order of time. I go back, then, to the Centennial year, for a glimpse at the Columbian Exposition in Chicago, and especially at the Parliament of Religions, which was not only the most picturesque, but perhaps the most significant, religious assembly ever brought together upon this planet. The conception was a daring one; nowhere else but in Chicago could it have materialized. Such a comparison of religions could hardly help enlarging the range of many minds, and it must lead the advocates of all religions to emphasize that which is central and fundamental in their forms of faith. All this tends to unity and fraternity. That the opportunity for such a comparison was offered by Christianity is of great significance; no other form of faith would have suggested such a thing; this, in itself, indicates the likelihood that Christianity will be the solvent and unifier of faiths.

It was a strange and somewhat disheartening fact that in the year of the Parliament of Religions our country should have been visited by an astounding outbreak of religious bigotry. Whether the fraternization of the religions at Chicago had anything to do with this, I do not know; it is possible that some small souls were disturbed by what seemed to them a dangerous lowering of barriers between religionists, and may have been spurred to dig deeper the chasms which sympathy and good will were filling up. The outbreak occurred in the domain of ultra-Protestantism, and was directed against the Roman Catholic Church. Several secret orders, whose object was hostility to Romanism, either sprang into existence or awakened to new activity, about this time. The movement began with the wide dissemination of literature of the most surprising character. The document most extensively circulated was entitled "Instructions to the Catholics." It purported to have been issued by the order of the Pope; the headlines generally made that assertion; the names of eight archbishops were signed to it, and the countersign of Cardinal Gibbons was appended. This document, in the form of a tract for general circulation, was brought to me by dozens of men, — most of whom supposed that it must be genuine. The "Instructions to the Catholics" included such admonitions as these: "We view with alarm the rapid spread of educated intelligence, knowing well that wherever the people are intelligent the priest and prince cannot hope to live on the labor of the masses whose brains have been fertilized by our holy catechism. . . . We view with alarm the rapid diffusion of the English language. . . . In order to find employment for the many thousands of the faithful who are coming daily to swell the ranks of the Catholic army, which will in due time possess the land, we must secure control of all the cities, railways, manufactories, mines, steam and sailing vessels — above all, the press — in fact, every enterprise requiring labor, in order to furnish our newcomers employment; this will render it necessary to remove or crowd out the American heretics who are now employed. You need not hesitate; it is your duty to do so. You must not stop at anything to accomplish this end. There are many ways to consult your father confessor, but be careful to do nothing that will create scandal."

The astounding fact is that this document was freely circulated for many months, and that it was published in scores of anti-Catholic papers. No exposure of its fraudulent nature, so far as I know, was made in the religious or secular newspapers. Probably most of the editors may have supposed that its absurdity would be evident, but in fact it was accepted as genuine by hundreds of thousands of American citizens who are able to read and write, and who assume to be educated persons. It was possible for them to believe that the high prelates of the Roman Catholic Church are stupid enough to issue a document like this and sign their names to it. And, believing that such were the purposes of the Roman Catholic authorities, it was easy to rope these hundreds of thousands into a secret organization whose purpose was a bitter warfare, political, social, and industrial, against all members of the Roman Catholic Church. Such an organization sprang into active existence and spread itself over the country in 1893. Its members were bound by a solemn oath never to favor or aid the nomination, election, or appointment to office of a Roman Catholic, and never to employ a Roman Catholic, in any capacity, if the services of a Protestant could be obtained. Such an attempt as this, not only to disfranchise Roman Catholics, but to prevent them from obtaining an honest livelihood, — to starve them to death, — was deemed the proper and Christian thing by tens of thousands of our Protestant church members and hundreds of our Protestant ministers in the last decade of the nineteenth century. This organization swept the state of Ohio, and several of the western states; most of the local governments were in its power; our own state legislature was under its control; candidates from both parties rushed into it, to get its support; men swore this hideous oath in order to get themselves elected to judgeships.

As the madness spread, the tales respecting the malign purposes of the Roman Catholics became more and more harrowing. They were importing arms in coffins, and other ghostly packages; they were drilling every night in the basements of their churches, — this was confidently affirmed respecting many churches which had no basements. One Protestant minister in Columbus announced from his pulpit that he had bought a rifle to defend his home, — evidently wishing to suggest to his congregation the wisdom of adopting the same precaution. Scores of newspapers, with large circulation, fanned the flame of suspicion and spread the panic. A forged encyclical, to which the name and title of Pope Leo XIII was prefixed, released all Catholics from any oath of allegiance which they might have taken to the United States government, and gave specific orders that "on or about the feast of Ignatius Loyola, in the year of the Lord 1893, *it will be the duty of the faithful to exterminate all heretics found within the jurisdiction of the United States.*" This forged encyclical was kept standing for weeks in the papers representing the order. To arm themselves against this threatened slaughter, the lodges of the society in Toledo ordered a large consignment of Winchester rifles, which were distributed among their members. The fact was subsequently brought out in an action at law, in

BOUQUETS AND BRICKBATS 363

which the seller of the rifles sought to recover the cost of them.

Such was the epidemic of unreason and bigotry which was raging in free and enlightened America, during 1893 and 1894. It cannot be said that the Roman Catholics had recently done anything to excite this antipathy; all their tendencies had been in the direction of more friendly relations with their Protestant neighbors. And while this fury was in the air, their behavior was, for the most part, altogether admirable. They endured, with great forbearance, the monstrous falsehoods which were told about them; they waited patiently for the day when the mists of suspicion and fear would clear away.

When the movement first began to gather strength in Ohio, I lost no time in bearing my testimony against it. In an evening sermon I took up and analyzed its literature, proving from its own documents its fraudulent character, and seeking to show how radically it was at war not only with truth, but with justice and honor and fair play and every dictate of Christian morality. In my own congregation the society gained no foothold; I did not know of one member of my church who united with it; but the case was very different with most of the Protestant congregations.

My sermon brought down upon me the denunciation of the anti-Catholic crusaders; by some of them it was charged that I was in the pay of that church. One of my ministerial brethren stated, as of his positive knowledge, that my sermon was the result of a definite bargain between myself and the Roman Catholic bishop;

he gave, minutely, the conversation between myself and the bishop over the telephone the Saturday evening before, which was, substantially, as follows: —

Myself. "Is this Bishop Watterson?"

The Bishop. "It is."

Myself. "Well, that sermon is ready."

The Bishop. "All right; preach it to-morrow night and your thousand dollars will be ready for you on Monday morning."

No comment is needed on the fertility of the imagination which could evolve such a fiction; the only thing notable is that any man should find it prudent to tell such a tale in an intelligent community. This is, indeed, the amazing thing, that such monstrous fabrications — stories so palpably at war with every element of probability — can be circulated by human beings who, in ordinary matters, must be credited with possessing common sense. Apparently it is only when their religious prejudices are excited that men completely part with their rationality. And it must be remembered that this obsession cannot be charged against "ignorant foreigners"; the vast majority of these zealots were English-speaking people.

I might naturally have hoped that, in my testimony against this fraudulent and mischievous organization, the pulpits of Columbus would be with me; but such was not the case. Five or six of them — not more, I think — spoke out clearly and bravely; the rest were either silent or openly defending the pestilent order. Quite a number of the ministers were known to be members of it; most of those who were not were either in sympathy with it or afraid of it. Several of them told me that while they did not approve of it, there were so many members of it in their congregations that it would not do for them to say anything about it.

It is asking too much to expect us to believe that all those who circulated these astounding reports about their neighbors were unaware of their falsity. The most intelligent of them must have known that these tales were lies. Probably they governed themselves by the philosophy which is rudely expressed in the maxim, "Any stick is good enough to beat a dog." The stories were slanders; but the Roman Catholics were dangerous people, and therefore any reports which tended to discredit them, whether true or false, might be useful. It did not appear to these pious Protestants that in this kind of casuistry they had adopted the worst maxim ever credited to the Jesuitic teaching.

It was surprising to see how quickly this proscriptive movement collapsed, for within two years it disappeared from sight, and those who had availed themselves of it to climb into power were eager to hide all traces of their connection with it.

I have lived through two of these epidemics of religious rancor, about forty years apart; I sincerely hope that our country has seen the last of them. Our Roman Catholic fellow citizens have earned the right to be protected from such proscription. There is no reason to suspect them of any unpatriotic purposes. They are bearing their part in the promotion of thrift and order and intelligence. Any attempt to discredit or disfranchise them on account of their religious beliefs ought to be resisted by every intelligent American.

CHAPTER XXIV

THE NEGRO PROBLEM

> And ye shall succor men;
> 'T is nobleness to serve;
> Help them who cannot help again:
> Beware from right to swerve.
>
> I cause from every creature
> His proper good to flow:
> As much as he is and doeth,
> So much he shall bestow.
>
> But, laying hands on another
> To coin his labor and sweat,
> He goes in pawn to his victim
> For eternal years in debt.
> *Ralph Waldo Emerson.*

THE reader of these pages will not need to be told that the writer of them has not been unmindful, through his lifetime, of the interests of the negro race in this country. When the negroes were emancipated, and opportunities were opened for their education and preparation for citizenship, that philanthropy appealed to me as one of the most enlightened and most urgent of all. It happened that there was an organization for missionary work, affiliated with the Congregational churches, which seemed to be specially fitted to take up this work among the negroes. This was called "The American Missionary Association"; it had been formed by men who were in revolt against certain pro-slavery complications of the Congregational Mission Board; its attitude toward the negroes had always been sympathetic; and when the contrabands were gathered by thousands at Fortress Monroe and in the camps of the northern armies, this society immediately entered the field and began among them the work of education. With the coming of peace and the swarming of the negroes in the southern cities the opportunity was indefinitely extended; and it was not long before many schools had been established in different parts of the South. Thus it was that the religious body to which I have always belonged was a pioneer in the work for the Freedmen. Other Christian denominations have been engaged in the same enterprise and have done excellent work, but the Congregationalists, whose interest in education has always been deep and active, were the first in this field, and have always been among the foremost. To their enterprise is due a very large provision for negro education in the southern states. The great institution at Hampton was founded by them; it has, however, for many years, been on an independent foundation. The same is true of Berea College in Kentucky. Fisk University at Nashville, Atlanta University, Tougaloo University in Mississippi, Talladega College in Alabama, Straight University at New Orleans, Tillotson College in Texas, are institutions which have been planted and are maintained by the American Missionary Association; and added to these is a considerable group of normal schools, and other secondary schools in different parts of the South. In connection with these schools, in places where graduates of these schools are gathered, and in many other places, Congregational churches have also been formed.

In this work of the American Missionary Association I have had a deep interest from my earliest ministry; most of its officers have been my friends. For several years I was one of its vice-presidents, and in 1901 I was honored by being chosen its president.

It is not improbable that some of those who read these pages may find themselves questioning whether such an institution as this has now any proper work to do. The southern states, it may be said, are making provision for the education of the negroes, and it is better to leave the business in their hands. It may be that they have done all that could be reasonably expected of them, but the provision is yet, in most of these states, wholly inadequate. The Southern Education Board, which has been formed to aid the southern states in extending and improving their educational facilities, is a witness to the fact that such aid is needed, even by the whites. Among the blacks the need is far greater.

The truth is that the emancipation of the slaves threw upon the people of the South a tremendous burden, which, in their impoverished condition, they were utterly unable to bear; and it was and still is the duty of the people of the North to share it with them. For the burden is not yet lifted, nor has it ceased to press, with crushing weight, upon the southern people.

See what the problem is, as it presents itself to the mind of one southern educator, Professor Woodward, of Trinity College, North Carolina: "To state the terms of this problem is to indicate its unexampled difficulties; here are nine millions of aliens, doubling about every forty years, fixed as to habitation, socially ostracized,

THE NEGRO PROBLEM

politically disfranchised, morally undeveloped, — in a word, a race, a thousand years behind, who must somehow be built into this national fabric and organically incorporated with the national life and character. Evidently such a consummation will severely tax the intelligence and the patience of the whole people for generations to come."

No better statement of the task could be asked for. But to whom does it belong? Let the same voice teach us: "The negro problem is a national problem, however southernly located, to be solved by the whole people of the South, the whole people of the North, and the negroes, getting together and working together on common grounds; for on such agreement and co-work the solution of it depends."

This southern gentleman is inclined to decline help from the North in the education of white children; "but the North owes the black," he insists, "as much as the South owes him, and that is the great debt. . . . Helping people whose best education is self-help and who have the means of self-help within reach, degrades both giver and receiver. It is to be hoped that the North, in its southern movements for negro education, will correct this initial mistake, this confusion of duty and charity, and fix organization on the safe basis of northern obligation for the education and civilization of the negro."

We may feel that the southern gentleman is too sensitive on this score. One reason why northern help is extended to southern whites is that the southern whites are overburdened by their task of providing elementary education for the vast numbers of illiterate blacks. It is not an impulse of charity, but a sense of justice, which prompts northern men to share with them the burden. So also testifies another brave southern man, the Reverend Edgar Gardner Murphy, of Alabama: "The Nation, including the South as well as the North, the West as well as the South and North, has to do with every issue in the South that touches any national right of the humblest of its citizens." That is surely the statesmanlike distribution of responsibility for this business.

But what is the nature of the task? The negro is on the hands of the nation. What shall we do for him? What shall we make of him? Here the voices divide. The prevailing sentiment at the South to-day undoubtedly insists that he must be kept in a subject, if not in a servile position. Governor Vardaman declares that he must be educated, but that his education must be industrial and moral, not intellectual. We must educate his hands and his heart, says this philosopher, but not his head. There is a problem in pedagogy for you! Governor Vardaman reminds us of the English mechanic who brought his boy to the night school, saying, "I want this boy to learn to write; I want him to write my letters and keep my accounts." "Very good," said the master; "we will teach him to write and to read." "No, no!" said the father. "I don't want him to know how to read. Teach him to read, and he'll be wastin' his time with books and papers and all such. Teach him to write, that'll be of some use." The notion that education can be put up in air-tight, non-communicating compartments, and that the negro's heart and hands can be adequately trained without developing his brain, deserves a place in the museum of psychological curiosities.

If the main thing to be done for the negro is to keep him in ignorance and subjection, that is a task which requires no great amount of art, — nothing but hard hearts and brutal wills. There is physical force enough in the nation to hold him down for a while; how long that dominion would last, I will not try to tell. The civilization built on that basis will fall, and great will be the fall of it. We have had our admonition already, — a war that cost six hundred thousand lives and twelve billions of dollars, — and the bills are not paid yet. That is a slice of the retribution due for trying to build a civilization on prostrate manhood. If we are not satisfied with that, if we insist on trying the same experiment over again in a slightly different form, another day of judgment will come, and will not tarry. We shall get it hammered into our heads one of these days that this is a moral universe; not that it is going to be, by and by, but that it is moral now, moral all through, in tissue and fibre, in gristle and bone, in muscle and brain, in sensation and thought; and that no injustice fails to get its due recompense, now and here. The moral law admonishes us not to make our fellow man our tool, our tributary. "Thou shalt treat humanity" — it is Kant's great saying — "ever as an end, never as a means to thine own selfish end." Disobey that law, and the consequence falls. Evade it no man ever does for so long as the wink of an eyelid. Its penalty smites him with lightning stroke; he is instantly degraded, beclouded, weakened by his disobedience. Virtue has gone out of him; the slow decay is at work by which his manhood is despoiled.

The same law holds in all realms. It is as sure and stern in its dealing with races as with persons. The stronger race that tries to treat the weaker not as an end, but as a means to its own selfish ends, plucks swift judgment from the skies upon its own head. On such a race there will surely fall the mildew of moral decay, the pestilence of social corruption, the blight of its civilization.

This is not northern fanaticism. It is a truth which has been uttered more than once, with the emphasis of conviction, by strong men in the South. It is not the view which prevails there to-day, but it is a view which is held there by a strong minority of the ablest men, and it must prevail. The luminous studies of the negro question which have been given us by Mr. Ray Stannard Baker in the "American Magazine" bring before us the elements which will finally rule in the working out of this problem. There are men at the South to-day who know and say that the task which the negro presents to the South and the nation is not the task of keeping him in subjection, but the task of lifting him to manhood and giving him the rights and responsibilities that belong to a man. "The best southern people," says President Alderman, of the University of Virginia, "are too wise not to know that posterity will judge them according to the wisdom they use in this great concern. They are too just not to know that there is but one thing to do with a human being, and that is to give him a chance." In the same vein President Kilgo, of Trinity College, North

Carolina, insists that the negro must have the right and the opportunity to make of himself all that God meant him to be. "He lifts his dusky face to the face of his superior, and asks why he may not be given the right to grow as well as dogs and horses and cows. For a superior race to hold down an inferior one that the superior race may have the services of the inferior was the social doctrine of mediævalism. Americans cannot explain why they shudder at the horrors of the tenth and eleventh centuries, and are themselves content to keep the weak in their weakness in order that the strong may rule better."

To this southern testimony some northern men would do well to give good heed. Its implications are large. It means that while the primary need of the negro is industrial education, the scheme which stops with that will not do at all. It is this southern college president who says again: "The education given at Tuskegee and Hampton is founded in wisdom. However, industrial education does not and cannot develop the highest and broadest moral character. If the negro is only capable of learning the lesser morals, and filling the lesser spheres of moral duty, then industrial education will prove sufficient for all his development. . . . If he is to be judged by the higher standards of moral life, then he must be given those things which will fit him to meet the duties and tasks of the higher moral life. To shut a race within narrow limits forces it to develop a contentment with a low order of things."

There is a further truth which these far-seeing southern men do not fail to seize and emphasize. If, as seems to be determined, there is to be social separation between the races, that is itself a decisive reason why the black man must have access to the highest culture. "For the very reason," says Mr. Murphy, "that the race, in the apartness of its social life, is to work out its destiny as the separate member of a large group, it must be accorded its own leaders and thinkers, its own scholars, artists, prophets; and while the development of the higher life may come slowly, even blunderingly, it is distinctly to be welcomed."

These southern witnesses make it clear that the kind of work which those with whom I have been associated have been trying to do for the negro is not unnecessary or superfluous work. Much ill-considered criticism has been expended upon the "universities" and "colleges" maintained in the South for the benefit of the negroes; but these are for the training of leaders and teachers; and if the races are to be socially separate, the nine millions of blacks must have their own teachers and leaders, and they must be well trained and competent. If all social contact between the races is to be prevented, then it will not be seemly for a white physician to practice medicine in a black man's home, nor for a white lawyer to do business for a black client; the race must have its own doctors and lawyers, and they must be men of skill and learning. Is there any good reason why a black physician should not be as well educated as a white one? No less imperative is the demand for thoroughly educated schoolmasters and preachers.

What is more, it is abundantly proved that it is only where the higher education flourishes that primary education can be efficiently maintained. Teachers who know no more than is taught in the primary schools cannot teach primary schools. And those who are teaching in the industrial schools must know more than is taught in those schools. Mr. Washington's school at Tuskegee is one of the noblest institutions on this continent; but the men and women who are working by his side were largely trained for their work in the colleges which our American Missionary Association has been maintaining, and in others like them. It is not needful to plead the cause of industrial education; that is abundantly vindicating itself, and such work as Hampton and Tuskegee are doing deserves the enthusiastic support of all men of good will. Industrial education is part of the curriculum in all the institutions whose names I have given, and of which our Association has the care. I have only desired to call attention to another aspect of the question which the superficial observer is apt to overlook.

There is no reason why there should be any quarrel between these two classes of educators; each needs the other's aid. Much less reason is there why the northern men who have been working since the war for the uplifting of the negroes should fail to honor the glorious company of southern men whose eyes are open to the ethical principles involved in our most serious social question, and who are setting their faces steadily toward the only goal which American civilization can keep in view. "The thinking men and women of this section," says Professor Woodward, "are ready to grant to the negro opportunity to win, as he may be able, full citizenship and all it implies, educationally and politically. But this opinion is not generally influential as yet, whatever strength it may win in the future." No; it is not generally influential yet; but it is the opinion that must prevail, because this is a moral universe. The words which I have quoted from these southern men are true words; the breath of God is in them; they ring with the accent of conviction. They are not going to be taken back. They cannot be gainsaid. They will force the assent of honest men, here and there, who will take them up and repeat them. They will form, little by little, a body of opinion at the South which will assert and maintain the right of the negro to be a man, with all that that implies.

CHAPTER XXV

A POLITICAL RETROSPECT

> For art and labor met in truce,
> For beauty made the bride of use,
> We thank Thee; but, withal, we crave
> The austere virtues strong to save,
> The honor proof to place or gold,
> The manhood never bought nor sold!
>
> Oh, make Thou us, through centuries long,
> In peace secure, in justice strong;
> Around our gift of freedom draw
> The safeguards of thy righteous law:
> And, cast in some diviner mould,
> Let the new cycle shame the old!
> *John Greenleaf Whittier.*

LET me turn back and gather up a few memories of the fortunes of the nation during the days since I found my home in Columbus. The disappearance of politics from this narrative at about the time of the removal of the narrator to Ohio would be a phenomenon needing explanation. It might, indeed, be attributed by scoffers to the fact that an over-supply of political pabulum furnished by Ohio had caused a surfeiting of the appetite for politics. The absence from the Mosaic literature of all reference to the future life has been by some critics explained as the reaction of Moses against the excessive other-worldliness of Egypt; and some similar inference might be drawn from the omission of politics from these Recollections since 1883. I must, therefore, make haste to disavow such an imputation against my Ohio neighbors. We are, indeed, in this commonwealth, somewhat actively concerned about politics; next to baseball it is, perhaps, the most engrossing interest of our lives, and the nation will admit that the Ohio politicians have made good. The strenuosity of political allegiance in this neighborhood seemed at first, I confess, somewhat excessive. I had worn, rather loosely, the party uniform, in Massachusetts; but Republicanism had never been a religion with me, and I had never felt that a refusal to vote for an unfit Republican could be counted as apostasy. When I found that Ohio Republicanism was inclined to put that construction upon independent action, I saw that I must not pretend to be a Republican.

In the campaign of 1884, when my parishioners discovered that I did not intend to vote for Mr. Blaine, some of them were concerned about my soul; but most of them learned, before long, to let me pass as a probable recipient of uncovenanted mercies. I ought then to have voted for Mr. Cleveland, and it has always been a matter of sincere regret to me that I did not; the misgiving with respect to his moral soundness which then withheld me was not justified. The behavior of the man in that ordeal should have reassured me. His entire subsequent career won for me the heartiest conviction of the essential integrity and greatness of his character. Few men in public life have inspired a more profound confidence in their ruling purposes.

The non-partisan attitude which from this time forward I was constrained to maintain has sometimes caused me inconvenience; there have been times when

A POLITICAL RETROSPECT

I should have been glad to belong to a party, but, on the whole, I am inclined to think that, for me, it has been the right attitude. There are decided advantages in not being a member of any political party.

Once I was asked to serve as one of the four election judges of my voting precinct, and, as a citizen who wishes to do his share of the hard work, I promptly accepted. When, however, I came to qualify, I found difficulty. The law required that not more than two of the judges should be members of any one political party. Two Democratic judges and one Republican judge had been sworn in, and the document presented to me to sign made me state that I was a citizen of the state and of the precinct, and that I was a Republican. "But I cannot sign that," I said. "Are you not a Republican?" asked the official. "No." "Are you a Democrat?" "No." "Will you swear that you are not?" "Certainly." "Very well." So the words "he is a Republican" were erased from the certificate of appointment, and the words "he is not a Democrat" were written in. This seemed to fulfill all righteousness, and I was permitted to serve the state in the capacity of an election judge by solemnly swearing that I was not a Democrat.

Let me here recall a later experience in practical politics which may have interest for amateur politicians. In the late winter of 1903 we were confronting the municipal election, and, in view of conditions then existing in the city, the decent people were "under conviction," and were saying among themselves as they are wont to say periodically, "Men and brethren, what shall we do?" There was a proposition that the men's clubs in the churches form a federation to take part in the campaign. Such a suggestion was made in our own men's club, but it was not cordially received; the impression was that any combination of the churches as such would be inadvisable. After the meeting of the club had adjourned, three or four of us tarried and formed a plan of operations. Each was to invite three or four men, whose names were agreed upon, to meet on a subsequent evening at a room in one of the business houses. About fifteen men came together, and a pledge was framed by which the signers agreed to vote in the coming election for candidates selected from the nominees of the two leading parties by a committee of twenty of their own number, — this committee to be equally divided between the two political parties. The pledge was not to be published, and the canvass was to be quietly made; no one was to be invited to sign whose name had not been approved at our meetings. We wished the signatures of no active politicians, and sought only the coöperation of those who would stand together in the fulfillment of our non-partisan pledge. The attendance upon our weekly meetings increased, but our lists grew much more rapidly; before the newspapers got wind of our scheme, we had nearly two thousand men pledged to vote for the ticket which we should recommend. This was before the nominating conventions, and while the party machinists were discussing candidates. As soon as the nature of our operations became known, we were beset by intending candidates, who wished to secure our indorsement before their nomination; but we positively refused to commit ourselves to any of them, insisting that our selection must be made from the actual nominees. The fact that twenty-five hundred men were pledged to ignore party ties and to vote solidly in this election for candidates selected by themselves from the two tickets was a fact of some significance to the managers of the two machines, and gave us, no doubt, a better list of candidates to select from than we should have had otherwise.

It appeared to most of us beforehand that the pinch of the problem would come in the selection of our committee of twenty, and in the ability of that committee, if it could be chosen, to agree upon their selection of candidates. Greatly to our surprise, neither of these difficulties proved serious. We easily found twenty men who agreed to serve, and they were men whose names would carry weight in the community. The only question that was raised in this selection concerned myself. I declined to serve for the obvious reason that I was not a member of either party. But here again my non-partisan attitude failed to protect me, and the Republicans insisted on electing me, probably on the ground that I was "not a Democrat." The committee was composed of business men, professional men, one or two university professors, two clergymen, and two sensible workingmen.

I have rarely participated in a more interesting task than that which was presented to this committee. We canvassed fully and amicably every candidate named on the two tickets, looking up the record of every one; in a few cases, where there was little choice, we indorsed both candidates, and, in every case, we reached a unanimous decision. An address was prepared, signed by all of us, and published in the newspapers, submitting our list of recommendations, explaining that twenty-five hundred men had pledged themselves to disregard their party connections and vote for these candidates, and asking others to do the same. The result was the election of all our candidates with the exception of one constable, and generally by heavy majorities.

The organization, which styled itself "The Municipal Voters' League," had no permanent officers except this "Committee of Twenty," which was by vote continued in office, and authorized to fill its own vacancies and to proceed along the same lines whenever occasion might serve. That committee, or the nucleus of it, is still in existence, but the time seems never to have come for calling it together; that time may, however, arrive at no distant day. There seems to be no good reason why such a committee, like the famous Municipal Voters' League of Chicago, might not perform for any community a most valuable service. Its usefulness and permanence would depend, of course, on the honesty and thoroughness with which its work was done. If it could gain the confidence of the community, so that intelligent voters felt that they could safely follow its recommendations, it could largely control municipal elections; for there is an increasing number of voters who are ready to ignore party in municipal affairs and only wish to be guided in their choice of the best men.

As an indication of the growth of independency, the story of our League is significant. It is not a local condition, either. Ohio, which is strongly Republican in national elections, has twice elected Democratic governors; Minnesota offers a still more striking illustration, and all over the land the day of the independent voter seems to have arrived.

One finds, in a survey of the political progress of the last twenty-five years, much that is reassuring. The political morality of the present decade, as compared with that of the Cleveland and Harrison administrations, is clearly of a higher grade. This judgment applies to the executive departments; anything more immoral than the general attitude of the national legislature as displayed in the tariff debate of 1909, it would be difficult to imagine.

It was during the administration of Mr. Harrison, in 1890, that Mr. McKinley succeeded in carrying through Congress the tariff bill which bears his name. No one who knew Major McKinley can doubt that he believed this measure to be fraught with blessings to the American workingman; it was his ambition to create in this country an aristocracy of labor. He was not a profound thinker, and these intricate problems of economics were sometimes beyond his grasp; the naïveté of his reasonings upon them was frequently more engaging than convincing. There must, however, have dawned upon his mind, now and then, as he was trying to adjust the schedules, a suspicion that some other motives besides the good of the country were finding expression in the scramble for rates that should be prohibitory. But Major McKinley's simple faith and superficial logic strongly appealed to the multitude, his tariff measures gave him the leadership of his party, and, when he was defeated for Congress in 1891, made him the Governor of Ohio.

We had him in Columbus for four years, and he commended himself to all our citizens by the benignity and grace of his deportment, and the sweetness and nobility of his personal character. The Governor of Ohio, at that time, was not an important factor in the life of the commonwealth. He had not the veto power, and the legislature was not in the habit of seriously considering his recommendations. There was a little petty patronage at his disposal, and Governor McKinley appeared to be making the most of this in the way of strengthening his hold on the political machine, evidently with his eye upon the future.

Certain scandalous raids were made by some of the great corporations upon the legislature about this time, engineered by some of our great statesmen, and while the Governor had no power to prevent this, he did not, so far as I remember, exert that positive moral influence against it which might well have been expected of him. On the whole, I must confess that Mr. McKinley's career as Governor did not inspire me with high expectations of his success as an administrator of national affairs, and in this, I own, I was happily disappointed. William McKinley, as President of the United States, was a much larger figure than William McKinley as Governor of Ohio. When the heavy responsibilities fell upon his shoulders, he stood up under them with a firmness and a dignity that many who had watched his career in the lower position hardly expected of him. The

A POLITICAL RETROSPECT

men whom he gathered about him were, as a rule, men of great ability and high character, — John Sherman, John Hay, John D. Long, William H. Moody, Elihu Root, E. A. Hitchcock, James Wilson; no President could be suspected of selfish or sinister purposes who called into his Cabinet such men as these.

One sometimes wonders whether a little stiffer fibre in McKinley's will might not have averted the Spanish War. To those who now read over the documents which detail the negotiations with Spain regarding Cuban affairs, it seems clear that the Spanish government was ready to concede all that we had a right to demand. But the clamor for war, from the beginning of the incident, was fierce and brutal; there was a powerful sentiment, much of it outside the President's party, for war at any price. One shudders to recall the temper of the time as it found expression in the newspapers, and in Congressional oratory. I heard an eminent statesman saying in the streets of Columbus that it was time we had another war; it would give to many of our young men the opportunity of a career which they were never likely to find in the walks of peace. I wonder if we have not moved forward a little since that day; it seems to me that a sentiment as atrocious as that could hardly be ventured in these times by persons claiming to be civilized.

Doubtless there was much in the conduct of Spain which ought to have kindled indignation; and when the tragedy of the Maine occurred, it was hard to restrain the popular wrath. Still, the action of Spain regarding this, as we now know, was all that we could have desired, and the hot haste with which our Congress insisted on making ready for war was, to say the least, unseemly. It is clear that Mr. McKinley did his best to restrain the rampant jingoism of Congress, and but for the report of Mr. Proctor upon the condition of the *reconcentrados* in Cuba, he might have succeeded. But that testimony of a sober-minded man concerning the enormities of the Spanish administration in Cuba swept away the ethical restraints and let the elemental passions loose.

There was food for much reflection in the movement of the popular mind in that series of events. All kinds of motives mingle to produce effective public opinion; the ferocity of the brute, the greed of the trader, the ambition of the self-seeker, the narrow patriotism of the jingo, the antipathies of race, the bigotries of religion, the passion for freedom, the hatred of cruelty, the sentiment of humanity, — all these were seething together in the public mind in those early days of 1898.

I am sure that the baser passions would not have prevailed in that hour; that the final word for war was spoken by the impulse of humanity. Yet I do not think that those who uttered that word were so fully acquainted as they should have been with the attitude of the Spanish government; and I have doubted whether President McKinley gave the people all the information they ought to have had in that critical moment.

It was the parting of the ways with this nation. From that hour she has been constrained to be a world-power. Her intervention on behalf of Cuba launched her upon a new career. From this destiny she had steadily drawn back, but it is now inevitable, and she has no right to shrink from it. The well-being of the world is to be settled, more and more, by consultation and coöperation among the world-powers, and this nation must take her share of the responsibility. Into this august business Mr. McKinley introduced us. It was good judgment and good fortune that guided him to the choice of John Hay, first as ambassador to England, and then as Secretary of State. Nothing finer in the way of diplomacy has ever been recorded than Hay's management of the Chinese question. What worlds of confusion and misery might have been let loose in the far East, during the last ten years, if it had not been for that far-sighted intervention! And what a glorious new note it is that we hear resounding in Hay's state papers — that the Golden Rule is and must be the foundation of international law!

We must give Mr. McKinley's administration due credit for these great achievements. And while its record is not flawless, and sinister forces were gaining strength here and there, yet the President's grasp upon affairs seemed to be strengthening, and his last utterance, his speech on reciprocity, the day before his assassination, was by far the most convincing word that he had ever spoken. What a tragedy it was that he should be stricken down at the moment of his life when his outlook was widest and his purpose strongest! And what a pitiful commentary it is upon the blindness of the insurrectionary elements in our society, that they should select for slaughter such a man as William McKinley, — a man whose deepest sympathies were with the lowliest classes, and who could not, intentionally, have added a straw to the burden that any poor man was bearing! Some things are so horrible that they are simply absurd.

With the passing of President McKinley there moves promptly to the centre of the stage the most forceful figure yet seen in our national history. I believe that I can trust myself to speak soberly of Theodore Roosevelt, for, though my admiration and affection for him are deep and large, I am not unconscious of his limitations, and, in some things, I find myself in sharp disagreement with him. With his eagerness to increase our armament I have no sympathy; I believe that the day of disarmament is nigh, even at the doors, and that our nation is called of God to take the initiative in it. We are not in danger of aggression from any power under the sun; and it is perfectly safe for us to stop our shipbuilding and lift up the standards of peace before all the nations. The peoples everywhere will respond to that call with a mighty enthusiasm, and they will compel their governments to give heed to it. When the British Foreign Secretary declares that the increase of armaments, within the past ten years, is a satire upon civilization; when the whole world sees that the mere dread of war is driving all the great nations into extravagances of expenditure that are crippling industry everywhere and threatening national bankruptcy, it is time that some great nation should pause in this mad race to ruin and call a halt to the rest. Our nation is the one that can speak with most commanding voice. It is her manifest destiny to lead the nations in the paths of peace, and her opportunity is here, for peace has already become not merely a possibility, but a stern economic necessity.

In his strenuous insistence upon multiplying the big ships, Mr. Roosevelt seems to me, therefore, to be setting

A POLITICAL RETROSPECT

himself against the things that he most strongly stands for. I like it not, any more than I like his present pastimes in Africa: these exhibitions seem to me something other than his best self. His best self appears in that glorious deed by which he put an end to the war between Russia and Japan; in the return of the indemnity money to China; in the convention with Japan, negotiated by Mr. Root, but giving expression to Mr. Roosevelt's good will. No man has ever done so much to promote peace on earth. And this is the kind of work he is going to do for the world in the days that are left to him.

It would not be difficult to name a number of things in which Mr. Roosevelt has fallen below himself, in the seven years of his public service. But I wonder whether any man with such tremendous energies, always in full play, ever made fewer mistakes. And certainly no man since Lincoln has poured into the life of this nation such a stream of vitalizing influence.

My interest in Mr. Roosevelt began a long time ago. On the night of Mr. McKinley's first election, a little group of men, waiting in our church parlors for returns, balloted for the next President. When the votes were counted, there was one for Theodore Roosevelt, which was plausibly charged to me. When he was police commissioner in New York, something that I had said or done drew from him a friendly letter, which opened the way for me to meet him, on my next visit to the metropolis, and the acquaintance then begun has been of great profit to me. He came once, at my invitation, to Columbus, and spoke to our citizens on the problem of the city; and while I have never belonged to the inner circle of his intimate advisers, I have known him well enough to feel sure of his ruling motives.

In one of my early conversations with him he spoke of the insecurity of his tenure of office, saying: "I don't know how long I shall be in public life. The politicians may not continue to want me; and they have effectual ways of getting rid of a man when they are done with him; but I shall try to do what I think right, and when they are through with me, I think that I can get a living for my children with my pen, or in some other honest way." My answer was: "Nothing can keep you from going much further but your own default, and you are not a defaulter." Yet those who knew him best could hardly have dreamed that he would so soon be at the top of the world.

The essential loyalty of the man was at once revealed when he reappointed all the members of McKinley's Cabinet, and announced his purpose of carrying into effect, just so far as he could do so, the policy of his predecessor. It was a fine sense of honor which thus constrained him; the other Vice-Presidents who have been promoted by death have recognized no such obligation. The fidelity with which he kept this virtual trust has never been questioned.

For myself, I must confess that the elevation of this man to the place of power, just at this juncture, was a reason for profound thankfulness. That critical times had come upon this nation was evident enough. Vast combinations of capital were exerting a power of oppression such as no aristocracy of the Old World would dare to attempt; the railway managers were their thralls;

A POLITICAL RETROSPECT

some of the necessaries of life were largely under their control; by daring ventures in finance they had contrived to establish enormous "vested rights" in the form of inflated capital of public-service companies; every year they were finding new ways of creating gigantic debts, the interest of which would be a perpetual charge upon the producing classes. The extent to which this exploitation of the whole population had been carried by "big business" was something fearful. The process went on noiselessly; silken toils were silently spun and woven about the limbs of the workers in their sleep, and there were few who knew why their progress was impeded. That the burdens thus imposed would at length become intolerable, and that revolution would be the issue, was plain to all who could discern the signs of the times, but their voices fell on deaf ears. Fortunate it was for this country that the arrival of Theodore Roosevelt at the head of the nation was no longer deferred. Here was a man with eyes to see the extent and the enormity of this veiled injustice, with words to describe it, and with an arm to smite it. The service which he has rendered to this nation in bringing into the light these furtive plunderings, in awakening the conscience of the land against them, and in setting the machinery of the law in motion for their prevention and punishment, is one of the greatest services that it has ever fallen to any man to render. He has not wrought alone; a multitude of others, some of them wisely and effectively and some noisily and passionately, have been exposing these injustices; but no one else has done a hundredth part of what Mr. Roosevelt has done to enlighten the people with regard to them, and to put them in the way of extinction. To his mind, it is entirely clear that the robbery which is effected by a rebate arrangement, or by the watering of the stock of a street railway, is just as heinous as that perpetrated by a burglar or a footpad, and far more dangerous to the peace of society; and he has contrived to get that idea into the minds of a great many Americans, — of so many that it is going to be increasingly unhealthy to carry on that kind of business in this country in the future.

The social conditions which Mr. Roosevelt confronted were such as had never before appeared. The ascendency of commercialism had assumed new and overshadowing proportions; the physical development of the continent had created conditions not clearly covered by statutory regulation, in which human greed found a large opportunity.

The great mass of wealth [says Professor Cooley] is accumulated by solid qualities — energy, tenacity, shrewdness, and the like — which may co-exist with great moral refinement or with the opposite. As a group, however, [men of wealth] are liable to moral deficiencies. . . . There is, especially, a certain moral irresponsibility which is natural to those who have broken away from customary limitations and restraints, and are coursing at will over an unfenced territory. I mean that business enterprise, like military enterprise, deals largely with relations as to which there are no settled rules of morality, no constraining law or public opinion. Such conditions breed in the actor a Machiavellian opportunism. Since it is hard to say what is just and honest in the vast and abstract operations of finance, human nature is apt to

A POLITICAL RETROSPECT 393

cease looking for a standard and to seize booty wherever and however it safely can. Hence the truly piratical character of many of our great transactions. And, in smaller matters also, as in escaping taxation, it is often fatally easy for the rich to steal. It must be allowed that such ascendency as the capitalist class has rests, in part at least, upon service. That is to say, its members have had an important function to perform, and in performing that function have found themselves in a position to grasp wealth. . . . At the same time, it is plain that a large part of the accumulation of wealth — hard, unfortunately, to distinguish from other parts — is accomplished not by social service, but, as just intimated, by something akin to piracy. This is not so much the peculiar wickedness of a predatory class as a tendency in all of us to abuse power when not under definite legal or moral control. The vast transactions associated with modern industry have come very little under such control, and offer a field for freebooting such as the world has never seen.[1]

Such were the conditions which Mr. Roosevelt faced, at the beginning of his administration. Vast combinations of wealth, created by the law and endowed with superhuman powers, were using these powers for purposes of spoliation — plundering the many for the enrichment of the few. To disentangle this piratical business from honest business, to protect legitimate enterprise and prevent and punish predatory schemes, — this was the task set before him. Clearly, this must somehow be done; unless it could be, democratic government was a failure. And Mr. Roosevelt addressed

[1] *Social Organization*, pp. 259–261.

himself to this Herculean task with a courage, a determination, and an enthusiasm which have won for him the admiration of the world.

The men who have been making enormous fortunes by piratical methods, and those who have wished to do so, have been greatly enraged by Mr. Roosevelt's activity; they hate him with a perfect hatred, and with honest cause; they have done what they could to discredit and destroy him. But the people know that he has made no war on honest industry; that he has only sought to put an end to plunder and to give every man a fair chance. The Roosevelt policies are fairly well understood by the people, and any attempt to recede from them will provoke a reaction which will not be profitable to the opposing interests. The Roosevelt policies mean simply honesty, justice, fair play; and any business which is too big to learn these lessons is too big to live in this country.

Even some of those on whom the heavy hand of the government has fallen seem to recognize the justice of the punishment. The New York Central Railroad has had, I believe, some drastic fines to pay for rebating, but the president of that railroad — a recently elected president — is now heard saying: "One of the crying evils of railway management in the past (and nothing but the strong arm of the law would ever have stopped it) was the practice of discrimination in favor of large shippers as against those that shipped little, the giving of rebates, and the distribution of passes to secure the business. We know better now. We know that the man who ships little, no matter how little, must have the same unit price, whether by the hundred pounds or by the

A POLITICAL RETROSPECT 395

carload, as the man who ships much, no matter how much." Yes, some of us do know better. And we shall not forget who taught us. For though we had laws enough to prevent all these robberies, they were practically a dead letter; it was the will of Theodore Roosevelt that gave them life and power.

To one episode in the administration of Mr. Roosevelt I will venture to refer, as it has a special interest for me. The strike of the anthracite coal-miners, in the summer of 1902, brought anxiety to all of us. It was the first thoroughly organized struggle of the miners of that region for improved conditions; their leaders seemed to have their forces well in hand, and on the other side the temper of the railway presidents appeared to be exceptionally obdurate. Their positive statement that there could be no arbitration was a defiance which the men could scarcely decline, and the entire army of bituminous miners stood behind the anthracite men with strong assurances of support. The terrible consequences of the prolongation of this struggle to the poor of the eastern cities made the outlook most disquieting. That something must be done to break the deadlock was evident, and all hearts naturally turned toward President Roosevelt as the one man who could undertake, most hopefully, this work of mediation. The editor of the "Cincinnati Post," a daily newspaper circulating largely among the working-classes, came to Columbus to consult with me about this. He wished to circulate, widely, a petition to the President, asking him to intervene, and he desired me to frame the petition. Realizing that much depended on the way in which this appeal was made, I shrank from taking this responsibility. There was a question, too, whether the President would undertake such a task; and it might embarrass him to put upon him the necessity of refusing it. If he should undertake it and should fail in it, that would be unfortunate for him. I asked the editor to let me think about it an hour, at the end of which time I found myself convinced that Mr. Roosevelt would neither refuse the task nor fail in it; and that a strong demand laid on him by the people might enable him to do what he would not feel like doing on his own initiative. I therefore wrote this petition: —

To His Excellency Theodore Roosevelt, *President of the United States:*

We whose names are underwritten, citizens of the United States, most earnestly ask you to use your good offices in bringing to an end the unhappy strife now prevailing in the coal regions.

Some of us are men and women who work with our hands; some of us are earning our livelihood in other ways; many of us are losers now by this conflict; all of us are appalled by the prospect of suffering before the country if it be not speedily terminated; and we feel that we have a right to call upon you as our representative to see what you can do to make peace.

We do not ask you to use any official power in the matter, for you have none to use; we only ask you as the first citizen of this nation to mediate between these contending parties.

You can speak as no one else can speak for the plain people of the country. Every workingman knows that you are his friend; no capitalist of common sense can

A POLITICAL RETROSPECT

imagine that you are his enemy. The fact that others have spoken without effect does not shake our faith that your words of counsel and persuasion would be heeded.

We want no injustice done to either party in this conflict. We want no coercion to be used or threatened. Coercion is the game both sides are now playing; we want them to stop that, and reason together. No question of this kind is ever settled rightly or finally by coercion.

We recognize the fact that you would hesitate to interpose, even in the interests of peace and good will, lest you should seem to be exceeding your prerogative. But if the voices of hundreds of thousands of your fellow citizens should summon you to such a task, you would not, we are persuaded, shrink from undertaking it.

This is not business, Mr. President, it is not politics; it is something much higher and finer. May God help you to render this great service to your country, and crown you with the blessing that belongs to the peacemakers.

I have put this petition on record here because it is part of the history of the time. The newspaper which suggested it printed and circulated widely the petition; many church congregations and other assemblies adopted it; large numbers of copies of it went to Washington. Many other appeals were made to the President; this was one of numerous influences which induced him to take up this task, the successful performance of which fills one of the bright pages in a great record of patriotic service.

CHAPTER XXVI

PARTNERSHIP WITH PLUNDERERS

> Shall not that Western Goth, of whom we spoke,
> So fiercely practical, so keen of eye,
> Find out, some day, that nothing pays but God,
> Served whether on the smoke-shut battle-field,
> In work obscure done honestly, or vote
> For truth unpopular, or faith maintained
> To ruinous convictions, or good deeds
> Wrought for good's sake, mindless of heaven or hell?
> Shall he not learn that all prosperity,
> Whose bases stretch not deeper than the sense,
> Is but a trick of this world's atmosphere,
> A desert-born mirage of spire and dome,
> Or find too late, the Past's long lesson missed,
> That dust the prophets shake from off their feet
> Grows heavy to drag down both tower and wall?
> *James Russell Lowell.*

I AM often inquired of respecting the beliefs and practices of "the Congregational Church." I can only answer by asking another question: "Which Congregational church?" At the last account there were 5989 Congregational churches in the United States, each of which is free to frame its own creed, and organize its work in its own way. There is no such body as "The Congregational Church of the United States," as there is a Presbyterian Church of the United States, or a Methodist Episcopal Church of the United States. The Congregational churches coöperate in many ways for missionary and philanthropic purposes; they give and take advice, through councils called for the purpose; but they have no central government with authority to make laws for them or impose creeds upon them. There is not, and cannot be, as I have explained on a former page, any uniform creed to which all Congregationalists must subscribe. There is, however, a general agreement in teaching, and a good measure of uniformity in practice; and there has always been a large coöperation in Christian work. About the middle of the nineteenth century the need of a closer affiliation of these churches began to be strongly felt, and in 1871 "The National Council of the Congregational Churches" (not of the Congregational Church) was formed, its object being to bring the churches into closer fellowship, and to give greater efficiency to the enterprises of evangelization and philanthropy which they were prosecuting together. That Council meets every three years; it brings together about five hundred representatives of the churches; it consults respecting our various missionary enterprises; it studies the ethical and social problems with which the churches are grappling; it considers how friendship and helpful relations may be promoted between Congregational Christians and Christians of other names. It has no power whatever; it cannot ordain or depose a minister, it cannot establish or dissolve a church, it cannot define or punish heresy, it can only recommend to the churches and the benevolent societies represented in its organization such measures as seem good to the majority of its members. Such moral influence as this has been found to be adequate for all the purposes of a Christian organization. It is about all that any ecclesiastical body possesses in this day and age; not many churches are seeking to enforce their decrees or their dogmas by guns or clubs. The National Council has done much to promote the solidarity of our fellowship; it has enabled us to value more highly the things we have in common; it has brought some of us almost to the point of being willing to call our communion the American Congregational Church.

The presiding officer of this body bears the ancient title of Moderator, and to this office I had the great honor to be chosen, at the meeting in Des Moines, Iowa, in October, 1904. The office is one in which no power is vested, and to which no emoluments are attached. The moderator presides over the meeting at which he is chosen; becomes, *ex officio*, a member of the Standing Committee of the Council for the next three years; calls the next meeting of the Council to order, and presides until his successor is chosen; and on the first evening of that meeting, delivers an address. This has generally been regarded as the extent of his function. But my predecessor, the Reverend Dr. Bradford, of New Jersey, had ventured to enlarge this function. He had visited, by invitation, the churches in many localities, had spoken at various Congregational assemblies, and had done much to strengthen the bonds of fellowship among the churches. So grateful had this service been that the Council which elected me by resolution requested me to continue the same kind of work, exercising a kind of ministry at large, as opportunities might be given me. That proved to be a large order. Such opportunities were numerous, and the next three years were busy years. The care of my church could not, of course, be re-

PARTNERSHIP WITH PLUNDERERS 401

linquished, and I managed to be in my own pulpit most of the Sundays; but if to be "in journeyings often" is the proof of an apostolate, mine was well established. My itinerancy took me to twenty-five states of the Union, led me four times across the continent, — going and coming, — each time by a different route, and called on me for many addresses before state and local associations, conferences, and clubs. It was a laborious, but a delightful service; the moderator, as the symbol of the unity of the denomination, and a witness to a desire to draw the churches into a closer fellowship, was welcomed everywhere with great cordiality.

It was not, of course, the business of the moderator to meddle with the business of the various assemblies which he was called to address, or to attempt to exercise any influence in local affairs; all that he could do was to discuss the larger interests which were common to all the churches, and to point out as best he could the lines in which the Spirit was leading them.

In the early spring of 1905 our churches were surprised by the announcement that a gift of one hundred thousand dollars had been made to our Foreign Mission Board by the president of the Standard Oil Company. The donor was not a member of our communion. The first statements respecting the gift conveyed the impression that it had not been solicited, that the only agency of the Board in the matter had been that of a passive recipient of a gift brought to its doors. The explanations of the authorities, and all the earlier newspaper comments, assumed that this was so. It was admitted by some of these apologists that it would not have been right for the Board to seek contributions from such a source; but that when they were freely offered, they could not be rationally refused. These representations and admissions clearly indicated some uneasiness of mind on the part of the recipients, and made it plain that the nature of the alliance into which they had entered was not altogether satisfactory to them.

For there had come, very promptly, an emphatic declaration against the acceptance of money from this source. As soon as the gift was announced, I wrote a letter to the "Congregationalist," protesting against the action by which the Mission Board was drawing our churches into a dishonorable alliance; declaring that the money thus bestowed had been iniquitously gained, and that we could not accept it without being partakers of the iniquity. Similar protests came from a considerable number of the best men in our denomination. A strong group of ministers in the vicinity of Boston took up the matter with vigor and united in a dignified and temperate memorial to the Board against the reception of the gift. Presently, however, it transpired that the money had been paid over and most of it expended before any announcement was made; the protest against the acceptance was therefore futile. That the money should be returned was the clear dictate of sound morality, but of that there seemed little hope. The practical question concerned the future action of this Board, and of our other missionary organizations. That a great wrong had been done and a serious injury inflicted upon the churches represented in this society seemed to some of us very clear; that wrong must be confessed with shame; the question was whether it should be repeated. On that question there arose a debate in which the whole country was enlisted. It must be said that the debate revealed a widespread need of elementary instruction in the first principles of ethics. It exhibited, in a startling manner, the extent to which the moral perceptions even of leaders in the church have been blunted and confused by the worship of money. So much have we all become accustomed to think and say, in our religious, educational, and philanthropic enterprises, — "The one thing that we need is more money," — that it has become quite too easy to subordinate many of the higher considerations for the sake of getting money.

The prompt answer of many amateur moralists to our protest was that money has no moral character; that one man's dollar is as good as another man's — will buy as many Bibles, pay as many missionary salaries, do as much good. When we replied to this by asking whether money contributed by highwaymen and pirates — booty which they were known to have taken from their victims — should be received with thanks by churches and missionary societies, it was generally admitted that that would be inadvisable. Even the law would discourage this kind of benevolence.

The plea was then made that money to which the owner had a clear legal title must be taken without questioning. But there is much to which there is a clear legal title which differs but little, when weighed in the scales of a sound morality, from stolen money; and the proposal to stand on a bare legality did not commend itself to sensitive consciences.

It was then asserted that a good share of the money contributed for religious and charitable purposes has been obtained by doubtful means, and that it is impossible for us to make discriminations. To this, the answer was that we proposed no quixotic inquisition into the character of the offerings which are thrown upon the contribution plate; we would assume that all these are honest dollars unless we knew the contrary. Moreover, when any man makes an offering in a wholly impersonal way, without calling attention to his gift or seeking recognition for it, we have no call to investigate his motives or his character. The case in which the moral difficulty arises is that of a man who is known to have accumulated his wealth by unsocial or flagitious methods, and who, in bestowing it, wishes the grateful recognition of those who receive it.

The real question which emerged from all this haze is simply this: What is the right relation between moral teachers and the possessors of predatory wealth? It is impossible to deny the existence of a considerable class of persons who have obtained great wealth by predatory methods, by evasion and defiance of law, by the practice of vast extortions, by getting unfair and generally unlawful advantages over their neighbors, by secret agreements, and the manipulation of railway and government officials; by such violations of law as have been brought to light in thousands of indictments in the rebate cases; by the use of trust funds for private gain; by manifold arts that tend to corrupt the character and destroy the foundations of the social order. The national government has been expending much of its strength, during the past three years, in the detection and punishment of crimes of this character. And it is a notorious fact that some of those who have gained great wealth by such methods have been diligently and in many cases successfully seeking to establish close relations between themselves and the moral teachers of the country. The question is what these moral teachers ought to do about it. What attitude should they maintain toward such men as those whom our government has, for the last three years, been persistently endeavoring to convict and punish? Ought they to go into partnership with them in the business of religion or of education or of philanthropy?

To the suggestion of partnership those thus challenged are apt to demur. "We have proposed no such thing as partnership," they protest. But what else shall it be called? If you persuade a man to invest one hundred thousand dollars of his capital in your business, is he not, to all intents and purposes, a partner in your business? Will he not be, in his own eyes, and in yours, and in the eyes of the whole community, associated with you in your business? And can the moral teachers of the community afford thus to associate themselves with men who are setting the laws at defiance, and trampling on all the principles of justice and humanity in their ruthless pursuit of gain?

It would seem that if the churches and the colleges of the land have any clear calling, it is that of making abhorrent and detestable, in the sight of the youth, the conduct of men who are amassing great wealth by methods which tend to the overthrow of free government and the destruction of the social order. They will not fulfill this calling by building churches or endowing mission boards with money contributed by such men, or by erecting college halls that bear their names. No amount of money that such givers can contribute can compensate for the lowering of ideals and the blurring of consciences which this kind of partnership involves. Is it really very wonderful that such a moral cataclysm as that which appeared in the insurance investigation should have taken place in our American society?

Such were the convictions which led to the protest against the acceptance by our Mission Board of Mr. Rockefeller's gift. The question was debated, at the beginning, as I have said, on the understanding that it was a voluntary gift; but it afterward transpired that such was not its character. Mr. Rockefeller had not thrust his offering upon the Board, and he naturally declined to have the case so represented; it was at his demand that an explicit and extended statement was finally made, showing that the officers of the Board had been engaged for more than two years in soliciting this gift. This exhibit disclosed some lack of ingenuousness in the previous conduct of the discussion. If this fact had been clearly stated at the outset, the attitude of many minds toward the transaction would have been different. The question now before the churches was whether this policy should be commended and continued. In answer to this question I gave early notice that a resolution would be offered, at the annual meeting of the Board at Seattle, in October, to this effect: "Resolved, that the officers of this Board should neither

PARTNERSHIP WITH PLUNDERERS

invite nor solicit donations to its funds from persons whose gains have been made by methods morally reprehensible or socially injurious."

At the meeting in Seattle this resolution, and the "Statement of Principles" made by the officers of the Board in defending its action, were submitted together. The address which I made in support of my resolution, upon the question, "Shall Ill-Gotten Gains be sought for Christian Purposes?" is published in the volume entitled "The New Idolatry." The debate was not a protracted one. The "Principles" submitted were not, apparently, such as the corporate members present cared to defend. Yet they were not ready to adopt my resolution, with its practical reproof of the conduct of their officers. To vote it down, and thus officially consent that ill-gotten gains should be solicited by their officers was more than they thought it prudent to do, and therefore the knot was cut by laying the resolution and the "Principles" on the table together. The issue was dodged. The officers of the Board were not reproved for what they had done, and they were not authorized to continue their practice. So far as the action of the corporate members was concerned, it was a drawn battle. But there was no question about the verdict of the people. The great audience that listened to the discussion spoke its mind most emphatically. The newspapers of the region, some of which had sneered at the protest before the meeting, were united and enthusiastic in their testimony that it was a righteous protest and ought to be heeded.

I had no expectation, when I went to Seattle, that

I could get my resolution adopted; I knew that the majority of the corporate members who would be present were committed against it, and the last words of my speech were these: "Some of you have been kind enough to assure me that I am in a very insignificant minority. That may be; I do not know about that; I leave that to be decided by you. It will not be the first time that I have been in a very small minority, even in this Board; but I have seen such small minorities, in a very few years, grow to overwhelming majorities. 'The safe appeal of truth to time' is one on which I have learned to rest with hope, and I therefore commit with confidence what I have said to you, and to the people of the Congregational churches, and to the kindly judgment of all honorable men." Within three months after the meeting, the officers of the Board, though taking no public action in the matter, were ready to give assurances that the spirit of my resolution would govern their future conduct. The protest was justified and the battle was won.

There can be no doubt that this discussion has cleared the air. Even the man in the street is able to see that the alliance of churches and colleges with public enemies is not a good thing; that one man's money is decidedly not as good as another man's — when the acceptance of the money involves partnership with evildoers or condonation of nefarious conduct. Even the politicians are able to see the point. A society was formed in Cincinnati, not long ago, for the protection of the ballot; and George B. Cox, of that city, sent the managers his check for five hundred dollars. They sent it back. Why? Was not George Cox's money as good as any other man's money? The treasurer of the National Republican Committee, in the campaign of 1908, announced that contributions from corporations would not be received, and that those which had been sent in would be returned. Why? Is not a corporation's money as good as the money of a private person? Is there any justification for these scruples? Probably there is. Probably there are compromising relations here that had better be avoided. The politicians are becoming sensitive about such matters. I have no doubt the churches and the colleges will be more so, one of these days.

The response of the people to this protest was one that touched me deeply. Letters from all parts of the Union literally poured in upon me, for months. One could never have guessed that such an issue would stir the people so profoundly. Among these hundreds of strangers who wrote to express their approval were men and women of all ranks and classes, but the testimony that was most grateful came from those outside the church, who had been repelled from it by its seeming subserviency to Mammon, and who were glad to welcome any signs of the breaking of that yoke. I could not reply to all those friendly letters, but I have kept them all; and I trust that some of those who then stretched forth to me a kind hand may read these words and find in them some sense of my gratitude for their words of comfort and good cheer.

CHAPTER XXVII

OCTOBER SUNSHINE

Ay, thou art welcome, heaven's delicious breath,
    When woods begin to wear the crimson leaf,
    And suns grow meek, and the meek suns grow brief,
And the year smiles as it draws near its death.
Wind of the sunny south! Oh, still delay
    In the gay woods and in the golden air,
    Like to a good old age released from care,
Journeying, in long serenity, away.
In such a bright late quiet, would that I
    Might wear out life like thee, mid bowers and brooks,
    And, dearer yet, the sunshine of kind looks,
And music of kind voices ever nigh;
    And when my last sand twinkled in the glass,
    Pass silently from men, as thou dost pass.
                      William Cullen Bryant.

I AM writing these words at the end of May, in the year nineteen hundred and nine. The record of the family Bible and the reflection of gray hairs in the looking-glass would make out that with me it is late October; but the tingle in my blood and the scenery of the garden and the heart insist that it is "the high tide of the year." It seems a good time to gather up a sheaf of miscellaneous memories and reflections for which no place has been found in the discussions of larger affairs on preceding pages.

I should not like to leave on any mind the impression that the energies of my life have been wholly or mainly given to literature or politics or social reform. I have been — but for the four years of journalistic service — a Christian pastor; my interests have been centred in the churches I have been serving, and the life that I have shared with my parishioners and my neighbors has been the life best worth living.

I have often been asked how I have managed to do so much literary work. The easy answer is that I have done very little work of this kind outside of my preparation for my pulpit. Of the thirty-one volumes of which the encyclopædias accuse me, all but six have gone through my pulpit, and are printed as they were preached, with almost no revision. A number of these volumes are courses of Sunday evening lectures, originally prepared and preached with no thought of publication. "Did you ever hear me preach?" asked Coleridge of Charles Lamb. "N-n-never heard you do anything else," answered Charles. My friends are quite entitled to say the same thing about me, and I do not wish from them any other verdict. Only I insist that the pulpit in these days has a wide field open to it, and that everything which helps to prepare the Kingdom for which we pray is within the purview of the preacher. Furthermore, I maintain that good sermons may be and ought to be good literature; that the free, direct, conversational handling of a theme in the presence of an audience makes good reading in a book. If I am permitted to judge my own work, I should say that the best of my books, as literature, is the book of sermons, — "Where Does the Sky Begin?" My Sunday morning sermons have usually been devoted to the themes of personal religion, but in the evenings I have chosen to deal with wider interests, always, however, keeping the discussion close to the issues of life and character. I have steadily declined to go into the show business on Sunday nights, whether with music or with pictures, holding that amusement is not the crying need of any class in our city populations, and that the pulpit ought to maintain its dignity as a teaching function. These Sunday evening sermons and lectures have cost me, therefore, a great deal; I think that I have expended on them twice as much labor as on my morning sermons, though I have not meant to slight these.

Several of these courses of Sunday evening discussions have been given to religious themes, — the two books entitled, "Who Wrote the Bible?" and "Seven Puzzling Bible Books," the two volumes entitled, "Burning Questions," and "How Much is Left of the Old Doctrines?" the two little manuals, "Being a Christian," and "The Christian Way," and a number of smaller publications. There are several unpublished series of similar character. The social question in all its phases has been a constant theme, the effort being to present the Christian solution of such problems as they arise. Biographical studies have opened many productive fields; there is no more effective or convincing presentation of saving truth than that which is given in the life of a good man or woman, and nothing is more profoundly interesting to any sort of audience. I remember being invited by a minister in a neighboring town to give a lecture to his congregation, which was composed of unliterary people, and I offered him one that I had been giving in the colleges, on Thomas Carlyle. He objected, on the ground that his people would not care for it, but I insisted; and he afterward owned that I could have given them nothing that would have held their attention more successfully. Ethical themes of every variety, questions of conduct, problems of life, have been considered; the lessons of the great novels and the great poems have been studied. One course dealt with "Some Saintly Heretics," and one with the poets as preachers.

To poetry as the expression of the life of the Spirit, I have devoted much attention in my teaching. For several years I have given, in our chapel, on Friday afternoons in Lent, devotional readings from the poets, — readings with almost no comment; and these exercises have come to be regarded with much favor. From Milton and Wordsworth and Coleridge and the Brownings, from Tennyson and Matthew Arnold and Edwin Arnold and Jean Ingelow and Adelaide Procter and Christina Rossetti, from Bryant and Longfellow and Emerson and Whittier and Lowell and Sidney Lanier and Richard Watson Gilder and many other seers and singers, messages have come to us that opened the gates of heaven and made plainer the paths that lead thither.

It will be fifty years next January since I began my work as a Christian minister, and I wish to bear testimony that I am not yet tired of my work, and have not begun to doubt whether it is worth while. Save for that brief episode in journalism, I have kept steadily at it; and that was hardly an interval, for I was preaching nearly every Sunday, and for almost two of those years I had much of the care of a parish. I have been sometimes tempted by college work. In the spring of

1886 the presidency of Western Reserve University was vacant, and a friend of mine, on the board of trustees, was solicitous that I should consider a call to that position. Other members of the board were also interested, and it was settled that a delegation would visit Columbus for consultation. Just at this juncture the invitation came to speak at Cleveland, at that joint meeting of employers and workingmen to which I have referred in a previous chapter. When I told my friend of the invitation, he shook his head: "You had better not go," he said. "Why not?" "Well, I would rather you would not raise such questions, just now." "Just now is exactly the time to raise them," I answered. "It is better that everybody should know just now where I stand on this issue." So I went to Cleveland, and heard no more from that board of trustees.

In the early spring of 1893 ex-President Hayes, who was then the president of the trustees of the Ohio State University, had several interviews with me, in which he informed me that the board wished to elect me to the presidency of that institution, but desired to wait until the legislature should remove the limitation upon the amount of the president's salary. In June of that year I was invited to make the Commencement Address at the Illinois State University, whose presidency was then vacant; and, shortly thereafter, was surprised by the notification that I had been elected to that office. Such an offer had to be respectfully considered, and I visited Champaign and looked over the field, but concluded that I would rather remain in Ohio. During this summer the anti-Catholic eruption broke out, and I made no delay in freeing my mind about it. The next legislature, as I have explained, was dominated by this proscriptive organization, and notice was promptly served upon the university trustees that they could get no appropriations without the guaranty that nobody in Columbus should be made president of the institution. The appropriations were secured, and I was not made president. Free speech, it is clear, is sometimes a costly luxury to those who indulge in it; but it is worth all it costs. Such martyrdom as this is not worth whimpering over. I should have been a caitiff if I had hesitated to speak my mind freely on either of these occasions, and any promotion which silence would have purchased would have been degradation.

Several other propositions to enter upon college work came later, but they had ceased to interest me. I began to prize the freedom of my pulpit. There was some misgiving about the kind of work which would be required of a college president, and about the kind of restraints which would be laid upon him. This misgiving has never arisen to the height of apprehension indicated by the remark of President Andrew D. White, of Cornell, to my friend, Professor Moses Coit Tyler: "Moses, if any man ever offers you a college presidency, shoot him on the spot!" But there has been enough of it to make me, on the whole, rather thankful for the fortunes that have shut me into the calling to which my life has been given.

I do not believe that there is any place of influence in the world in which a man can be as free as in the Christian pulpit. There are churches, no doubt, in which limitations would be imposed upon the preacher, if the preacher would submit to them, and there are preachers who habitually wear the halter and are waiting to be told what they must not say. Unquestionably there is cowardice and subserviency in the pulpit, as everywhere else. But there need not be. A minister with a clear sense of his vocation, and with a fair amount of common sense, who can make allowances for differences of opinion, and discuss critical issues with a reasonable degree of moderation, can speak his mind more freely than most moral teachers. I have been saying things, with no sense of restraint, during the last fifty years, that I should not have been so likely to say if I had been a journalist or a college professor. I have not always commanded the assent of all my auditors, but they have recognized my right to speak, and have never sought to muzzle me. I doubt if any other kind of work, in which a living was to be made, would have given me so large an opportunity as my churches in North Adams and Springfield and Columbus have given me to speak my deepest thought.

But it has not all been criticism or controversy. How far from it! The great themes of the ideal life are, after all, the supreme interests. The insights, the aspirations, the consolations, the convictions, the hopes, the purposes which flow into our lives from the realms about us and above us — how much our peace and our strength depend upon them! These things of the Spirit are the great realities. The existence of that world in which our higher nature dwells and from which we draw our inspirations is not a matter of conjecture. Herbert

Spencer himself, the great agnostic, declares that we are more sure of the Unknown Reality, out of which all physical forces and laws proceed, than we are of our own existence. By our scientific logic we cannot define it, but we cannot think without assuming it. And that which our scientific logic cannot define is made known to us in our religious experience. It is with these realities of the unseen realm that our faith makes us acquainted. And these, after all, are "the fountain light of all our day, the master light of all our seeing." It is in the light of them that everything else gets value and significance. They are the only certainties. Everything else is fleeting and illusory. Continents subside and mountains explode and crumble, but no moment can ever come when truth will not be better than falsehood, and fidelity than treachery, and trust than suspicion. How much better? Infinitely better. No measurements can express the difference. Thus we know ourselves to be children of the Infinite; elements enter into our lives which lift us out of the realms of time and space, and reveal to us our larger parentage. It is only as we are able to draw into our life these great elements, to transfigure our human relationships and duties with the light that never was on sea or land, that life becomes significant and precious. Nothing can save our social morality but a constant infusion of this idealism. Where it is wanting, trade becomes piracy and politics plunder, the walls of the home collapse, and the state rests upon a volcano.

I wonder if any one thinks that these things which the eye cannot see and the ear cannot hear are any less essential to human life to-day than they were in a former generation. I wonder if any one imagines that any scheme of social reconstruction can be devised which will enable us to dispense with faith and hope and love, with the things that we think of when we pray.

For my own part, I have no such expectation. These things are much more real to me, much closer to my life, than they were fifty years ago. It never before seemed to me so well worth while to try to make men see them. Religion, at the beginning, was largely a matter of tradition; to-day I am resting in what I have verified. Of some things I am much less sure than once I was, but what Jesus has taught us about the Father in heaven and the Brother on the earth looms large. I want to get to understand it and to do it. The things that men have said about him concern me less and less; the things that he himself has said concern me more and more. A correct theory of his person is of much less consequence than obedience to his words. Has he not told us so? "Why call ye me Lord, Lord, and do not the things which I say?" The only way to find out what he is, is to obey his commandments. "If any man will do his will, he shall know of the doctrine." Yet there are millions who are deeply exercised over metaphysical theories of his nature, but who are utterly skeptical concerning his explicit counsels about living together.

There is much earnest questioning in these days respecting the alleged decadence of the church. Such an exhibit as that which Mr. Ray Stannard Baker has just made of the religious conditions in New York city is not comforting. Nor is this state of things wholly exceptional. What is the matter with the church? The matter is that it has concentrated its energies upon believing things about Christ, and has ceased believing him. It has forgotten its commission: "Go ye and make disciples of all the nations, *teaching them to observe all things whatsoever I commanded you.*" If the church would dare to teach and to practice the things which Jesus Christ has commanded, she would soon regain her lost power.

It is the belief, the assurance, that the church must return to the simplicity that is in Christ, must begin to take his teachings seriously, must learn what he meant by seeking first the Kingdom of God and his righteousness, that has made the preaching of the gospel such an intensely interesting business to me, during the last quarter of a century. It begins to be evident that the church is envisaging her own failure, and is inquiring with contrition and solicitude, what it means. I cannot help hoping that she will be able to see, before long, that the way of Jesus is the way of life for the individual, for the church, for the industrial order, for the commonwealth, and that she will find a way to enforce that truth upon the thought of mankind.

All the signs indicate that modern society is being forced by the disastrous failure of the methods of strife to entertain the possibility of coöperation as the fundamental social law. The multiplication of armaments has become not only an enormity, but a howling farce; it is impossible that the nations should go on making fools of themselves after this fashion. The industrial conflict is no whit less irrational. And the terrible collapses in big business during the last decade have reduced to absurdity the scheme of the graspers. Who wants to climb to their bad eminence? If there are still many who do, there is certainly an increasing number of those who feel that such success is a dismal failure. And the conviction grows that the Golden Rule is, after all, the only workable rule of life; that we must learn how to live by it. This is the sign of promise. Is He really coming to his Kingdom? One would like to live fifty years longer just to see.

I wish that I might draw the attention of some of the young men who will live through this period of fifty years, and who are cherishing the purpose of service, to the work of the Christian ministry. I am far enough from thinking that the church is perfect, or from imagining that all the work of the Kingdom is done by the church. But the church has been, and in increasing measure will be, the vitalizing and inspiring agency in the social movement. Unless the ideas and forces which the church stands for are at the heart of that movement, it will come to naught; and it will not come to naught. There is no place in which a man can get nearer to the heart of that movement than in the Christian pulpit. It is sometimes supposed to be a narrow place, but, as a rule, it is as wide as the man who stands in it chooses to make it. And I know no other position in which a man has so many chances to serve the community; in which he is brought into such close and helpful relations with so many kinds of people. The field of the church, under the right kind of leadership, is as wide as the world, and the force of the church is more responsive to-day than ever before to the right kind of leadership. There are, it is true, too many churches which are sponges rather than springs of influence, — which devote their energies to building themselves up out of the community instead of pouring themselves into the community in streams of service; which have not learned that it is as true of churches as of men, that they who would save their lives lose them. But it is quite possible for a brave and warm-hearted leader to put a new spirit into such a church as this, and a conversion of that sort makes joy among the angels. And the man who gets the confidence and affection of a group of people who are enlisted in such work as properly belongs to a church of Jesus Christ; who can live among them, for a generation or two, sharing their fortunes, giving and receiving comfort and inspiration and courage and hope, leading them in such enterprises of good will as are always inviting them, has got about as good a thing as any man can pray for.

CHAPTER XXVIII

LOOKING BACKWARD AND FORWARD

> The airs of heaven blow o'er me;
> A glory shines before me
> Of what mankind shall be, —
> Pure, generous, brave, and free.
>
> Ring, bells in unreared steeples,
> The joy of unborn peoples!
> Sound, trumpets far off blown,
> Your triumph is my own!
>
> Parcel and part of all,
> I keep the festival,
> Fore-reach the good to be,
> And share the victory.
>
> I feel the earth move sunward,
> I join the great march onward,
> And take, by faith, while living,
> My freehold of thanksgiving.
>   *John Greenleaf Whittier.*

I FIND myself, as I approach the close of this record, meditating on the words of the old prophet: "Go thou thy way till the end be: for thou shalt rest, and stand in thy lot at the end of the days." I am not, indeed, disposed to admit that my work is all done; these Recollections have been written while my life is in full vigor, because I did not wish them to reflect the judgments of decrepitude. When a man is seventy-three years old, it is natural for him to feel that the time has come to take in sail. Yet that feeling may be too freely indulged. The Psalmist's estimate may have been reasonable for his time; but since that day the average term of human life has been greatly prolonged. That recent impressive exhibit of the work done by the master minds of the centuries after the seventieth milestone has been passed, is full of encouragement. I believe that when we shall have learned how to live, centenarians will be dwelling on every street, and septuagenarians will be counted as hardly past their prime. I am not, then, concerning myself greatly about the future; I only hope that I may be able to stand in my lot until the end of the days, working as long as I can help, and ready to step aside as soon as I begin to be in the way.

There is some interest, however, to me in a backward look from the point which I have now reached, over the years whose experiences I have been trying to trace. It is not the verdict of egotism which makes them fruitful and memorable years.

Since my life began, the entire face of the world has been changed. Africa, which, seventy years ago, was, but for a fringe along the Mediterranean and a tassel at the southern cape, cloaked in densest darkness, has been invaded from every side by the forces of civilization, and now promises to be, within the present century, the scene of vast industries and mighty transformations; Asia is quaking in the throes of great overturnings; but it is the map of Europe on which the most marvelous changes have been recorded. The boundaries of most of the states have been moved again and again since I began to study geography, and the entire fabric of political society has been reconstructed.

In England, four years before my life began, the Reform Bill had enfranchised a considerable portion of the population, but a vast majority of the people were still without the suffrage; in successive reform measures I have seen this right extended to one section after another of the English people, until now the suffrage is practically universal, and England is about as near to being a true democracy as any country in the world. France, in 1836, was under the milk-and-water monarchy of Louis Philippe; I remember well the downfall of that Orleans dynasty, in 1848, and the blare of trumpets that proclaimed the flamboyant and short-lived Second Republic, whose house of cards was so soon toppled over by the cynical usurper who vaulted into the saddle and rode ruthlessly over the liberties of Europe for twenty years. The bursting of the bubble of the Second Empire and the rise and steady progress of the Third French Republic, which now bids fair to give France enduring peace with freedom, are among the great historic events of my recollection.

In the meantime the *disjecta membra* of the German states have been erected into a mighty empire; Italy, so long a group of quarreling principalities, has become a people with a national consciousness; Spain has dwindled to a third-class power; Bulgaria has come to her own; Russia, the last stronghold of absolutism, stands dazed and helpless in the presence of that populace on whose necks her autocracy has so long been standing; and the Sick Man of the Bosphorus is taking the medicine which promises to save his life.

What a gallery of portraits might be drawn, if one had time and skill, of the men who have been marching across the map of Europe during the last seventy years, — of Peel and O'Connell and Cobden and Bright and Disraeli and Gladstone; of Louis Blanc and Thiers and Gambetta; of Garibaldi and Mazzini and Cavour; of Castelar and Prim and Serrano; of Bismarck and Von Moltke; of Menshikoff and Gortchakoff, —not to speak of those poets and painters and sculptors and musicians who have lifted into the light the real and enduring things, — the things of the Spirit.

The changes in the world of thought which have taken place during the past seven decades have been more radical and more momentous than any which have taken place in the industrial or the political realm. What goes on in the outer world, in truth, only registers the movements of mind. The astounding progress in the practical arts is the result of scientific discovery, and science belongs to the world of thought, not to the world of things. Civilization is a spiritual, not a physical fact.

It was the emancipation given to the life of the Spirit by the great masters of modern philosophy, Kant and Fichte and Hegel, that set men to thinking about the life of mankind, that led to explorations into old records of humanity's earlier experiences, that developed the historical sense, that showed the present to be the child of the past, that prepared the way for that doctrine of development which was to revolutionize human thought.

Lyell's geological researches, which showed that the earth's crust had been slowly modified by age-long processes, first brought home to the popular mind the significance of this new theory. It would be difficult for the younger generation to understand with what amazement, yea, what indignation, this new teaching was received. The outcry against the Higher Criticism has been feeble compared with the denunciations hurled against the geologists from pulpit and sanctum and platform. Soon, however, it began to be evident to all who could think, that the records plainly written on the rocks by the Creator Himself can be no less veracious than those written upon parchment by human hands; that science gives us the word of God no less authoritatively than revelation; that the infidelity which disputes the truth that God has revealed in his works is quite as heinous as that which questions the truth of a statement in a holy book.

Thus, little by little, the truth began to be dimly apprehended — it is not yet, by any means, fully understood — that God is in his world to-day as really as He ever was; that the work of creation is not yet finished, and never will be. The work of creation is a continuous process, and so is the work of revelation. All that we call Nature is but the constant manifestation of the divine power; and the Spirit in whose image our spirits are fashioned, and with whom we are made for fellowship, is here, all the while, as close to us as He ever was to any men in any age; as ready to give inspiration and wisdom to us as He has ever been to any of his children. This is the truth which is slowly breaking through the mists of tradition, and is beginning to light up the world with a new sense of the nearness and the reality of the living God.

Good men are sometimes anxious lest we should lose our religion. It looks as though we were going to lose the husk of it and find the kernel; to lose the chrysalis and win the butterfly. The trouble has been that our laborious thinking has put our God far away from us. "He *was* working here once," we have said, "in the morning of the Creation, but He finished his work then and went away; since then He has only appeared now and then to work a miracle; all we know of Him in Nature is through the report that comes to us from those far-off times. He *was* speaking here, once, in the days of prophets and apostles, but He finished what He had to say and sealed the book; since then there is no open vision, no authoritative word."

All this puts Him far away. Our religion, whatever we call it, becomes mainly a tradition. We are climbing to heaven by ladders of testimony to bring God down, we are descending into the abyss by our chains of logic to draw Him forth, when in very truth He is near us, in the very breath of our life, in the thrill of our nerves, in the pulsations of our hearts, in the movements of our minds, living and working in us and manifesting Himself in every natural force, in every law of life. This is the truth which the world is beginning to understand, the truth of the immanent God; and when it gets to be a reality we shall not be afraid of losing our religion.

We hear people, in these days, denying the supernatural. It is a little as if the planets should proclaim that there is no such thing as space, or as if the rivers should declare that there is no such thing as water. We cannot lay our hand on life anywhere without feeling the thrill of that SOMETHING MORE which underlies all law and eludes all physical analysis.

It is toward this larger faith that the movements of thought have been leading on through all the years of my pilgrimage. It is a far cry from those old legal and mechanical conceptions of the relation of God to the world which prevailed in my youth, to this vital faith in a living God of which I have been trying to tell, and it must not be supposed that the whole church has arrived at these convictions. I have shown where the head of the column is marching; the rest of it is moving along.

These changes in the underlying philosophy of religion are not so obvious to the multitude, but the changes in the popular teaching of the church are evident to all. The message which is spoken to-day fom the most orthodox pulpits is a very different message from that to which I was accustomed to listen in my boyhood. The motive of fear, of terror, was then the leading motive; this motive is not employed now as it was then. It is not a moral motive. It does not appeal to human reason, or human freedom, or human affection; it seeks to overpower the human will. We have found a more excellent way. Mr. Moody was not an advanced thinker, but his appeal had little to do with the old terrorism; love was the motive on which he relied: "by the cords of a man" he drew men to God.

Another change of not less significance is that by which the emphasis is placed more and more upon the altruistic motive. It begins to be evident that that is the strongest motive. When I was a boy, the main reason urged for being a Christian was a selfish reason. It was insurance against loss; it was the personal gain, the personal happiness, the future blessedness of which it

LOOKING BACKWARD AND FORWARD 429

put you in possession, that were constantly kept before your mind. That motive has been steadily retreating into the background; the motive of unselfish service has been increasingly emphasized. Because the Christian life is the noblest life; because it is more blessed to give than to receive, and better to minister than to be ministered unto; because the good of life is not found by separating yourself from your fellows, but by identifying yourself with them, — therefore let us be Christians. This is what it means to follow Christ to-day, as the wisest preachers explain it; and this is an appeal which, when we learn how to use it, will have convincing power.

I am fain to believe that the time is drawing near when the Christian church will be able to discern and declare the simple truth that Religion is nothing but Friendship; friendship with God and with men. I have been thinking much about it in these last days, and I cannot make it mean anything else; so far as I can see, this is all there is to it. Religion is friendship — friendship first with the great Companion, of whom Jesus told us, who is always nearer to us than we are to ourselves, and whose inspiration and help is the greatest fact of human experience. To be in harmony with his purposes, to be open to his suggestions, to be in conscious fellowship with Him, — this is religion on its Godward side.

Then, turning manward, friendship sums it all up. To be friends with everybody; to fill every human relation with the spirit of friendship; is there anything more than this that the wisest and best of men can hope to do?

If the church could accept this truth — Religion is Friendship — and build its own life upon it, and make it central and organic in all its teaching, should we not see a great revival of religion?

I have thus, in a few words, tried to trace the path of religious progress through the seven decades of my recollections; it would be an equal pleasure to follow the growth of philanthropic sentiment and activity, the marvelous development of the æsthetic side of life, the progress of educational ideals and methods, and many others of the great human interests. For that there is now no room. But I should like to bear witness that the retrospect, from this point, confirms the remembered verdict of the years as they have been going by, that it is a good thing to live. There may be better worlds, but I should like to be guaranteed another seventy years in just such a world as this. There would be suffering and sorrow, struggle and privation, hard knocks and tough luck; they have not missed me, and if I had to go over the track again, I would not ask to be protected from them; I know that all this has been good for me. It is good for any man who will hold up his head and keep a trusting heart.

Of this I am sure: if it was ever worth while to live, it is worth while to live to-day. No better day than this day has ever dawned on this continent. Sometimes it may have seemed as if the foundations were crumbling under our feet, — the exposures of perfidy and dishonor have been so shocking. But the thing to fix the thought upon is the mighty revulsion of public sentiment against this rottenness and rascality. It is the sound and clear moral judgment of the nation which makes all this iniquity seem so horrible. The blackness of the shadow proves the intensity of the light. The annals of the future will mark these days as an epoch in the ethical awakening of the American people.

We turn our faces to the future with good hope in our hearts. There are great industrial problems before us, but we shall work them out; there are battles to fight, but we shall win them. With all those who believe in justice and the square deal, in kindness and good will, in a free field and a fair chance for every man, the stars in their courses are fighting, and their victory is sure.

BOOKS BY WASHINGTON GLADDEN

Plain Thoughts on the Art of Living. Ticknor & Fields, 1868; Porter & Coates.

From the Hub to the Hudson. New England News Co., 1869.

Workingmen and their Employers. Lockwood, Brooks & Co., 1876; Funk & Wagnalls, 1885.

Being a Christian: What it Means and How to Begin. Congregational Publishing Society, 1876.

The Christian Way. Dodd, Mead & Co., 1877.

The Lord's Prayer. Houghton, Mifflin & Co., 1880.

The Christian League of Connecticut. The Century Company, 1883.

Things New and Old. A. H. Smythe, 1884.

The Young Men and the Churches. Congregational Publishing Society, 1885.

Applied Christianity. Houghton, Mifflin & Co., 1887.

Parish Problems (edited and compiled). The Century Company, 1888.

Burning Questions. James Clarke & Co., London, 1889; The Century Company.

Santa Claus on a Lark. The Century Company, 1890.

Who Wrote the Bible? Houghton, Mifflin & Co., 1891.

Tools and the Man: Property and Industry under the Christian Law. Houghton, Mifflin & Co., 1893.

The Cosmopolis City Club. The Century Company, 1893.

The Church and the Kingdom. F. H. Revell & Co., 1894.

Ruling Ideas of the Present Age. Houghton, Mifflin & Co., 1895.

Seven Puzzling Bible Books. Houghton, Mifflin & Co., 1897.

Social Facts and Forces. G. P. Putnam's Sons, 1897.

Art and Morality. W. F. Ketchum, 1897.

The Christian Pastor. Charles Scribner's Sons, 1898.

How Much is Left of the Old Doctrines? Houghton, Mifflin & Co., 1899.

Straight Shots at Young Men. T. Y. Crowell, 1900.

Social Salvation. Houghton, Mifflin & Co., 1901.

The Practice of Immortality. The Pilgrim Press, 1901.

Witnesses of the Light. Houghton, Mifflin & Co., 1903.

Where Does the Sky Begin? Houghton, Mifflin & Co., 1904.

Christianity and Socialism. Methodist Publishing House, 1905.

The New Idolatry. Doubleday, Page & Co., 1905.

The Church and Modern Life. Houghton, Mifflin & Co., 1908.

Recollections. Houghton Mifflin Company, 1909.

INDEX

INDEX

ABOLITIONISM, 47.
Adams, Charles Francis, 210.
Advertisements, disguised, 233.
Alden, Henry M., 77, 184.
Allon, Reverend Henry, 355.
Allston, Washington, 353.
Amending the Ohio Constitution, 317, 318.
American Board of Missions, and the second probation question, 289; the question of gifts from plunderers, 401; is it partnership? 405; meeting at Seattle, 407.
American social life, in 1836–44, 12 ff.
Ames, Mary Clemmer, 191.
Amusements, controversy about, 168–171.
Anderson, Major Robert, 109.
Andrew, Governor John A., 179.
Andrews, Horace Lee, 29, 30.
Anthracite strike, 305.
Antietam, battle of, 128.
Anti-Slavery reform, 62.
"A. P. A.," 359, 365, 415.
"Applied Christianity," 297.
Arkansas, in 1837, 13.
Arthur, President Chester A., 280.
"Atlantic Monthly," 78.
Atonement, moral theory of, 266.
"Autocrat of the Breakfast-Table," 78.

Babcock, General O. E., 220.
Bacon, Reverend Leonard Woolsey, 190.
Baptism as a subject of controversy, 57.
Bartlett, Reverend William Alvin, 89, 98.
Bascom, Professor John, 74.
Beecher, Henry Ward, 58, 63, 89; Thanksgiving sermon, 1860, 99–102; 199, 214.
Beecher, Thomas K., 86.
"Being a Christian," 38, 257, 412.
Belknap, General W. W., 220.
Bermuda Hundred, 139.
Biblical revision and criticism, 259 ff.
Biography in the pulpit, 412.
Blaine, J. G., 316, 378.
Blair, Governor Austin, 210.
Bonner, Robert, 123.
Bowen, Henry C., 182.
Bowles, Samuel, 82, 240–248.
Boys in politics, 51.
Bradford, Reverend Amory H., 400.
Briggs, Charles F., 186.
Bristol, R. I., 3.
Brooklyn, N. Y., 89–91, 183, 214.
Brooks, Bishop Phillips, 325.
Browning, Robert, 316.
Bryant, William Cullen, 328, 410.
Buchanan's administration, 91.

438 INDEX

Buckley, Reverend James M., 215.
Bull Run, the first battle of, 117.
Burchard, Reverend Jedediah, 56.
"Burning Questions," 323, 412.
Burnside, General A. E., 124.
Bushnell, Reverend Horace, 119, 164–168.
Butler, General B. F., 220.

Cairnes, John Eliot, 256.
"Century Magazine," 174, 274.
Chadbourne, Professor Paul A., 73.
Chancellorsville, battle of, 129.
Chattanooga, battle of, 136.
Cheever, Reverend George B., 63.
Chicago, 13.
Chicago convention, 91.
Chickamauga, battle of, 136.
Chinese in North Adams, 171–173.
Christian Commission, 141, 142.
"Christian League of Connecticut," 274.
Christian rule of life, 299.
"Christian Way, The," 412.
"Christian World, The," of London, 323, 357.
"Christianity and Socialism," 324.
Church life at the middle of the 19th century, 57.
Church services in Owego, 33, 34.
Church work in city and country, 161, 162.
City, the problem of the, 90.
City Club of New York, 330.
City Point, Va., 139.
Civic Federation, 306, 330.
Civil Service Reform, rising demand for, 195; Grant's attitude toward, 195; first commission, 196; Curtis resigns, 219.

Classical studies, 64.
Clay and the tariff, 22.
Cleveland, President Grover, 316, 378.
Coal-miners, strike of, 29 ff.
Coan, Titus Munson, 188.
Cohoon, Jennie O., 98.
Cold Harbor, battle of, 136.
Colfax, Schuyler, 189, 214.
Columbian Exposition, 359.
Columbus, Ohio, 283, 284 ff, 286.
"Come-outers, and Stay-inners," 271.
Committee of Seventy on the Tweed ring, 206.
Compromise, the Clay, 31.
Compromise, Missouri, 48, 54.
Conferences of employers and employees, 304.
Congregational Churches, the, 398 ff.
"Congregational Quarterly," 266.
Connecticut Valley Theological Club, 272.
Connolly, Richard B., 197, 200, 207.
Cooley, Professor Charles H., 392.
Cornell University, 324.
Corporations, the first, 14.
Corporations and legislation, 219.
"Cosmopolis City Club," 329.
Cox, General J. D., 113, 194, 195, 210.
Creation, continuous, 426.
Credit Mobilier, 217.
Creed of 1883, 287 ff.
Crosby, Reverend Howard, 215.
Curtis, George William, 121, 196.

INDEX

Custom House scandals, 220.
Cuyler, Reverend T. L., 89.

Daniels, Ebenezer, 23.
Davis, Noah, 210.
Democracy in New England, 159–161.
Dickinson, Miss Anna E., 121.
Discipline by defamation, 268.
Disguised advertisements, 233.
Dodge, William E., 199.
Douglas, Stephen A., 48.
Draft riots in New York, 131–135.
Drew Theological Seminary, 324.

Eggleston, Edward, 182, 184.
Emerson, Ralph Waldo, 121, 122, 232, 366.
England, visits to, 353–358; in the 19th century, 425.
Erie Canal in 1844, 21.
Eternal punishment as a motive, 58.
Evarts, William M., 199.

Farrar, Archdeacon F. W., 354.
Federal plan of city government, 334.
Fish, Hamilton, 194.
Foss, Bishop Cyrus D., 215.
Foundations of belief, 322.
France in the 19th century, 424.
Fraudulent politics, 220.
Fredericksburg, battle of, 129.
Free Soil party, 54.
Fremantle, Reverend W. H., 357.
Frémont, John C., 66.
Friendship, the essence of religion, 429.
Fugitive Slave Law, debate on, 32; 45, 46.

"Gail Hamilton," 191.
Garfield, President James A., 73, 76, 113; election of, 278; assassination of, 279.
Garrison, William Lloyd, 191.
Gavazzi, Father, 279.
Geological discoveries, 425.
Germany in the 19th century, 424.
Gettysburg, battle of, 130.
Gilder, Richard Watson, 118, 136, 184.
Gladden, Amanda Daniels, 7, 12.
Gladden, Solomon, birth and education, 3; removes to New York and Pennsylvania, 4; letters, 4–6; religious life, 10; death, 11; souvenirs in Southampton, 18.
Gladden, Washington, birth, 8; early education, 9; removal to Owego, 12; journey to Massachusetts, 20; life on the farm, 23 ff; country school, 27 ff; early religious life, 32 ff; in the printing-office, 40 ff; in practical politics, 51; begins preparation for college, 57; enters Williams College, 67; is graduated, 84; begins teaching in Owego, 85; licensed to preach, 86; service in Le Raysville, Pa., 88; call to Brooklyn, 89; ordination, 97; removal to Morrisania, 115; hospital work with the Army of the Potomac, 137 ff; call to North Adams, Mass., 158; installation there, 166–168; on the staff of the New York "Independent," 187 ff.; removal to Springfield, Mass., 239; edits "Sunday After-

noon," 272; call to Columbus, Ohio, 283; service at Harvard University, 324; in the city council, 336; Moderator of Congregational Council, 400.
Gladding, Azariah, 2.
Gladstone, William E., 354.
"God in Christ," Bushnell's, 119.
Good Templars, 50.
Good will, the social law, 310 ff.
Grant, General Ulysses S., 131, 136, 142, 143, 151, 177, 193, 194, 210, 214, 216.
Greeley, Horace, 125, 126, 210–213.
Green, Andrew H., 207.
Guiteau, Charles J., 279.

Hall, A. Oakey, Mayor of New York, 197.
Hampton Institute, 373.
Harper, Fletcher, 200.
"Harper's Weekly," 200.
Harrison's Landing, Va., 138.
Harte, F. Bret, 191.
Hastings, Reverend Thomas S., 215.
Havemeyer, William F., 199.
Haven, Reverend Gilbert, 189.
Hay, John, 385, 387.
Hayes, President Rutherford B., 276, 277; 281, 414.
Hayes-Tilden contest, 275, 276.
"Herald," New York, 68, 110, 111.
Higher criticism, 318.
Hitchcock, Secretary E. A., 385.
Hitchcock, Professor Roswell D., 118.
Hoadley, Governor George, 210.
Hoar, Ebenezer Rockwood, 194.
Holland, Josiah Gilbert, 82, 174, 240, 274.

Holmes, Oliver Wendell, 67.
Hooker, General Joseph, 124.
Hoosac Tunnel, 174.
Hopkins, Professor Albert, 73.
Hopkins, President Mark, 71, 72, 86, 167, 265.
"How Much is Left of the Old Doctrines?" 412.
Howard University, 324.
Howells, William D., 44.
Hughes, Archbishop John, 112.
Hunt, Helen, 191.

Illinois State University, 414.
Immanence of God, 427.
Impeachment of Andrew Johnson, 180.
"Independent," New York, 63, 163, 182, 192.
Indian Orchard Council, 262 ff.
Industrial revolution, 294.
Industrial society, its foundation, 299.
International Council at London, 357.
Invasion of Pennsylvania, 130.
Iowa, 13.
Iowa College, 324.
"Is it Peace or War?" 301.

Jackson, Andrew, 14.
Jerusalem Chamber, 355.
Johnson, Andrew, 150, 154, 176, 180.
Jones, George, editor New York "Times," 200–202.

Kansas, 50, 65.
Kingsley, Charles, 176.
Knapp, Reverend Jacob, 59.
Know-Nothings, 52.
Know-Somethings, 52.

INDEX 441

Laissez faire, as a social theory, 295, 313.
Lanier, Sidney, 258.
Le Raysville, Pa., 88.
Leavitt, Reverend Joshua, 128, 185.
Lee, General Robert E., 129; surrender of, 145; 177.
Lenten services, 413.
Lewisburg, Pa., 10, 11.
Liberal Republican movement, 210.
Liberty party, birth of, 22.
Lincoln, Abraham, debate with Douglas, 90; nomination to the presidency, 91; election, 94; departure for Washington, 106; passes down Broadway, New York, 107; first inaugural address, 108; defense of Fort Sumter, 109; first call for troops, 109; advocates compensated emancipation, 124; answers Greeley's "Prayer of Twenty Millions," 125; issues Emancipation Proclamation, 128; at Petersburg, in 1864, 143; his attitude toward the Confederate leaders, 148; his assassination, 150; funeral services, 152.
Lincoln, Professor Isaac N., 74.
Long, Governor John D., 385.
Low, Seth, 329, 331.
Lowell, James Russell, 99, 109, 197, 209, 399.
Lyman Beecher lectures, 324.

McCarthy, Justin, 182.
McClellan, General George B., 124, 125.
MacDonald, George, 85.
McDowell, General Irvin, 117.

Mackenzie, Commodore Alexander Slidell, 76.
Mackenzie, General Ranald Slidell, 76.
McKinley, President William, 383 ff.
McVickar, Bishop, 215.
Maine prohibitory law, 50.
Mansfield College, Oxford, 324.
Manufactures, domestic, 14.
Martineau, Reverend James, 357.
Matthews, Stanley, 210.
Meade, General George G., 130.
Meadville Theological School, 324.
Merriam, Reverend James F., 261.
Michigan, 13.
Mill, John Stuart, 256.
Miller and Millerism, 59, 60.
Miller, Joaquin, 191.
Ministerial function, the, 416 ff.
Missionaries, as theological reformers, 290.
Missouri, 13.
Monopolies must be owned by the people, 309, 314, 345.
Moody, Dwight L., 428.
Moody, Secretary W. H., 385.
Moral theology, demand for, 223 ff.
Morrisania, N. Y., in 1861, 115.
Mount Tom, Mass., 3, 18, 240.
"Mountains, The," college song, 81.
Munger, Reverend T. T., 119, 265.
Municipal problem, the, 328 ff.; boards and commissions, 331; Galveston and Des Moines plan, 333; English system, 333; city transportation, 340; natural gas supply, 343; electric

lighting, 344; public service industries, 346; the spoils system, 348; water-supply, 349.
Municipal Voters' League, 379–383.

National Council of Congregational Churches, 399 ff.
National Municipal League, 330.
Nast, Thomas, 200–202; 212.
Nebraska Bill, 49, 50, 65.
Negro problem, the, 366 ff.; the American Missionary Association, 366; southern schools and colleges for negroes, 367; Southern Education Board, 368; testimonies of southern white men, 369 ff.; the negro needs a complete education, 334.
New Britain, Conn., 21.
"New Idolatry, The," 407.
New School Calvinists, 58.
New York city, 13, 67, 68, 110, 131–135.
Newspaper ethics, 234 ff.
North Adams, Mass., 68; life in, 158–173; amusement controversy in, 168 ff.; Chinese labor in, 171–173; ecclesiastical council in, 265.
Norwich, Conn., 3.

O'Brien, James, 200.
O'Conor, Charles, 207.
Ohio constitution, amending the, 317, 318.
Ohio State University, 323.
Oneida Community, 186.
"On to Richmond," 116.
"Outlook, The," 323.
Owego, N. Y., 4; 40 ff.

Owego Academy, 64.
Owego "Gazette," 40.

Page, William, 186.
Palmer, Governor John M., 210.
Parliament of Religions, 359.
Patton, Reverend Francis L., 225 ff.
Perry, Professor Arthur L., 74.
Petersburg, Va., invested, in 1864, 139.
Phillips, Professor John L. T., 74.
Pierce, President Franklin, 45.
"Plain Thoughts on the Art of Living," 173.
Platt, Thomas C., 66.
Plymouth, Mass., 3.
Poetry, its spiritual uses, 413.
Poland's Committee on Credit Mobilier, 218.
Polk and annexation, 22.
Pope, General John, 124.
Popular hysteria, 155–157.
Porter, General Horace, 143.
Porter, President Noah, of Yale, 265.
Porter, Colonel Peter A., 140.
Pottsgrove, Pa., 1, 7.
Predatory wealth and public teachers, 404; and politicians, 408, 409.
Printing-office, a country, 42–44.
Proctor, Lincoln Redfield, 385.
Progress in philosophy, 425.
Prohibitory liquor laws, 50.
Prostitution of the press, 236.
Public service industries, 309, 346.
Pulpit, the, and the labor question, 150 ff.; the freedom of, 415, 416; social leadership in, 420.

INDEX

Railways, the first, 13; railway journey in 1844, 20, 21.
Reading aloud, 24 ff.
Rebels and traitors, 178.
Reconstruction, the foolishness of, 176 ff.
Religion is friendship, 429.
Republican Party, origin of, 22; organization of, 66.
"Republican," Springfield, 49, 82, 83, 173, 242–245.
Rhodes, James F., quoted, 134, 143, 146, 148, 181, 192, 201.
Richardson, Charles F., 215.
Riis, Jacob, 1.
Robertson, Reverend Frederick W., 119.
Robinson, Reverend Charles S., 215.
Robinson, Governor George D., 303.
Rockefeller, John D., 401, 406.
Roman Catholic Church, 52, 359–365.
Roosevelt, President Theodore, 330; his naval policy, 388; his work as a peacemaker, 389; his accession to the presidency, 390; his attitude toward predatory wealth, 391–395; the anthracite coal strike, 395 ff.
Root, Secretary Elihu, 385, 389.
Roscher, Wilhelm, 297.
Ryder Lectures in Chicago, 324.

Saint-Gaudens, Augustus, 134.
"Salary Grab," 220.
Sanitary Commission, 141.
Schofield, General J. A., 144.
School, a country district, 27, 30.
School district libraries, in New York, 22.
Schurz, Carl, 1, 213.

Scientific progress, 425.
Scott, General Winfield, 45, 104.
"Scribner's Monthly," 174.
Scudder, Horace E., 77, 297.
Secession threatened, 97; peaceable, as a policy, 103–106.
Second probation, debate about, 290.
Secret societies in politics, 53, 54; 359–365.
"Seven Puzzling Bible Books," 412.
Seventh Regiment, New York, 112.
Seward, William H., 92, 128.
Seymour, Horatio, 130, 133.
Shaler, Professor N. S., 109.
Shaw, Colonel Robert G., 134.
Shelley, Percy Bysshe, 282.
Sheridan, General Philip H., 145.
Sherman, John, 385.
Sherman, General W. T., 144.
"Sigma Chi," a Clerical Club, 215.
Sixth Massachusetts Infantry, 111.
Slidell, John, 77.
Smith, Gerrit, 62.
Smith, Professor Henry B., 118.
Smith, Robertson, 319.
Smith, Roswell, 174, 274, 283.
Social changes, 16.
"Social Facts and Forces," 324.
"Social Salvation," 324.
Socialism, 306 ff.
"Something about manhood," 266.
Souls that need saving, 253.
South Carolina and Secession, 97, 102.
Southampton, Mass., 3; rural life in, in 1843, 18–20.
Spain in the 19th century, 424.

INDEX

Spanish War, the, 385 ff.
Spear, Reverend Samuel T., 187.
Spencer, John C., 77.
Spottsylvania, battle of, 136.
Springfield, Mass., 83; home in, 239; character of, 241, 242; industrial depression in, 248; lectures to workingmen, 250.
Springfield "Republican." *See* "Republican."
Standard Oil Company, 401.
Steamboats, the first, 13.
Stedman, Edmund C., 191.
Stevens, Thaddeus, 176.
Stoddard, Richard H., 191.
Stone River, battle of, 129.
Storrs, Reverend Richard S., 89, 98, 214.
Story, Joseph, 182.
Strike of coal-miners in the Hocking Valley, 29 ff.
Students in college, 325–327.
Sumner, Charles, 176, 213.
"Sun," New York, 213.
"Sunday Afternoon," a magazine, 272.
Supernatural, domestication of, 427.
Sweeney, Peter B., 197.
Swinburne, Algernon Charles, 40.
Swing, Reverend David, trial for heresy, 223 ff.; resigns from the Presbyterian ministry, 227; his subsequent career, 230.
Swollen fortunes, 315.
Symonds, John Addington, 294.

Talmage, Reverend T. De Witt, 214.
Tatlock, Professor John, 73.
Taylor, Bayard, 121, 122.
Taylor, Reverend William M., 215.

Texas, annexation of, 22.
Thomas, General George H., 144.
Thompson, Reverend J. P., 63.
Thurman, Senator A. G., 293.
Ticknor, George, 109.
Tilton, Theodore, 180, 182, 183.
"Times," New York, and the Tweed Ring, 198–204.
Todd, Reverend John, 167.
"Tools and the Man," 324.
Toynbee, Arnold, 95, 96.
Tracy, Secretary Benjamin F., 31, 50, 51.
Tremont Temple meeting, 303.
"Tribune," New York, 24, 31, 68, 94, 103, 112, 116, 126, 133.
Trumbull, Lyman, 210.
Tuskegee Institute, 373.
Tweed Ring, the, 197 ff.
Tyler, Professor Moses Coit, 86, 96, 415.

"Uncle Tom's Cabin," 45.
Union meeting in Cleveland, 301.
Union Relief Association of Springfield, 248.
Universalists, 37.

Van Dyke, Reverend Henry J., 93.
Vermont resolutions, 268.
Vicksburg, capture of, 130.

Wagner, Adolf, 297.
Walker, Francis A., 297.
War, its natural fruit, 221.
War prices, 124.
Ward, William Hayes, 182, 184.
Washington, Booker T., 1, 375.
Washingtonville, Pa., 9.
Western Reserve University, 414.
Westminster Abbey, 355.

INDEX

"Where Does the Sky Begin?" 411.
Whiskey Ring, 220.
White, Andrew D., 199, 415.
Whittier, John Greenleaf, 40, 223, 239, 353, 422.
"Who Wrote the Bible?" 320, 412.
"Wide-awake" movement, 92.
Wilderness, battle of, 136.
Williams College, in 1856, 69; its curriculum, 68–70; its instructors, 70–75; undergraduates in, 76–78; music in, 80, 81.
"Williams Quarterly," 79.
Williamstown, Mass., 68, 158.

Willis, Nathaniel Parker, 42.
Wilson, Henry, 189, 214, 216.
Wilson, Secretary James, 385.
Wilson, President Woodrow, 14, 48, 52.
Winthrop, Theodore, 112.
Wisconsin, 13.
"Witnesses of the Light," 324.
Wood, Fernando, 110.
Wool, General John E., 133.
Woolsey, Sarah C., 191.
Wordsworth, William, 1, 17, 158.
"Workingmen and their Employers," 250 ff.
World's Missionary Conference, 354.

www.ingramcontent.com/pod-product-compliance
Lightning Source LLC
Chambersburg PA
CBHW071433300426
44114CB00013B/1422